PC-MS DOS 4.0 for Hard Disk Users

PC-MS DOS 4.0 for Hard Disk Users

by
David D. Busch

BANTAM BOOKS
TORONTO • NEW YORK • LONDON • SYDNEY • AUCKLAND

PC-MS DOS 4.0 for Hard Disk Users
A Bantam Book / January 1989

ISBN 0-553-34600-8

Published simultaneously in the United States and Canada

Bantam Books are published by Bantam Books, a division of Bantam Doubleday Dell Publishing Group, Inc.
Its trademark, consiting of the words "Bantam Books" and the portrayal of a rooster, is Registered in U.S.
Patent and Trademark Office and in other countries. Marca Registrada, Bantam Books 666 Fifth Avenue, New
York, New York 10103

PRINTED IN THE UNITED STATES OF AMERICA

WAK   0 9 8 7 6 5 4 3 2 1

For David Jr., Michael, Jonathan and Cathy

Contents

Introduction

IBM Disk Operating System 4.00 (commonly called DOS 4.0) is only the latest edition of the basic software package that pervades everything we do with desktop computers. Certainly it was the invention of the microprocessor that made the personal computer possible. The development of the hard disk made such computers practical. However, sophisticated disk operating systems like DOS 4.0 and its predecessors provide PCs with their power. All three are essential components in the desktop revolution that is still in its infancy.

Few who have struggled to swap disks repeatedly with a floppy-based personal computer would argue that the hard disk drive has made it practical for individuals to access large databases of information. No one who has had to hunt through a stack of floppy disks to find a particular program file would contest the idea that today's large, complex programs demand fast, high-capacity mass storage.

In fact, the only "optional" component of a computer system that is more pervasive, or useful, than a hard disk are the (almost) twin operating systems that go by the names MS-DOS and PC-DOS. If a fixed disk drive is the PC's muscle, DOS is its brains.

Certainly, there are other control programs for IBM Personal Computers, IBM Personal System/2 micros and compatible systems. These range from various versions of UNIX to the venerable Concurrent DOS. For computers equipped with Intel 80286 and 80386 microprocessors, Operating System/2, usually called OS/2, is another option.

Yet, MS-DOS or PC-DOS is far and away the most popular software ever developed for computers designed for the IBM hardware standard (or standards). Millions of copies of LOTUS 1-2-3 are in daily use today, and WordPerfect becomes even more perfect (and popular) with each new release. Neither of these are as universally relied on as the champion of all software programs. If you operate an IBM Personal System/2, PC, PC-AT or compatible, the odds are overwhelming that you share that one piece of software with almost every other user of similar computers.

It's almost equally likely that you have some sort of hard disk drive installed in your computer. Fixed disk drives today cost little more than a floppy disk drive, and most computers are not available without a hard disk. In the IBM line, for example, only the PS/2 Models 25 and 30 can be purchased as a floppy-based computer. Among the compatibles, if you find a computer that doesn't have a hard disk, you are probably looking at a low-end laptop or a system used primarily for home/education applications.

Hard disks and DOS work together in a very synergistic way. DOS is a much more powerful and easy to use tool thanks to the fast access to large amounts of programs and data provided by hard disks. Hard disks themselves would be useless without a disk operating system to supervise their functions. Moreover, mass storage devices actually gain important new features that are built into DOS.

This book will explore the inter-relationship of DOS and hard disks from Version 2.0 through the latest Version 4.0. The emphasis, of course, will be on DOS 3.0 and later. Because DOS 4.0 is such a radical departure in many ways, we'll spend a lot of time discussing what is new. These releases are the versions in most common use today, and include features of most value to hard disk users.

WHY ANOTHER DOS BOOK?

For many months, DOS 4.0 was referred to in the computer press as DOS 3.4. That nomenclature was deceptive, and might have led you to believe that, judging from version number alone, the latest version of DOS is only a small upgrade from DOS 3.3. However, Microsoft had already introduced an operating system called MS-DOS 4.0 which was marketed only in Europe, so the DOS 3.4 designation persisted for some time. Just before it was finally introduced, the decision was made to go with the DOS 4.0 release number.

When comparing the new features of this latest edition of DOS, it will quickly become apparent that the changes rank with some of the most significant that have ever been added to the operating system. The pull-down menus and interactive dialog boxes, while hardly new to the PC community, represent a radical departure for DOS. An "installable file system," similar in concept to that provided with OS/2, allows scrapping the outmoded file allocation table-based file system of DOS that has limited users to 32-megabyte hard disk volumes. These changes alone warrant a new DOS book that helps users get the most from them.

Yet, even if you have no immediate plans to upgrade to DOS 4.0, this book still will be an important tool. Computers have the power to double or triple the productivity of the average worker, while making jobs more rewarding and perhaps a bit more fun. We all know that. What we may not know is *how* all that can be accomplished. As a result, the anyone who is interested in getting the most from a computer spends at least a little time haunting the computer book section of bookstores, looking for some clear, easy-to-understand instruction.

There have been dozens of books written on DOS that purport to do this. Most just repeat information found in the DOS manuals, or which is contained in one of the other books on using DOS. A few provide solid information that helps readers "turbocharge," "supercharge" or otherwise get more power from their operating system. I've written several books in this latter category, and know the validity of that approach from the inside.

There have also been many different books on hard disk management, such as my own "Hard Disk Solutions with Batch File Utilities" (Bantam, 1987). These books also concentrate on advanced techniques and generally have several chapters devoted to DOS.

What has been needed is a book that combines the two approaches to serve as a guide to DOS for hard disk users. The entry-level DOS books spend too much time explaining features, like DISKCOMP, that are really of use only to those who deal extensively with floppy disks. The hard disk user has to wade through all that to winnow out the information that is really of use: how can DOS make recovery from hard disk crashes easier? Isn't there a way I can back up only the files I worked on today without spending a lot of time? How does DOS really handle all these sub-directories?

Advanced DOS books may address some of these topics, but they don't always explain things in a way the beginner or intermediate user can understand readily. This book, on the other hand, should provide you with *all* the information you need to use DOS with your hard disks. Explanations will start at a simple level, and move on quite rapidly to more complex topics. The neophyte won't be left behind, and the advanced user shouldn't become bored. This was an ambitious goal to set for this book, but a challenge I took on eagerly.

IS DOS DEAD YET?

OS/2, at least in its Standard Edition 1.0 form, will have been on the market for nearly a year by the time this book is published. Isn't it foolish, then, to publish a DOS book in what may be the twilight months of the operating system?

OS/2-bashing was popular when the new operating system was first introduced. Most critics either didn't understand OS/2, or latched onto obvious "defects" such as its $325 price-tag, mammoth memory requirements and lack of applications. Even so, OS/2 is destined to become important in the future, unless it falls completely flat, as did TopView. However, the true usefulness of OS/2 may not come until the 25 megahertz, 80386-based $1500 desktop systems with 8 megabytes of memory that also lie ahead of us arrive.

Next year's computer won't process this year's workload. While the future may be fun to think about, most of us will handle today's challenges by finding new ways to wring the last bit of performance out of the hardware and software we have. So, DOS will remain the dominant operating system for several more years, at least. The reasons for this are readily apparent.

★ As mentioned earlier, DOS 4.0 includes some important new capabilities that will serve to extend the useful life of DOS, particularly for hard disk users. DOS has long been limited to a maximum partition size of 32 megabytes for a hard disk. This limitation was carried over to OS/2 for the initial versions, since OS/2 retains the same file allocation table (FAT) file system of DOS.

Both OS/2 and DOS 4.0 feature installable file systems (IFS), which, like installable device drivers, allow the user to replace a component of the operating system with a new version. New file systems can allow much larger hard disk volumes. For users with large amounts of storage who prefer to access larger disk drives rather than multiple logical drives, DOS 4.0 has some clear advantages.

The new user interface of DOS 4.0 should help allay the fears many have of approaching the operating system for the first time. Given the choice of sticking with an easier-to-use DOS or learning a whole new operating system (OS/2, even with the graphical Presentation Manager interface), a large number of users will elect to stick with DOS.

★ Applications for OS/2 still lag far behind DOS. You may not be able to get the software you want for OS/2 for some time yet. You may already *own* the software you want to use for DOS and want to avoid having to duplicate your investment. Many DOS programs can operate under OS/2's DOS compatibility mode, but only one at a time can be loaded. If you're going to operate in this fashion, why not stick with DOS?

★ Many of the features provided by OS/2 already are available for DOS through add-ons and utility programs. Do you *really* need multitasking? DESQview can provide multitasking of the DOS programs that are already available and, if you have an 80386-based computer, will use that microprocessor's memory management capabilities even better than OS/2 will.

However, multitasking is probably over-rated. Few users actually need to be able to run more than one program at once. If you can name more than two or three such instances, you're probably a computer programmer. Most of us use one foreground application at a time. We might want to be able to telecommunicate in the background, so that files can be transmitted or electronic mail accessed. Or, it might be convenient to print long documents in the background while doing something else. In rare instances, a spreadsheet might take so long to recalculate that it might be useful to go do something else in the mean time.

If those are the extent of your multitasking requirements, you are probably better off with DOS. Background communications programs and print spoolers abound that will let you set these tasks to work behind the scenes. Complex spreadsheets can benefit from a processor speed-up kit or math co-processor chip.

What most really have in mind when they drool over multitasking operating systems is the ability to go from the word processing document they are working on to a spreadsheet to check some figures. Perhaps they want to copy part of the spreadsheet and paste the information into the WP document. In any of these cases, the original application stops when the user jumps to a second for a moment or two. There is little need for any processing to take place while the user's attention is elsewhere.

Do you have your heart set on popping back and forth between applications in different windows? DESQview or Microsoft Windows can do just that. If you have a computer compatible with OS/2 anyway it is likely to be fast enough to operate any of a half-dozen different multi-tasking/windowing/applications-switching programs efficiently. If you end up with Microsoft Windows, you'll learn an interface that's almost identical to OS/2's Presentation Manager.

★ Some seven million or more computer users have systems based on the Intel 8088 or 8086 microprocessors. IBM continues to sell such computers in its PS/2 Models 25 and 30. These systems *can't* use OS/2, without a system board upgrade, or an add-on card of some type. Either option can cost up to $1000. If you're one of these folks, you'll be *very* interested in ways to get more out of your computer with good old DOS.

It would be foolish to insist that OS/2 won't play a major role in the future. However, most of us are living in the present. If you have this book, you have a considerable head start on the next two years or so—or beyond—when DOS will continue to perform reliably and effectively for millions of PC users.

WHY LEARNING DOS IS IMPORTANT

DOS is one of the oldest and most highly refined packages on the market, having been developed even *before* the IBM PC itself. DOS has to rank the best-supported software for the PC, as it is licensed and sold in various forms by the giants of the industry, including Microsoft, IBM, Tandy, Compaq, NCR and dozens of others. It is the only operating system these vendors have ever given their full support to for their personal computers.

If that isn't enough to insure continued long life for DOS as an operating system, it also may be the number one software bargain this side of the public domain. At $120—or less—per copy, DOS costs half to a third as much as most other programs of comparable complexity.

So, nearly every user of a PC will need to learn how to work with DOS. OS/2 aside for the moment, you may find islands of UNIX-like operating systems in some user environments where XENIX or AIX or UNIX V/386 allow using software originally written for larger multiuser systems. Digital Research Corporation's Concurrent DOS is popular among users looking for single-user multitasking. There are special operating systems called "control programs" for the latest generation of computers based on the Intel 80386 microprocessor chip. You may even find some users who interface only with a "shell" that insulates them from the operating system, such as Microsoft Windows. Large organizations may have written shells or menu systems of their own, particularly for networked systems. However, users in these environments are a distinct minority.

The rest of us need DOS on a daily basis, to manage files of information for ourselves and our applications software programs, such as word processors, speadsheets, or database managers. We use DOS to communicate with devices like the screen, printers and modems. Even if we spend the entire working day running a single application, DOS is there supervising and managing the operation of the computer. And should we need to do some housekeeping task, such as formatting a disk or copying a file, DOS will be the tool we rely on.

Unfortunately, many PC users know little about the software they use most. That is entirely understandable: DOS was written to be easy to use, but not necessarily to be easy to learn *how* to use. This book will make that job a little easier.

The effort on your part will be well worth it. Understanding how to use DOS will enable you to work better and more efficiently. You'll be able to install new software more easily, manage your hard disk, organize and back up your files more efficiently. Should a problem arise, a basic understanding of how different DOS commands function will let you troubleshoot the difficulty and avoid hours of headaches.

So, DOS is the operating system of the future, as well as the past, for most PC users. It's not too late to learn more about the latest commands of DOS 4.0 and beyond, and pick up some tricks that will let you work better, smarter, and more efficiently with your computer.

WHO CAN USE THIS BOOK

Those of you who have DOS 4.0 can benefit a great deal from this book. IBM, in its wisdom, has made the DOS Command Reference manual an optional $30 item. The supplied manuals will help you get started with the new DOS, especially considering the new, friendlier aspects of the operating system, such as the SELECT utility and the shell. However, as usual, a lot of information that you need to know is not presented clearly, buried deep within the manual, or relegated to the Command Reference.

For example, the casual reader might not deduce that, should they take advantage of DOS 4.0's much-touted ability to format disk partitions larger than 32 megabytes, they'll be unable to access that disk under earlier versions of DOS or with OS/2. Nor are they told in the accompanying documentation tidbits like FDISK's inability to partition a hard disk to exactly 32 megabytes—you must choose either 33 or 31 megabytes. While this information should be common knowledge by the time this book is published, neophytes who don't follow the leading PC publications will be at a disadvantage.

They'll find this book to be a helpful guide to DOS 4.0, providing a lot of the information IBM left out. This volume is particularly well-suited for those who are just learning DOS in any version, and who have been totally confused by the DOS manual supplied with their computer. Here, we'll explain some of the theories behind personal computers and operating systems in clear terms that even the beginner can understand. The depth of information is such that even old hands should find a lot of new, useful information.

Unlike the "alphabetical" command listings of some DOS guides, this book moves in a logical fashion from simple commands to the more complex. You won't learn about TREE until you understand directory structures and other aspects of hard disks.

Advanced users will find discussions of even the most esoteric, and little understood, commands. You may not *need* to know how to use DEBUG or EDLIN to work with DOS, but you will find that information here if you want it.

HOW TO USE THIS BOOK

Because of the tutorial approach taken, beginners are best advised to read the book from beginning to end, so that a solid foundation can be laid before complex topics are discussed. More knowledgeable readers can scan the table of contents or index to find the information they need quickly. This book should serve well both as a teaching tool and as a reference guide.

Ideally, you should read a chapter at a time, and then sit down with your computer and try out the new commands that you learn. You'll find this the easiest way not only to absorb information about DOS, but to retain it and put it to work for you.

The only exception to this rule is for DOS 4.0 users. We've put the chapter on installing DOS 4.0 on your hard disk in Chapter 7. We're assuming that all readers, whether you have DOS 3.x or

DOS 4.0 already have DOS installed on their hard disk, or will wish to read the background information in the first six chapters before they do install DOS on their disk. Since installing DOS 3.x is fairly simple to do, but difficult to understand without some background, putting the explanation on formatting and so forth a few score pages into the book seems like the best idea. At that point, you'll understand DOS better and will be better equipped to know what options you want when you install it.

DOS 4.0, on the other hand, is more complex to install but a bit easier to understand, because of the SELECT program. Therefore, it might well be feasible for a fairly new DOS user to go ahead and use SELECT to install the operating system even before completing the early chapters of the book. You DOS 4.0 users, then, might wish to skip ahead to Chapter 7 in order to get up and running quickly. Those with earlier versions of DOS who don't already have the operating system installed are better off reading the explanations in the initial six chapters first. You'll be more confident when you do get around to installing DOS on your hard disk.

VARIOUS DOS VERSIONS

As mentioned, this book will concentrate on the very latest versions of DOS, Version 3.3 and Version 4.0. For the most part, we'll assume that you have one of these. The descriptions of command syntax will also deal primarily with DOS 3.3 or DOS 4.0. In some instances where the differences are great, the commands as they worked under DOS 3.2 and earlier will also be described. The FDISK utility, for example, functions much differently under DOS 3.2, DOS 3.3 and DOS 4.0, so all three modes will be described.

In most other cases, the differences between command versions are small. Most of the DOS enhancements over the years have come as entirely new commands. So, if you find that the XCOPY command described in this book doesn't work at all, it may be because you have DOS 3.1 or earlier. Appendix B includes a DOS command guide that lists the version number when each command was introduced. You may use that as a guideline to which commands will work for you.

The alternative would be to present a tedious discussion of all the different DOS differences when presenting each command in the main body of the text. Instead, we'll point out only the differences likely to be of importance. DOS 1.1 and earlier versions, for example, will hardly be discussed at all.

In fact, we hope that this text will encourage you to go out and purchase the latest version of DOS so that you can benefit from some of the new features and capabilities. At $150 or less, depending on which version you buy and whether purchase it outright or pay only for the upgrade, DOS has to represent one of the best bargains on the software market.

SUMMARY

Whether you're using DOS 4.0 or an earlier version, you should find this book to be the first complete guide to using PC-DOS or MS-DOS with a hard disk. Everything from basics of computer systems to summaries of commands and syntax will be presented. Along the way you'll learn a wealth of tricks and techniques that will help you get the most from your computer and its most important software package.

PART

1

THE
BASICS

CHAPTER

The Personal Computer

INTRODUCTION

Many of us could care less about what's inside a personal computer, as long as it doesn't emit smoke or require feeding. The PC was one of the first tools of the modern age that is only used to a tiny fraction of its capabilities by the end-user. A computer can be programmed to do a wide variety of things. Yet, most of us aren't interested in programming at all. We want only to be able to carry out the tasks we are interested in—*applications*—and use a limited set of features possible on our computer. If sophisticated word processing capabilities are our main application, we aren't particularly interested that the exact same computer can also be used as a computer-assisted drafting tool, or as a window into a vast database of information.

This understandable orientation towards applications rather than hardware means that most of us know less about how a computer works than a dog knows how dogfood gets into cans. Yet, unlike dogs, humans have curiosity about how things work and the creativity to apply that knowledge in new ways. For that reason, this chapter has been included to tell you more than you might have known about the personal computer. The explana-

3

tions here will be brief and simple to understand, and will form a foundation for the information that follows. If your interest in hardware is nil, feel free to skim over the parts that don't catch your attention.

WHERE DID THE PC COME FROM?

Machines that perform calculations with numbers have been around for thousands of years. Just as you learned in high school that a lever is a simple mechanical machine, you might also have read that devices such as the abacus are simple computing machines.

Most trace the modern computer back only as far as Charles Babbage, a nineteenth-century British mathematician who was probably the father of "vaporware." Working models of his "difference" and "analytical" engines were never built. It wasn't until Herman Hollerith, an American engineer and inventor, conceived of the idea of using punched cards to store statistical information that computer science was really put into practice. It took the needs—and resources—of government to put these concepts to work, first for the census and eventually for military applications.

By the 1950s, computers had begun to be used for general-purpose business functions. In the 1960s, computers began to follow a course that many had not anticipated—distributed processing—which would lead to the personal computer as we know it.

Early computers, after all, were expensive, and required a great deal of maintenance as well as highly skilled operators. It made sense, then, to envision ever-larger computers with massive resources. Such computers would serve as central storehouses of information that could be accessed, in turn, by huge numbers of users. The logical conclusion of such a course was a single, worldwide computer of monolithic architecture and power. Science fiction novels of the 1950s and 1960s often featured such huge electronic brains.

Then something funny happened. People noticed that not every user needed access to every piece of information. In fact, most in business dealt with quite limited databases. They might want to look up invoice information on their own company, or access profiles of current customers' buying habits. Only rarely might someone in Wichita need to know, say, the current state of the olive crop in Spain. What *was* required in Kansas was fast access to the information that was relevant. And mammoth computer systems didn't lend themselves to efficiently sharing among thousands, or even hundreds, of users.

In fact, many computers didn't share their time at all. Programs were frequently run in *batch* mode. If you wanted to perform a task, you sent down a request to the computer system (this might be in the form of a stack of punched cards); there your job would wait in the queue until it was your turn.

Once a user saw how computers could process information efficiently, such waits became intolerable. Soon, people were demanding computers of their own. The first minicomputers were developed to meet this need for computing at a departmental or even an individual level. Science and engineering applications were driving forces behind the development of minicomputers. These users not only had heavy number-crunching requirements, but frequently could not proceed to the next phase of an experiment until the data from the last had been reduced and analyzed.

Even as minicomputers proliferated, the cost of processors remained high enough to make it hard for some users to justify.

By the mid-1970s, the transistor had begun to be replaced by integrated circuit chips, which incorporated thousands of transistor-like devices on a single wafer of impure silicon. The computers that once filled half a room could now be built of a size that would fit on a desktop. Just as importantly, the cost of the components needed to build a computer was slashed. Previous computer systems were designed in corporate labs by teams of engineers. Now PCs could be built in a garage workshop by anyone with the electronics savvy of the average ham radio operator—and many of them were. The first PCs were hobby computers built from scratch or from kits. Next came "turnkey" home computers that anyone could buy and use. As applications were written for these that made them suitable for business, these early Apple, Radio Shack, and Commodore systems found their way into organizations of all sizes. Often, microcomputers had to be put to work without the knowledge or consent of a large corporation's EDP staff.

It took the entry of IBM into the PC market in 1981 to fully legitimize the desktop computer in corporations, and introduce the term *personal computer* to the lexicon. A whole new industry today has developed around a tool that didn't even exist much more than a decade ago.

HOW DOES A PC WORK?

A microcomputer such as the IBM PC, PS/2, and compatibles is built around an integrated circuit chip called a *microprocessor*. This chip determines, to a large extent, what specific software the computer can run and how that software is handled. The first IBM-type PCs used the Intel 8088 microprocessor. That chip is found in IBM PCs, PC/XTs, PC Convertibles, and many "clone" PCs. The so-called "turbo" PCs may use a variation, the 8088–2, which can be operated at a higher speed. More recently, we've seen PCs, such as the IBM Personal System/2 Model 30 and Model 25, that use yet another variation, the Intel 8086 chip. More advanced systems use the 80286 or 80386 microprocessor. In the IBM line, for example, the Model 30 286, Model 50, Model 50Z and Model 60 use the 80286 (as did the PC/AT), while the Models 70 and 80 use the 80386 microprocessor.

The microprocessor contains individual memory locations called *registers*, and a set of built-in instructions—the *instruction set*—that can be accessed by the external programming. Depending on the values loaded into various registers, the chip will carry out one or more operations using the data located in other registers. For example, the microprocessor may be told to add the value in one register to that in another. The next step of the instructions may ask the microprocessor to compare the value now in that second register and do something if it is one value, or something else if it is not. The values that are moved into and out of registers are called *data*, while the instructions that tell the microprocessor what to do next are called the *program*.

BINARY NUMBERS AND MICROPROCESSORS

The information stored in these registers is manipulated in *binary* form. Binary is the base-two number system you probably studied in school and then immediately forgot. You won't need to relearn it to understand DOS. Most introductory books on computers feature at least a brief recap of binary arithmetic, so you can skip this section if you wish.

In computer systems, numbers are represented by zeros and ones, with each 1 representing a power of 2:

128	64	32	16	8	4	2	1
1	1	1	1	1	1	1	1

In this example, the number 11111111 (binary) represents a number with one in 2^0's place (a value of 1 decimal), one in 2^1's place (2 decimal), one in 2^2's place (4 decimal), etc. If you add these all together, you get 255, which is the largest value that can be represented by an eight-digit binary number.

These other examples should clarify further how the binary number system works:

```
00000001 binary equals 1 decimal
00000010 binary equals 2 decimal
00000011 binary equals 3 decimal
00000100 binary equals 4 decimal
```

Each of these examples uses leading zeros to "pad out" the numbers to an even eight digits. That's simply to illustrate that binary numbers as manipulated by computers usually consist of eight digits, which can only be either 1's or 0's. The computer, unlike humans, doesn't see the value of 2 (decimal) as 10 binary. Each of the memory bits that represent a number *must* be either 0 or 1, so 10 must be 00000010, and not simply 10.

As promised, you don't need binary arithmetic to use DOS, just as you don't need to understand the intricacies of electronic fuel injection to be able to drive a car. Yet, a basic understanding provides some insights into how computers work.

The first microcomputers had microprocessors that accepted data eight binary digits (*bits*) at one time. Each register had eight places to store 1's and 0's, so any combination of 1's and 0's from 00000000 to 11111111 could be handled in parallel. Such a microprocessor is said to have an *8–bit data path*, because all eight bits of information can move over separate, parallel electrical paths (rather than being loaded in single-file or *serial* fashion) within the chip.

The limitations of 8–bit microprocessors soon became apparent. The amount of information that can be handled by the computer is severely restricted by an 8-bit data path. If a certain *byte* (eight bits) of information needs to be loaded into a register, the microprocessor needs to know where to find it. In many cases, that byte must come from storage outside the microprocessor itself, since the number of memory locations within the microprocessor is limited.

Therefore, most of the data must be supplied from outside the microprocessor itself, generally from a temporary storehouse constructed of other integrated circuits and called *memory*.

To access data stored in memory, the program must first load into another set of registers the memory address of the data. As noted, the largest number that can be represented by eight bits is 11111111 binary, or 255 decimal. So, a single byte can keep track only of 256 different memory locations. Two bytes allow a 16–digit binary number and tracking 1111111111111111 (65,535 decimal) memory locations. This is the reason why the 8–bit systems of early computers were limited to 64K of memory.

However, the impact of an 8–bit microprocessor on performance goes beyond this memory limitation. The speed of a computer system is determined in part by how many operations it can perform each second. With an 8-bit microprocessor, much of the available computing time is eaten up simply by requesting and accessing data from memory.

Four operations are required simply to access a single byte of information from memory: two cycles for the microprocessor to provide memory with the location of the information required, and two to retrieve the information. Other operations within the microprocessor that involve numbers larger than 255 also require twice as many cycles as would be necessary if the chip had a data path wider than 8 bits.

The IBM PC improved on things by providing a 16–bit path internally for handling data. The first IBM PCs *could* have used the Intel 8086 microprocessor, which is the true 16–bit chip used today in the PS/2 Models 25 and 30 and other computers. However, in 1981, 16–bit memory was expensive, and the circuitry to support it was complex and costly to produce. So, a compromise was made: The Intel 8088 microprocessor was used in the IBM PC instead. This chip has only an 8–bit external data path for loading information from memory. Cheaper 8–bit memory chips could be used, along with simpler supporting hardware. The first IBM PC took just as long to access memory as the earlier 8–bit chips. Only as the data was moved around internally could the benefits of the 16–bit microprocessor be realized.

Even so, the improvements were significant. For example, the 8088 chip was designed to manage a full megabyte of memory. This was accomplished by providing a 20–digit binary number to allocate individual memory locations, instead of the 16–bit number used with earlier computers. You'll recall that the largest number that can be represented in 16 binary digits (1111111111111111) is 65,535. A 20–digit number (11111111111111111111) can count up to 1,048,475 different memory locations, or a full megabyte.

You might wonder how the microprocessor can efficiently keep track of 20-digit numbers, since its registers are only 16 bits wide. In practice, memory is divided into segments, and the microprocessor keeps track of segment number and the relative memory location within that segment. This may be clumsy, but it worked, and the new memory capabilities made possible a revolution in personal computing. As a bonus, the 8088 microprocessor operated faster than earlier 8–bit microprocessors from the same family, like the Intel 8085.

You may be interested to know that more than the width of the data path affects how fast your computer operates. An 8/16–bit computer based on an 8088 chip could theoretically operate faster than a 16/16–bit system. For example, the "clock speed" at which the chip is operated directly affects the speed at which calculations are made. The original IBM PC and compatibles operated at a speed, measured in megacycles per second or *megahertz*, of 4.77 MHz. The original PC/AT operated at 6 MHz.

Yet, we soon had "turbo" PCs that were designed to operate with chips like the 8088–2 at speeds as fast as 10 MHz. You can see that such a computer could actually outperform a 6 MHz PC/AT under the right conditions. Today, 80386–based systems commonly operate at 16 to 25 MHz speeds. The speed-demon IBM PS/2 Model 70 includes a version that functions at an incredible 25 MHz. Intel has already promised chips capable of 33 MHz and beyond.

The full performance potential of the PC became a reality a few years later, when computers based on the 80286 chip were introduced. Like the 8086 microprocessor, the 80286 chip offers true 16/16–bit internal/data paths. However, the 80286 microprocessor has two advantages over the earlier product. It can be operated much faster, at 10 to 16 MHz (some have even pushed this to 20 MHz). It also has a "protected memory" mode that allows reserving specific portions of memory for different applications, so they can be run simultaneously.

DOS only takes advantage of the first feature, in computers designed for faster operation with the 80286 chip. Multitasking can't be done with DOS in its unmodified form, even given the capabilities of the newer microprocessor. That's because DOS lacks some important capabilities, and was generally designed to assume that it had access to all the resources of the computer, including memory, at any given time.

DOS performs much the same in computers that boast the latest Intel 80386 microprocessor, which has a full 32/32 data path. DOS runs much faster at these computers' higher clock speeds, but gains no new capabilities.

The more efficient data path is nothing to discount. For example, for the 80286 chip, accessing memory requires only two clock cycles: one cycle for memory to accept the location of the information to be accessed, and a second for it to provide the microprocessor with the contents of that location.

Ideally, memory should be able to supply the information to the microprocessor within this minimum number of clock cycles. A 20 MHz 80386 chip has a clock cycle of about 50 nanoseconds (billionths of a second); and since two cycles are required to access memory, it can accept data 100 ns after requesting it. Memory that can meet this demand would be rated as 100 ns memory. This is also known as *zero wait states*, because the microprocessor does not have to wait more than the minimum number of cycles for the data. If the memory chip can respond no more quickly than three clock cycles (150 ms for the 20 MHz chip), then it is said to operate with one wait state.

Because zero wait state memory systems are more and more expensive as clock speeds increase, it is common to have at least one wait state in computers with clock speeds of 8 to 10 MHz or more. The PS/2 Models 50 and 60 both operate with one wait state, as does the 16 MHz version of the Model 80. The Model 50Z requires zero wait states.

OTHER HARDWARE COMPONENTS

A computer can have more than one microprocessor. Specialized *coprocessors* can take or *offload* part of the computational load from the main microprocessor. The most common coprocessor is the math chip, such as the 8087 or 80287. Software that involves a great deal of number crunching will run considerably faster on a computer equipped with a math coprocessor. This also demonstrates that *software* is another factor affecting computer speed. If the software is being run on a computer with a more powerful instruction set or with a math coprocessor, the program has to be written to take advantage of those resources.

Other types of coprocessors handle different functions. IBM included a special type of microprocessor called the Intel 82385 cache controller in its PS/2 Model 70–A21 (the 25 MHz 80386–based system). This microprocessor, which is installed on a daughterboard with some supporting circuitry, includes its own memory (64K worth) that happens to be very, very fast—on the order of 30 nanoseconds. Programming in the 82385 determines what data will be stored in the fast cache memory. Ideally, DOS will find information it needs there in the cache without needing to access the hard disk. The more often this happens, the better the system performance.

Among the resources that your software can draw on are various "modes" of the microprocessor chip. The 80286 chip, for example, has both *real* and *protected* modes, mentioned briefly above. Real mode is the familiar mode used by DOS and today's software. One task, such as a program, can be operated at one time, and DOS assumes that it has access to all the memory available in running that task. Protected mode is an additional way of using the microprocessor to allow multiple tasks to operate simultaneously. Each has its own protected area of memory. As noted, DOS generally doesn't have provisions for this sort of operation, although some add-ons and special operating systems, such as Concurrent DOS and DESQview, do provide something along these lines. OS/2, which will be touched on from time to time in this book, is specifically designed to use the protected mode of the 80286 and 80386 chips.

The 80386 adds a "virtual 8086" mode, which neither DOS nor OS/2 takes advantage of. This in effect simulates more than one 8086 chip, each of which can be used independently by different software. Where protected mode divides up the resources of the microprocessor among several separate tasks at one time, virtual 8086 mode makes it seem as if there exists an entire group of microprocessors, each of which can be totally dedicated to the task at hand. A simple way to compare the two modes is to think of protected mode as providing multitasking for one user, while virtual 8086 mode allows multiple *users*. At this writing, there is no operating system or software that takes advantage of the 80386 chip's virtual 8086 mode.

The next generation of microprocessors, the 80486 series, is not expected to be available much before late 1989, and will not see widespread use until the early 1990s. These will be 32–bit microprocessors that are three to four times faster than the 80386 of today, and have improved direct access to memory.

According to Intel, the 80486 will have the equivalent of one million transistors (compared to 275,000 in the 80386), and something called a *virtual 80286 mode*. This will allow the microprocessor to run multiple sessions to an extent not possible with the

80386. For example, multiple copies of DOS could be run—something that even OS/2 can't handle today. Such microprocessors are likely to be put to work for *multi-user* applications rather than for single users.

Computers must consist of more than a microprocessor. The "brains" of the computer must be supplied with information, in the form of programs and data, and some place to store that information when it is not being actively used. As we've seen, one storage place for data is called *memory*. How fast the memory is capable of accepting and supplying data can also affect the speed of a computer.

Main memory consists of sets of chips that reside on the main circuit board of the computer, or on add-on memory cards. This random-access memory (RAM) is usually of the "dynamic" type, which must be electrically "refreshed" many times each second to keep the chip from losing the information that has been stored. Laptops that retain their memory contents even when they are turned "off" actually use a special type of RAM memory with very low power requirements. A trickle of electricity from the laptop's built-in battery is sufficient to preserve memory contents.

True nonvolatile "static" RAM is not widely used in PCs because of its added expense. However, because static RAM can be accessed faster (since there is no need to interrupt access to the memory to provide refreshing signals), this more costly form of memory has found application in some high-speed 80386–based systems.

Because dynamic RAM is volatile, it is generally used to store information temporarily. Programs and important data are transferred to some other medium, such as the hard disk, for permanent storage.

A second type of silicon memory exists: read-only memory, or ROM. Like static RAM, ROM does not require an electrical voltage to retain its contents. However, unlike all forms of RAM, the information in ROM cannot generally be changed by the user. ROMs are usually programmed at the factory, and contain information (usually programs) that rarely, if ever, needs to be altered. When that does become a necessity, the old ROM chip needs to be removed and a new one inserted.

ROM programs include the power-on self-test that the PC performs when the computer is switched on, part of the control program that supervises the computer and, in IBM PCs, and PS/2s, part of the BASIC language. There are several different types of ROM, which differ chiefly in the methods used to program them. Some ROMs can be erased by various means and then reprogrammed, although this is generally beyond the capabilities of the end user. Erasable programmable read-only memory (EPROMs) and electrically erasable programmable read-only memory (EEPROMs) are used in some specialized applications.

Other hardware components of the typical PC include mass storage devices, such as floppy disks, hard disks, CD-ROM drives, optical disk drives, and tape systems. These may be built in or attached through peripheral cards that fit in slots included in the computer. Hard disks in particular will be explained more fully later in this book. Expansion cards can include interfaces for printers, modems, fax machines, terminal emulators, local area networks, or other peripherals.

All these components are integrated through the supervision of the disk operating system.

SOFTWARE

Other than peripherals such as disk drives and printers, the final link in determining the power and speed of your computer is the disk operating system, DOS. The functions of the microprocessor, memory, and the peripherals are supervised by DOS.

A small portion of this operating system is built into the computer on a ROM chip, in the form of the read-only memory/basic input-output system (ROM/BIOS). This has as part of its functions bootstrap instructions that tell the computer what to do when it is first powered on. In addition to performing certain diagnostic tests on the computer, the ROM/BIOS also tells the system to look for DOS, either on the floppy disk drive A: or on the hard disk, drive C:. This process will be covered in more detail later.

For now, all you need to know is that one of the first things a computer does when powered on is to load DOS. From that point on, most functions are controlled and supervised by DOS. Your other software is said to operate "under" DOS. More specifically, DOS is loaded first and then directs loading of your application program. While the program is operating, DOS remains in the background. Tasks such as disk input/output (I/O) are supplied to the software, in most cases, through *calls* to various DOS services.

SUMMARY

In this quick explanation of how computer systems work, we've seen that a control program like DOS is needed to supervise the many complex functions of the computer's hardware and software. This control is needed to make it possible to perform useful work with the computer. In the next chapter, we'll look more closely at what DOS is, and how it helps us use hard disks.

CHAPTER

2

The Basics of PC-DOS/MS-DOS

INTRODUCTION

So far, we've considered the PC only as a collection of components. The microprocessor is at the heart of the system, and does useful work by loading information from memory, performing calculations based on the values found in some of its registers, and directing the results, or *output*, back to memory. That's really all that is needed for a functioning computing machine. Humans could, theoretically, program a computer by manually throwing switches, and obtain results by reading the status of memory registers. In fact, something on that order was done in the early days of microcomputing by those who put together their own machines.

However, few end users today can "speak" machine language. Some system is needed to translate our instructions to a form the computer can understand, and then convert the microprocessor's output to some human-readable format. That is the role of the PC's software.

This chapter will explain just how software interacts with the hardware through an intermediary, the disk operating system.

INTRODUCING DOS

Each software program that we run could easily be stuctured to communicate directly with all the components of your PC, from the microprocessor itself to the CRT screen, keyboard, printer, and hard disk. That would, however, be an extraordinary waste of human and computer resources. Each time a programmer began developing software for a personal computer it would be necessary for that programmer to develop routines to handle common chores, such as input/output to the disk, writing to the screen, etc. Even if a programmer actually developed such a code only once, and then re-used it over and over within a program, or even among several programs, there would be a great deal of duplication of effort, since each programmer in turn would be reinventing the wheel. The programs themselves would be longer than necessary, since many of them would incorporate routines that duplicated that found in other programs.

Another problem exists. As you know, hardware configurations of PCs can vary, even among those conforming to the IBM standards. One computer may be equipped with an EGA color monitor, 640K of memory, and a 20-megabyte hard disk. Another may have a VGA monitor, 3 megabytes of memory, and a 44-megabyte drive. Some of these differences can be accommodated by the computer's hardware. PCs do, in fact, have provisions in ROM for handling various types of hard disk configurations, or *geometries*. However, there are other, much more subtle differences. Software that addresses different types of hardware must allow for these complex variations among equipment configurations.

Such situations can be easily avoided. A program interface can be written to fit between the hardware and the software applications. When a program wants to fetch information from the hard disk, it needn't interrogate the disk to see how it happens to store information, or how that information is cataloged. Instead, the request for data can be sent to the software supervisor, which accesses the hard disk and forwards the information—or perhaps an explanation of why it couldn't be found—back to the program. All the software a user might have can use this method, allowing the common software interface to replace their own program modules.

There are several advantages to this scheme over and above simplifying software applications. The supervising program can be changed, if necessary, by the manufacturer of the computer to compensate for significant differences in hardware. The commands received from the applications programs remain the same. The only thing that needs to change is how the interface program puts them to work with a specific hardware configuration.

For example, a computer may use a monochrome display adapter (MDA), color/graphics adapter (CGA), enhanced graphics adapter (EGA), or professional graphics adapter (PGA) such as commonly found in IBM PCs, PC/ATs, and compatibles. Or a computer may use the multicolor graphics array (MCGA) in the PS/2 Models 30 and 25, the video graphics array (VGA) introduced first for the PS/2 Models 50, 60 and 80, or even the ultra-high resolution 8514/A display adapter board. This list shows that IBM surely must love standards, because it created seven of them just for its desktop computers. Other graphics standards, including the Hercules monochrome graphics guidelines, exist for PCs.

All these can easily be accommodated by a standard program interface, either through built-in provisions or by means of add-on modules called *drivers*. Again, the software application doesn't need to concern itself with all the details of displaying text or graphics on the screen if it uses the *services* provided by the supervising program.

As you have guessed, this program is called the disk operating system, or simply DOS, even though its functions go far beyond simply supervising the disk drives. Most of the functions of the programs you run are, in fact, handled by DOS.

Some software bypasses DOS and does access the hardware directly. For example, DOS is notoriously slow in writing to the screen. When all PCs were sluggish 4.77–MHz 8088–based models, it was tempting to write to the screen using routines in the BIOS, rather than those provided by DOS. However, the programmer risked having software fail to run on near-compatible computers. A few years ago, such "ill-behaved" programs, such as Flight Simulator, were often used to test the compatibility of clone computers.

Today, most PCs run so much faster that it is not as necessary to bypass DOS as before. Moreover, the ROM-BIOS found in almost all compatible computers closely duplicates the functions of the code of the IBM BIOS. So, compatibility problems have been greatly reduced.

THE BIRTH OF MS-DOS/PC-DOS

Microcomputer disk operating systems predate the IBM PC by almost a decade. The early CP/M operating systems were developed by Digital Research, Inc. for 8–bit computers based on the Intel 8080 family of microprocessors. Although other DOSs came along for systems like the Radio Shack Model I and Apple II, CP/M was the most widely used control program for microcomputers. It seemed logical, then, to adapt CP/M to the 16–bit 8086 microprocessor, which, after all, was a member of the same family and upwardly compatible in many ways. Such systems were already being developed for business computers that used what was known as the *S-100 bus*. A bus is simply a way of standardizing a computer system's control lines so they can be accessed by add-on hardware, such as peripheral cards.

However, CP/M-86 didn't arrive soon enough to suit Tim Paterson, a hardware engineer and co-owner of Seattle Computer Products. Paterson began developing an operating system called 86–DOS that was designed to look like CP/M to the end user, although the program code itself was entirely different. He used a similar structure and *calling conventions*, which are the rules programmers use governing the interface with the hardware. Even so, Paterson managed to overcome some of the serious technical limitations of CP/M.

Microsoft Corporation, already well established in the industry because of its *de facto* standard BASIC, had been approached by IBM to provide the operating system for its upcoming personal computer. The company licensed Paterson's DOS, which was renamed PC-DOS and introduced in 1981 along with the first PCs.

Since that time, DOS has undergone eight significant revisions, generally in connection with the introduction of new hardware. The most significant was the unveiling of DOS 2.0 in March, 1983. This was the first release of DOS to support hard disks, and the change that really launched the growth of the personal computer in business.

The revisions have involved both IBM and Microsoft. DOS 3.3 was the first upgrade prepared entirely in-house by IBM. Microsoft later incorporated IBM's changes into its own 3.3 release of the operating system. The most recent release, DOS 4.0, added only a few new features; but as we will see, the upgrade is an interesting one.

A quick look at the DOS versions will show how the system has evolved through the years:

Release	Date	Hardware Product
1.0	08/81	IBM PC
1.1	05/82	Double-sided drives
2.0	03/83	IBM PC/XT, hard disks
2.1	10/83	PCjr, half-height drives
3.0	08/84	PC/AT, 1.2-megabyte drive
3.1	03/85	IBM PC Network
3.2	12/85	PC Convertible, 3.5–inch drive
3.3	04/87	PS/2, 1.44-megabyte drive
4.0	07/88	New interface, 32M barrier removed

While this growth has paralleled the maturization of the hardware, each new release of DOS also provided new enhancements that have made software more functional. Until DOS 3.3, each version of the operating system was prepared by Microsoft, which licensed the software to IBM. IBM sometimes made its own modifications to the operating system, but in general MS-DOS and PC-DOS have been very similar and compatible.

DOS 3.3, which heralded the "next generation" Personal System/2 computers, was prepared by IBM and the changes licensed back to Microsoft. There was a gap between the time IBM's version was introduced and the appearance of Microsoft MS-DOS 3.3, but again the versions were very similar.

The same course was taken by IBM for DOS 4.0, which was developed in-house and then turned over to Microsoft, who marketed it to its OEM customers. Let's quickly review the changes between the four major releases of DOS. Some of the terminology in these summaries may not mean much to you now, but all of them will be covered in detail later in this book.

Version 1.0 to Version 2.0

The original DOS 1.0 was on the market only about nine months. However, keep in mind that those were also the early days of the IBM PC; the number of *users* of the disk operating system at that time could be measured in thousands. Version 1.1 is actually the release that first saw widespread use. It added the capability of using double-sided drives. Instead of a paltry 160K of disk space, each disk was given the capability of storing 320K of information on 40–track, eight-sector disks.

Less than two years after the introduction of the IBM PC, it was being considered as a serious business computer. In March, 1983, IBM introduced the IBM PC/XT, which was equipped with a 10–megabyte hard disk drive. DOS 2.0 was introduced at the same time with some features designed to make use of a hard disk more efficient. Other new features were also provided. (These will all be discussed later in the book. For now, some of them may not mean much to you.) The new features added for DOS 2.0 included:

★Provision for a special file of commands that DOS will read each time it starts up. This file, called CONFIG.SYS, is different from the AUTOEXEC.BAT file. It allows defining special *drivers* for peripherals such as RAM disks, the keyboard, or screen.

★Enhancement of the operating system to support one or more fixed disk drives, which can be used to start up or "boot" the system. The fixed drives can be divided into more than one operating system, so one may be partitioned for PC-DOS, and another for Concurrent DOS or XENIX.

★Increased potential disk capacity, thanks to the ability to use nine–sector 5.25–inch disks, rather than the eight–sector formatting used previously. Instead of 320K, floppy disks could now be formatted to hold 360K of information.

★Tree-structured directories, allowing subdirectories within any given directory or subdirectory. This feature allows dividing up a disk into separate logical areas and grouping programs or data in convenient order.

★Disk volume labels—the ability to name disks, but only during FORMAT (in version 2.0 of DOS), or through the use of a special utility program not included with DOS.

★Extended keyboard and screen control. Starting with DOS 2.0, the user is able to redefine keys from DOS, control the color of the screen, and move the cursor with special character sequences.

★Redirection of input and output. DOS may cause a program to receive its input from a source other than the keyboard, such as a file, or to send its output to a destination other than the screen, e.g, another file. In between, you may use "filters" which can sort or otherwise manipulate the data.

★New commands, such as CLS (clear screen), ASSIGN (reassign disk drive letters—e.g., change drive A: into drive B:), PATH (used with tree-structured directories), and PROMPT (change the system prompt).

★Enhancement of previous DOS 1.1 commands. CHKDSK, DIR, ERASE, and FORMAT were among the commands with new features.

Enhancements from DOS 2.0 to DOS 3.3

When the second-generation PC/AT was introduced in August,

1984, a new generation DOS, version 3.0, was unveiled. At the same time, version 3.1 was announced for use with the IBM PC Network. A new whole number release usually indicates a major upgrade, and in the case of 3.0, there were many new features beyond those necessary to provide for the 1.2-megabyte disk drives in the PC/AT. These included:

★ATTRIB, which marks files as read-only.

★LABEL, used to add, change, or delete a volume label.

★SELECT, enabling the user to choose the keyboard layout and date and time format he or she wants to use.

★COUNTRY, which can be included in the CONFIG.SYS file to "permanently" install a date and time format.

★Virtual disks or "RAM" disks that can be automatically installed when DOS is booted. Previous versions of DOS also allowed RAM disks, but the user had to provide the software from another source, such as the vendor of a multifunction or memory board. Starting with DOS 3.0, the VDISK.SYS device driver was supplied, with the capability of installing such disks automatically with statements in CONFIG.SYS.

★The capability of specifying the maximum number of drives that can be accessed, using the LASTDRIVE statement in the CONFIG.SYS file.

★Provisions for 1.2-megabyte 5.25 –inch high capacity disks. DOS 3.2 and 3.3 added 720K, and 1.44-megabyte 3.5–inch disks, respectively, on computers equipped with those drives and the proper controller.

★Enhanced commands to support the higher capacity disk drives. FORMAT, BACKUP, RESTORE, DISKCOMP, and

DISKCOPY all allow for the 1.2-megabyte drives and, later, 3.5–inch drives.

★DATE, now supporting additional date formats.

★In DOS 3.2, the XCOPY command to allow new copying features as well as the DRIVER.SYS device driver, which allows users to create an alternate identifier for a drive.

★Also in DOS 3.2, the APPEND command, which allows users to specify path searches for all types of files, not just system files ending in .EXE, .COM, and .BAT extensions.

★In DOS 3.3, features like CALL, which allows batch files to call other batch files, and @, which prevents a command (for example, one in a batch file) from being echoed to the screen.

Changes Introduced in DOS 4.0

DOS SHELL   DOS 4.0 offers an optional menu-oriented interface that can be loaded when you boot the computer, or called from the command line with the DOSSHELL command. The pull-down menus can be manipulated by using the keyboard or a mouse to run programs and perform various DOS functions. HELP screens, a feature of OS/2 but absent from DOS until this version, have also been added.

File management has been made simpler, allowing users to mark files and copy, move, or delete them quickly. The shell allows you to change the colors DOS uses to present it, and lets you load program names into the main menu for faster access.

Expanded Memory   DOS 4.0 is now furnished with new device drivers to allow extended memory to be used as expanded memory. XMAEM.SYS is intended for the IBM PS/2 Models 70 and 80; XMA2EMS.SYS can be used with other computers.

Installable File System   The IFS capability allows replacing the file allocation table system with others that support new types of devices, including media with volumes larger than 32 megabytes.

TSR Programs The proliferation of memory resident utilities (the so-called "terminate-and-stay-resident" or TSR programs) has been recognized by DOS. These previously had to be loaded from the DOS command line, either manually or through a batch file like AUTOEXEC.BAT. Now, DOS will look for the INSTALL command in the CONFIG.SYS file to load specified programs automatically on boot-up. The advantage? CONFIG.SYS can't be accidentally or deliberately interrupted by the user (like AUTOEXEC.BAT can), so the person configuring the system is assured that the desired TSRs are loaded.

MEM.EXE This new DOS external command augments CHKDSK. Unlike CHKDSK, MEM reports on extended and expanded memory as well as conventional memory, and lists the names of the programs loaded into memory.

SWITCHES Command A new SWITCHES command for the CONFIG.SYS file prevents your computer from using its extended keyboard functions (if available), providing extra compatibility with older software applications.

ANSI.SYS Parameters ANSI.SYS now has three new parameters. The /X parameter lets you redefine the "extra" keys provided with extended keyboards such as those found on later PC/ATs and the PS/2 line. The /L parameter lets you over-ride your software and retain the greater number of screen rows that MODE can now set for display with EGA and VGA graphics adapters. The /K parameter is another way to turn off the extended keyboard functions.

Other Changes APPEND, BACKUP, BUFFERS, CHKDSK, COUNTRY, and a host of other commands have been changed slightly. There are many more enhancements like these to DOS

4.0 that will be covered later in this book. These are only the highlights.

HOW DOS STARTS UP

By now you are aware that DOS serves as the interface between your hardware and your other software programs. You may be wondering exactly how this operating system shell sets itself up as the supervisor of your system.

When the computer is switched on, some very simple programs located permanently in the ROM-BIOS perform a series of tasks. Some diagnostic programs run, making checks of various system resources such as memory. If all is well, the ROM-BIOS next tries to turn over control to a more complete operating system. It doesn't know what that OS is; all the ROM-BIOS has is a set of instructions that tell it where to look for the next data.

It will first try to find this information on the floppy disk in drive A:. The ROM-BIOS's instructions contain the code that direct the PC to start up the drive's motor and move the read/write head to a predetermined position where, by convention, another start-up program is stored. If there is no disk in drive A:, or if the door to the drive is open (or the mount/demount button is not depressed with 3.5–inch microdisk drives), the ROM-BIOS won't find the program it is looking for. In that case, it will proceed to the next section of its boot-up program, which tells it to activate the read/write head of the first hard disk in the system. If there is no hard disk, or if a non-system disk is loaded in drive A:, the computer will be unable to load DOS. If a non-system disk is loaded in drive A:, the computer will inform you of the error and offer the chance to replace it with a bootable disk. If DOS cannot be found, the system will instead load its one built-in program, Cassette BASIC.

Happily for most readers of this book, DOS will already have been installed. So the ROM-BIOS will direct the read/write head to the first sector of the hard disk and load into memory a short bit of code called a *partition loader*.

A *partition* is any of several discrete sections of the hard disk that can be set aside by DOS. The partition loader tells the computer which of these partitions contains the actual code to boot DOS. The read/write head moves to the first sector of the bootable partition, accesses yet another section of loader code, and proceeds to load the full operating system. Information needed to do this includes the sector size of the hard disk, the number of sectors grouped together in a single *cluster*, the number of *cylinders* (stacks of tracks), and the size of the disk directory and file allocation table. All these will be explained in more detail shortly. For now, you need only keep in mind that, since any of these variables may be changed by modifications to DOS, the system needs to know their current values before it can continue with the boot-up process.

THE DOS SYSTEM FILES

Only three core programs, called *system files*, are needed for DOS to run. Two of these are not generally seen by the end user because DOS makes them "invisible" on the hard disk, and further protects them from accidental erasure. If you ask for a directory of files on your disk, you'll never see these invisible programs, IBMBIO.COM and IBMDOS.COM. (These are the names of the files under PC-DOS; the MS-DOS equivalents for earlier versions of DOS are IO.SYS and MSDOS.SYS.)

A third, called COMMAND.COM (in both versions of DOS), is stored as an ordinary visible file on your hard disk.

The two invisible files, plus two other optional files, CONFIG.SYS and AUTOEXEC.BAT, must be in the root directory of the boot disk. COMMAND.COM may be located somewhere else if you include a SHELL statement in the CONFIG.SYS file telling DOS where to find it. These special files will all be discussed in detail later in this book.

DOS imposes some further restrictions on exactly where the invisible files are located on the disk. IBMBIO.COM must be the first file listed in the root directory. The booting code reads only the first sector of the directory, and interprets only the first 11 bytes. It ignores the directory entry pointing to the first sector of the program. As a result, IBMBIO.COM must always reside starting at the first data sector on the disk, and continue as consecutive sectors. The booting program doesn't contain the necessary logic for jumping around the disk to locate scattered sectors of a file.

These system files vary from one release of DOS to the next, and so are incompatible. It is actually these files that you must replace on your hard disk when you upgrade from one DOS version to another. Most other DOS files must also be replaced, but DOS will kindly let you know that with a WRONG DOS VERSION error message. However, if you try to mix system files on a single hard disk, DOS won't boot at all.

IBMBIO.COM and IO.SYS contain a core of routines that allow the operating system to interface with the PC's hardware. These include codes to handle the clock, CRT, keyboard, printer, and the drive used to boot the operating system.

IBMDOS.COM and MSDOS.SYS contain the application program interface, or API. You'll see the term API used a great deal in the future, particularly in connection with OS/2. The API provides all the key DOS services that are called on by your software. This interface in effect insulates the programmer from the hardware by accepting and providing requests for disk, file, or CRT services.

The user doesn't need to know how to make those requests of the operating system. The third system file, COMMAND.COM, serves as a *command processor*. When you type commands at the keyboard, such as DIR, and press Enter (or Return), the characters you typed are intercepted by COMMAND.COM. The command processor will examine the command line that was typed in, and try to make sense out of it. If the command was:

```
DIR C:
```

COMMAND.COM will recognize that as a valid command sequence and activate the services needed from IBMDOS.COM to move the read/write head of the hard disk to the directory track, read in the information, and display it on the CRT screen.

You may type additional information on the command line, such as /P or /W. COMMAND.COM will see if either is allowed for the

DIR command. In this case, the /P and /W are valid parameters, called *switches*, that tell DOS to display the directory in either a *paged* (24 lines at a time) or *wide* (five columns of file names) mode. Had you typed an invalid parameter, or typed in the name of a file or command that DOS could not locate (say, DRI instead of DIR), DOS would let you know.

To be 100 percent accurate, COMMAND.COM is non-optional only to the extent that DOS must have *some* program in place to serve as the command processor. The user can substitute another program for COMMAND.COM, if desired. There are, in fact, several programs on the market that provide extensions to DOS's command capabilities through a substitute for COM-MAND.COM. However, 99.9 percent of us never use anything other than COMMAND.COM as the operating system shell. A method for changing from COMMAND.COM to another command processor will be explained later in this book.

When you load a program, that program will seem to take over for DOS. However, DOS is still present in the background, accepting requests from your program for services, and handling the myriad tasks of a well-run computer system.

OTHER DOS FILES

Many of the commands that you'll learn about, such as COPY and DIR, are *internal* DOS commands. That is, they are loaded into memory when the system boots up and can be accessed at any time by COMMAND.COM. Other DOS commands are stored in the form of files on your hard disk. FORMAT, for example, is actually a utility program called FORMAT.COM or FORMAT.EXE and must reside on a disk in your system for DOS to use it. Commands like FORMAT are called DOS *external* commands.

We've been talking about files without really defining what they are. A file is a collection of information that DOS treats as a separate logical entity. Physical features are those that exist physically: Your hard disk is a single physical disk drive. A logical feature is one that exists only by agreement or convention. A hard disk drive that has a capacity of 60 megabytes may be divided, or partitioned, into two 30–megabyte drives by DOS. You

still have a single 60M physical drive; however, it now consists of
two 30M logical drives, which have been given the logical drive
designations of, say, C: and D:.

Similarly, your hard disk consists of a mass of information that
really is nothing more than a series of reversals in the direction
of the magnetic poles coated on the disk surface. DOS sets these
aside as tracks and sectors and allocates sets of them as specific
files. We'll get into more detail about how files are stored on the
disk later when some of the nuts and bolts of hard disks are
covered. For now, all you need to know is that files can consist of
either programs or data. Programs are usually *DOS executable*
files. Data may be collections of information, such as the information in your spreadsheet or the text loaded by your word processing program.

Some collections of data also resemble DOS executable
programs in that they contain a list of instructions. However, DOS
cannot carry out those instructions directly. Instead, the instructions are read in, one at a time, by a program that *can* be executed
by DOS. For example, what you might think of as a BASIC
"program" is actually a data file that is interpreted by
BASIC.COM, BASICA.COM, GW-BASIC.EXE, or some version
thereof.

Another data file of this type is the *batch* file. In this case, batch
files consist of lists of instructions that are carried out by the command processor. For example, a batch file might consist of these
lines:

```
DIR A:
DIR B:
DIR C:
```

COMMAND.COM will open the file, read in one line, close the
file, and carry out the command. Then the batch file will be opened
again, the next line read, and that command carried out. This particular example would cause DOS to display directories of drives
A: through C: (if available).

You can activate a batch file directly from DOS, but the instructions in the file don't directly call DOS services, as is the case with an executable file. However, because batch files are interpreted by the DOS system, they are grouped along with executable files as *system* files. We'll learn more about these shortly.

SUMMARY

This chapter provided an introduction to the basics of DOS. We looked at how DOS starts up, and the various types of system files. We also looked at the difference between DOS internal and external commands.

The next chapter will explore the idea of files further, including DOS's file-naming rules and the conventions commonly applied along with them.

CHAPTER

3

File Types, File Names, and Conventions

INTRODUCTION

In this chapter, we'll look more closely at how DOS handles files.
We'll explore the different types of files, as well as the ways DOS
allows us to name them. We'll provide a typical scheme for
naming files so that those who tend to be a bit disorganized can
tell something about them just by looking at the file name. Let's
begin by looking at some of the different types of files.

TYPES OF FILES

At the end of the last chapter we finally got around to defining
just what a file is, and explained the difference between DOS executable files and data files. However, it will be useful to delve
into a little more detail.

Files consist of zeros and ones that the computer interprets to
represent individual codes. Those codes, in turn, are interpreted
by programs in the computer to mean something else. Generally,

the code numbers themselves are digits in the range 0–255, since a single 8-bit binary byte (00000000 to 11111111) can represent any number in that range.

Some of the codes are interpreted by the supervising software programs such as DOS or BASIC as *program code*, or instructions. Other codes are interpreted as data. What a given code number means to the computer at any given time is determined by the meaning assigned by the supervising program.

For example, if DOS is executing a program and encounters the two codes 205 and 33 as the next two to carry out, it will interpret them in a certain way. Those two code numbers happen to form a pair of instructions that tells DOS to carry out a DOS function. The particular function desired is conveyed to DOS just prior to the 205,33 instruction through another code number (which is loaded into a certain microprocessor register). In this context, the 205 and 33 mean only one thing. (The programmer probably entered as a mnemonic into the assembler as INT 21; the assembler then translated that to the hexadecimal equivalent, CD 21, which the computer then sees in binary as 11001101 100001. Aren't you glad the computer takes care of all this for you?)

Under other conditions, the same two code numbers could be interpreted as something else. In the ASCII code, the numbers 205 and 33 decimal represent an = graphics character (not the equals sign) and the exclamation point (!) respectively. So, any program that interprets ASCII code would see those two characters instead.

The point is that the actual numbers found in a file are not as important as how they are interpreted by the software that uses them. Files all contain codes from 0 to 255.

When you use the TYPE command to tell DOS to print out a file's contents to the screen, what you actually see are the characters that correspond to a set of codes called the American Standard Code for Information Interchange (pronounced ASKEY). The ASCII code is a standard that defines what common alphanumerics and symbols correspond to the numbers from 0–127. The other characters to 255 are undefined by the ASCII code, but vendors like IBM have chosen their own characters for them.

So, if you TYPE a program file, with DOS instructions like 205 and 33, you will see instead the ASCII and IBM characters that correspond to those numbers, since the "program" interpreting them (in this case DOS'ss COMMAND.COM command processor) sees them under those terms.

Files that contain only the printable, conventional ASCII characters are called ASCII files, quite logically. Other files may contain any of the 256 possible codes that their software requires. Some files may even contain a combination of ASCII and other characters, because the software uses the extended codes as formatting information. DOS executable files may contain both the program instructions (codes like 205 and 33) and the ASCII text that will be printed to the screen by the software.

In this book, you'll have occasion to use various ASCII files. These include batch files as well as special files like CONFIG.SYS. It will be useful to list the most common file types, so you'll know what they are when you need them.

ASCII Records

These are ASCII files generated by a software program as a means of storing data. Each individual record will be separated by a *delimiter*, such as a comma. Such files may be generated by database management programs, spreadsheets, or other software. The chief difference between an ASCII record file and a plain ASCII file is that the former will be structured, while the latter (such as letters or documents) will have no particular structure to the information.

.COM Files

These are files that contain nothing but machine-language instructions. DOS always looks for .COM files first in the current directory when a file name is entered at the command line (unless you precede the name with a path name). If such a file is found, DOS will load that file into memory and transfer control to the machine language instructions it contains.

Since .COM files contain nothing but the program instructions, the entire file must fit into the single segment of memory that DOS knows how to handle unaided. Therefore, .COM files must be 64K or smaller.

You might be interested to know that OS/2 more or less does away with .COM files entirely, since this simple method of program execution is incompatible with a multitasking system where programs may be swapped in and out of memory constantly. OS/2's invisible files *do* have the .COM extension, but are actually .EXE files given the .COM name for compatibility reasons.

.EXE Files

These files are also DOS-executable files. DOS will look for a file with an .EXE extension to match a command entered at the DOS prompt if no .COM file is found.

.EXE files contain more complex instructions that allow them to operate over several memory segments, and therefore be longer than 64K. As the .EXE file is loaded, DOS encounters a number that tells it what type of file it is. Next, there is a series of numbers that provide DOS with information needed to load and run the file, including the number of bytes used in the last sector of the file, and the number of 512–byte segments in the file. This allows DOS to determine exactly how long the file actually is.

That's important because DOS must be able to relocate the .EXE file in memory, and know where the various segments of the program reside. Versions of DOS prior to 3.3 included a utility called EXE2BIN that would convert some .EXE programs to .COM format. The source program, of course, had to be able to run in less than 64K, and other conditions had to be met. More recently, the small gains provided by this utility have become less important, and EXE2BIN has fallen into disuse.

.BAT Files

Batch files are simply a special type of ASCII file with the .BAT extension. DOS will search a directory for a .BAT file if no .COM or .EXE file is located. COMMAND.COM can carry out the instructions in the .BAT file, although the allowable commands are fairly limited. We'll discuss batch files more thoroughly later in this book.

FILE NAMES AND CONVENTIONS

Files are always given a file name or *specification*. This name consists of three parts: the drive/path designation, the file's root name, and its extension. The format is as follows:

```
drive/path:filename.ext
```

The drive/path may consist only of the drive letter, such as A:, B:, C:, etc., or can include the *path* to the *subdirectory* where the file is located. Both drive and path may be included, if desired; however, they are optional. We'll discuss paths and subdirectories more fully later. To keep things simple for now, we'll consider the drive/path designation as if only the drive letter is significant.

The root file name is any name you choose, up to eight characters. Any of the alphabetic characters from A to Z may be used, as well as the numbers 0 to 9. You can also incorporate any of these punctuation symbols in a file name:

```
& # @ ! % [ } _ ' ( )—^ ~
```

The extension is optional for most types of files, at least as far as DOS is concerned. Your applications software may demand that a given extension be applied to the data files that it works with. In most cases, the software will supply an extension only as a default or preferred value. You can usually substitute another if you wish. Extensions are often used to show what type a file is. Most DOS files do include an extension. Certain DOS files—those ending in .EXE, .COM, and .BAT extensions— must have that extension to be recognized properly by DOS.

The extension can be any three characters that are legal for the root file name, separated from the root by a period. You probably know this from reading various DOS manuals. What you may not be aware of is that certain special or even *invisible* characters can also be incorporated into a file name. These are the characters with codes numbered from 127 to 255. There are some special uses for file names incorporating these characters, as we shall see. Since there is no key labeled with these characters, how can you type them in?

Each character on the keyboard has been assigned an individual ASCII code. You may enter a character by typing that key, or by entering its ASCII code at the keyboard through a special provision of DOS. For example, the uppercase letters A to Z are represented by ASCII codes 65 to 90. Lowercase a to z are 97 to 122. Numerals are 48 to 57, and punctuation marks have their own codes. To let DOS know you are typing an ASCII code and not the number itself, you need to hold down the Alt key and type the number on the numeric keypad. For example, to produce the letter A, you can hold down Alt and press the 6 and then the 5.

This isn't a very good way of typing the usual characters; however, it is the only way to enter some of the special characters that don't have corresponding keys on the keyboard. For example, Alt-255 produces a null character that is not displayed on the screen but that can be used as part of a file name. A file named:

```
MYFILE<Alt-255>
```

could not be copied, erased or accessed in any way if the user typed only

```
MYFILE
```

at the keyboard. (The brackets < >are not typed, but indicate a key combination.) We'll see a way around this shortly as we further explore file naming conventions. The tricky part is that DOS will more or less ignore such characters if typed in from the command line. So, you not only could not create such a file name easily, you'd find it impossible to type the character in to ERASE it, COPY it, or perform any other function with it—even if you knew it was there.

However, where there's a tricky part, there is usually a way to circumvent it. Many text editors allow entering these characters through the Alt key method, and enable you to write special files that will create files or even subdirectories with these names. We'll explore this option more later on. This chapter will even show you a way to erase or copy these sneaky files using ordinary DOS commands.

A file name obviously may *not* contain a period, since the period is used to separate the root name from the extension. For the same reason, a colon, used for the drive designator, cannot be used. Since DOS sees a space as a delimiter for commands, you generally can't include one in a file name (there are ways around this, too; for example, BASIC can create a file name with an embedded space). DOS also uses the equals sign, semicolon, comma, and tab character to delimit commands, so they are eliminated as well. Other illegal characters in file names include:

```
*  ?   \  <  >  |
```

These are all used by DOS for other purposes. Although DOS will allow the following characters, you probably should avoid using these symbols in your file names if you can:

```
%  &  (  )
```

The reasons behind this recommendation are complex. The ampersand and parentheses in particular have special uses under OS/2. Since file structures are compatible between OS/2 and DOS, you probably don't want to create any file names that could cause some problems or confusion should you need to exchange files with an OS/2 user.

DOS won't allow you to use certain file names, since it has reserved them for its own use to name its devices. These include:

```
CON
PRN
AUX
```

```
NUL
LPT1, LPT2, LPT3
COM1, COM2, COM3, COM4
```

The rule applies only to the use of these as root file names. You may use any of the three character reserved names as file name extensions if you wish. These are all legal file names:

```
TESTER.CON
ACCTS.PRN
OUTPUT.AUX
JUNK.NUL
```

There are some conventions to creating file names that you will want to be aware of. The *underscore* character is often used to connect parts of a file name into one "word." The main use for this convention is to make the file name easier to read. You'll see files named like these:

```
JUL_88.WKS
BACK_UP.EXE
WORK_DOC.TXT
```

It's a good idea to use all eight characters of the root file name if you'll have many files that must be clearly differentiated. A short file name just gives you less information to work with in identifying a file. The extension should also be used to provide identifying information.

As noted, some extensions have special meanings to DOS. You can legally use them for files that aren't of the type DOS is expecting to see, but you may not like the results. These extensions are as follows:

.BAK	backup file
.BAS	BASIC program file
.BAT	batch file
.COM	type of executable file

.EXE   another type of executable file
.HEX   file used with DEBUG
.MAP   special listing file used with LINK
.OBJ   object code from a compiler
.REL   object code file from an assembler
.TMP   temporary file

In addition, you should know that OS/2 names its batch files with the .CMD extension. If you'll be sharing files with OS/2 users, avoid this extension if at all possible.

Some application programs either prefer or require that the extension be constant. Some of the most common extensions of this type are:

.ARC   compressed file, which can be extracted
        using ARC.EXE or another utility program
.TXT   word processing file, used by
        DisplayWrite 3 and other programs
.DOC   another word processing file, used by
        DisplayWrite 4, PC-Write, and other
        programs
.BAK   backup files, used by Sidekick, WordStar,
        and many other programs
.WKS   Lotus 1–2–3 Release 1 and 1A worksheet
.WK1   Lotus 1–2–3 Release 2 worksheet
.WKQ   Quattro worksheet
.PRN   Print file
.PIC   Graphics file
.PIX   Graphics file, used by Inset and others
.DEF   definition file used for program setup
        by programs such as PC-TALK, Quattro, etc.
.PIF   program information file, used to supply information
        to Microsoft Windows, OS/2, etc. about applications
        programs

You can also create your own extensions that have special meanings for you and allow you to find files more easily. Thus, if your applications don't pre-empt the extension, you can read the following section for more ideas.

A DOS FILE-NAMING METHOD FOR HARD DISK USERS

Depending on your viewpoint, DOS is either remarkably flexible or horribly unstructured. When it comes to file naming, DOS's flexibility allows the user a great deal of leeway in choosing monikers for files. This unfortunately results in many nonstandard or even haphazard ways of applying those names. For a single user, this may not matter much. In a business, it can lead to disaster.

For example, you as an individual have decided to write a letter to Robert Smith outlining a proposal for his company. You may choose to name the document SMITH.DOC or, if you were smarter, SMITH.LET. After the document is composed, you copy it to a floppy disk (or send it over your network) so a word processing operator can print it out and put it in the mail. You keep the original on your hard disk.

A month later, someone in your organization sees the file SMITH.DOC on the massive hard disk of your company's "main" word processing computer. What does the file name tell her about the file? She might guess that it contains a word processing document instead of a spreadsheet (because of the extension), and even that it was either created by someone named Smith or intended for an individual or company named Smith. Other than the date it was last modified and the size of the file in bytes, that's all the directory listing will tell anyone.

If someone happens to create *another* document called SMITH.DOC, you may have a problem. At best, it will be possible to get the two confused. At worst, one may be copied over the other somewhere along the line, leaving you with half as many documents as you want to retain.

Of course, DOS's stingy eight-character name plus three-character extension limitation makes such a scenario possible. But even with operating systems that do allow longer file names, users still tend to use shorter ones that are easier to type. The problem is that users generally don't have a system for naming their files. They use whatever name occurs to them at the time the file is created.

You're obviously free to choose whatever file naming scheme you wish. The following description may provide you with some guidelines and ideas for establishing a system of your own. Particularly if you work in an organization where files are exchanged with other users, we'd encourage you to come up with some sort of logical method for selecting file names. Later on, we'll see how the hard disk's subdirectories can also be used to keep various files separate and organized.

There are three things to keep in mind for getting the most from your eight-character limit. First, you don't have to use whole words or even lengthy abbreviations to stand for significant data. Initials, code numbers, or other conventions can be used to represent longer words. If everyone in your work group has unique initials, you can mark files belonging to them using only two characters of the file name. The other characters can be reserved to mean other things.

Second, to take advantage of a special DOS facility for searching for file names (discussed next), you should try to make each descriptor occupy the same position in the file name each time. You may have to "pad" out a file name with null characters (not blanks) to do this, if all the descriptive information is not required. That will allow you to look for all files matching a given specification.

Finally, try not to waste space in your file name. The fewer positions used up needlessly, the more available to store descriptive information. Examine a typical file name "code":

```
DB89B8RS.TXT
```

In this case, we'll assume that the extension, .TXT, has been preempted by the word processing program. The other characters have been prescribed by the end user in a logical manner. Here's how the eight-character file name is broken down into separate *fields*.

`IIYYDMAS.ext`

II These two characters are the initials of the author of the document. In this example, the author was DB, or David Busch. If two or more people in your organization have the same initials, you may want to use nicknames, or just assign arbitrary letter combinations. The characters AA to ZZ can be put together in more than 350 combinations, while adding the numbers 0 to 9 results in more than 300 *more* combinations. If you want to cut down this field to a single character, A–Z and 0–9 can be used to represent 36 unique individuals.

YY These two characters represent the year the document was initiated: 88, 89, 90, etc. Since most files won't remain useful longer than three or four years, you could trim this field further as well just by limiting the significant information to the last digit. An 8 would stand for 1988, a 9 for 1989, and so forth.

D This represents document type. In this example, B stands for Bid. You can use P for proposal, L for letter, M for memo, or any other mnemonic characters you wish. As with author name, A–Z and 0–9 can represent up to 36 different document types.

M The M represents the month the document was created, in this case month 8 or August. September would be 9. How do we indicate months 10, 11, and 12 without taking up another valuable position in the file name? Although a zero could be used for October, it makes a certain amount of sense to stick with the same numbering scheme used in hexadecimal notation. That is, A equals 10, B equals 11, C equals 12.

A The A field, here with an R, stands for approval status, or some other information of use to your organization. Possible values might be R for in revision, A for approved, I for inactive, etc.

S This field marks the current status of the document, such as Sent to customer, Rejected by customer, etc. You can use mnemonics or other codes to indicate up to 36 different status conditions.

.ext The extension can be used to show what type of applications program created the document. TXT would mean word processing, WKS a spreadsheet program, etc.

Since this example has two "wasted" characters, plus the extension, you can see that a great deal more information can be included: as many as five additional fields if your application software allows using the extension.

The main drawback to using such a file naming system is that most organizations will require a "key" to allow users to find the documents they want by reconstructing the file name from the information at hand. This chart will list all the document types and their codes, author or user codes, basic subdirectory structure, and other information. If you have a memory-resident notepad, the chart can be placed there ready for instant access at the press of a hot key. It may simply be more convenient to print out the code and tape it near the computer.

USING WILD CARDS

The real power of such a system involves a DOS feature that hasn't been discussed yet: wild cards in file names. Many commands don't require that you name a file explicitly. You may instead substitute so-called wild card characters. As with wild cards in games, these characters may stand for any valid file name character. The two wild cards recognized by DOS are the question mark and the asterisk.

The ? may stand for any character in the specified position. The * can replace any number of characters from that position onward to the end of either the root file name or the extension.

For example:

```
DB89B8RS.WK?
```

could represent all files that start with the indicated characters. So, these would all match:

```
DB89B8RS.WKS
DB89B8RS.WK1
DB89B8RS.WKQ
```

We could also have typed:

```
DB89B8RS.WK*
```

to achieve the same effect. The ? stands for one character only, while the * can represent one or more characters. As a result, if we wanted to see all files starting with DB, we could use any of these commands:

```
DIR DB??????.???
DIR DB*.???
DIR DB??????.*
DIR DB*.*
```

This capability becomes particularly powerful when file names have been constructed, as recommended, with standardized positions. To see a directory of all the worksheets belonging to DB, we could type:

```
DIR DB??????.WK?
```

If we wished to see only those for 1988, we could type:

```
DIR DB8?????.WK?
```

Interested in finding all the proposals that have been rejected? If your file names are set up properly, you can do it. Try this command:

```
DIR ???P???R.*
```

Judicious substitution of wild cards and careful file name selection will allow you to locate, erase, copy, and otherwise manipulate files in powerful ways. Later in this book we'll find out how subdirectories can also be used to segregate files in useful ways.

You'll also be interested to know that wild cards can be used to manipulate files that happen to contain odd characters—those you normally can't type in from the DOS command line.

Imagine you suddenly find a file on your hard disk that looks something like this:

```
REM OVE.COM  254 05-19-89 4:22p
```

Oops. Where did that come from? You do remember typing in a utility from a magazine the day before. It involved a BASIC loader that wrote various bytes stored in DATA statements to the disk to create the working .COM file. It looks like you made a mistake when you typed the line that contained the file name. The space you inserted was passed along by BASIC to DOS when the file name was created. Now, how do you fix this?

You probably guessed by now that the command:

```
COPY REM OVE.COM REMOVE.COM
```

won't work. DOS will tell you that you have entered too many parameters after the COPY command. It sees the space between REM and OVE as a delimiter. You've in effect told DOS to copy the file named REM to a new file named OVE.COM, but included an extra parameter, REMOVE.COM, on the same line.

Instead, substitute the ? wild card for the space:

```
COPY REM?OVE.COM REMOVE.COM
```

DOS will send your disk churning for a few minutes, then respond:

```
(0) File(s) copied.
```

Oops again. What happened? DOS *really* doesn't like spaces in a file name, and won't let you copy such files even if you do use a wild card.

However, you *can* RENAME or ERASE such files with wild cards. If you want to keep the file, simply rename it with a command like this one.

```
RENAME REM?OVE.COM REMOVE.COM
```

Or, you can delete it entirely by typing:

```
ERASE REM?OVE.COM
```

However, you should make certain there are no other file names that match the wild card specification, since they will be erased as well. For example, the previous command would also delete REMLOVE.COM or REM-OVE.COM. While such an occurrence may seem unlikely, it's *always* best to doublecheck before deleting any files on your disk with wild cards of any type.

SUMMARY

In this chapter we learned a bit about the different types of DOS files, and how DOS uses them. Files and file-naming conventions were explained, along with a sample system that will be of particular use to hard disk owners. We also saw how wild cards can be used to make access to files more efficient. There are a number of DOS commands that can be used with file names in this way, including ERASE, COPY, XCOPY, etc. However, before we can really put these to work with our hard disk, it might be a good idea to explore just what a hard disk is.

4

Hard Disk Basics

INTRODUCTION

Before we jump right into DOS commands as they apply to hard disks, it makes sense to look at what a hard disk is. This chapter will serve as your introduction to the technology behind hard disks, and will serve as a basis for understanding how they operate and how they work with DOS. There will be some nuts-and-bolts discussions, but nothing really too complex. Hard disks are, in fact, easy to understand. In theory, they resemble the familiar floppy disk. In practice, there is a lot more to them.

WHAT'S A HARD DISK?

The hard disk itself is like a floppy disk in that a circular magnetic surface is used to record information, and a read/write head, something like the heads found in tape recorders, is used to record and retrieve information.

However, on closer comparison, a floppy disk and disk drive are relatively large, imprecise components. That's the case, in part, because floppy drives and their disks must be built to tolerate wide variations in operating environments and in the components themselves. Floppy disk drives must function in somewhat dirty surroundings (such as ordinary dusty room air), and allow repeated mounting and dismounting of cheap, mass-produced disk media.

With hard disk drives, the media, read/write heads, and other drive components as well as interface circuitry (and sometimes the controller) are built as a single integrated unit. This allows a higher degree of precision in fitting together the components that make up the hard disk drive. As a result, some special techniques can be used that result in much higher information densities.

One such technique is to have the read/write head *fly* over the surface of the disk at a very small distance, supported by a cushion of air, instead of resting directly on the disk surface as it does with floppy disks. The head does not touch the hard disk surface, except when the disk is stopped, or because of an accident called a *head crash*. As a result, the disk surface does not wear, and rotational speeds can be much higher. Just as speed-reading techniques allow you to absorb information faster, simply making a hard disk rotate faster allows the read/write head to access data more quickly. Where floppy disk drives rotate at 300 revolutions per minute, hard disks commonly rotate at 3,600 rpm, with correspondingly higher data transfer rates.

There are other differences between a floppy disk and a hard disk. The magnetic coating of a floppy disk is applied to a flexible polyester support or *substrate*. Fixed disks, in contrast, use a rigid aluminum platter. This platter is diamond turned. Then a magnetic coating is applied. Until recently, iron oxide particles were applied onto the media in a very smooth layer. Today, so-called *thin-film* techniques are used to coat the media with a much thinner (and tougher) layer that has smaller, denser magnetic particles. The thin films can be applied either by plating (something like the way paint is applied by a roller) or sputtering (similar to using a paint spray can).

Both thin-film techniques allow placing more tracks per inch of radius and recording more bits per inch of track, when compared to the older iron oxide coating method. This is because the newer coating methods provide higher values of *coercivity*, which is a measure of the strength of the magnetic field required to switch the magnetic patterns in a material. As coercivity increases, the size of the particles that can be practically used in magnetic media grows smaller. Thin films allow densities up to 15 or 30 million bits per square inch using normal linear recording techniques.

However, there are drawbacks to both the newer technologies. Sputtering has traditionally been the more expensive method, and was too costly to use for the least expensive hard disk drives. Plating can produce disks that hold more data than sputtered disks, and can be the lower-cost technique. Unfortunately, plating sometimes allows the disk media to corrode, which almost always means lost data.

Plated disks also suffer from *striction*, which is a physical property that causes two smooth surfaces to tend to stick together. Higher data densities call for smaller flying heights (the closer the read/write head is to the disk surface, the smaller the magnetic particles can be and still be successfully detected). These can range from 15 to 17 microinches down to 12 to 14 microinches (millionths of an inch). At such flying heights, special lubricants may be needed to prevent striction from causing the heads to crash into the disk surface.

Because even a particle of dust can loom as an impassable object, given the low flying height of a hard disk read/write head, the platters and heads must be sealed inside a mini "clean room" that provides an environment free of contaminants. If this protection is breached, the user is exposed to the dreaded head crash. A grain of dust, or sometimes an external vibration, can cause the read/write head to strike the disk platter forcefully instead of gliding over smoothly. Should the head crash take place when the head is passing over an information-containing area, data can be permanently lost. In the worst cases, damage can occur in the directory track, whereupon the disk controller no longer knows where to find *any* of the information on the disk.

Gradually, we've moved from hard disks with 5.25–inch aluminum platters to those with 3.5–inch (or even smaller) diameter surfaces. This is because the smaller drives require smaller components, which can in turn be made more rugged. In addition, smaller drives allow faster access to the data, since the read/write head has to travel a smaller distance to reach a given track. Thin-film media are making these smaller drives possible with no sacrifice in storage capacity.

With all magnetic disks, information is recorded on the magnetic surface by a read/write head that causes changes in the orientation of the particles or *domains* on the surface. Before the data is recorded, all the magnetic particles on the disk are aligned in the same direction. As information is written, electric currents in the read/write head produce appropriate flux changes in the magnetic orientation of these particles. When the data is read back, these changes in the disk *induce* electrical currents in the read/write head, producing electrical signals that can be amplified and interpreted by the controller and passed on to the computer system.

The distance between these flux changes on the disk determines the density of information that can be recorded on the disk. The distance can be measured both radially, out from the center of the disk (how many different tracks can fit on the disk, or tracks-per-inch) and along the track itself (bits-per-inch).

In general, the flux changes are recorded along the surface of a given track. This is called *linear* recording. However, another recording method, called *vertical* or *perpendicular* recording, allows storing information even more densely. With this technology, the particles are positioned vertically rather than horizontally. The disk media must be coated in a special way. The magnetic layer must be soft on the bottom and hard on the top, to allow the particles to move in the desired direction, yet resist damage at the surface of the disk. In addition, the read/write heads must be specially designed, and fly closer than ever to the disk surface.

With perpendicular recording, densities of 30 million to 60 million bits per square inch—double that of longitudinal or linear recording methods—are possible. This translates into 20,000 to 40,000 bits per inch of track, and 1,000 to 2,000 tracks per inch. A typical hard disk using conventional recording may have 345 tracks per inch, with 17 or 18 sectors per track, and a 360K floppy disk only 48 tracks per inch, with only nine sectors per track.

These narrower, denser tracks require read/write heads that are much smaller than those found in floppy disk drives. The heads are moved across the surface of the disk by a head-positioning device. Cheaper systems use a stepper motor. More expensive (and more desirable) is the voice-coil motor. These may use rare-earth elements such as cobalt and neodymium in the track sensors, allowing the heads to be positioned more accurately, translating into greater potential capacity. Voice-coil motor actuators also boast faster access times.

For simplicity's sake, in the discussion that follows, we'll talk about the hard disk as if it consisted of a single platter with a single surface on which have been recorded magnetic tracks and sectors. In truth, hard disks generally have several platters, each with two surfaces, and read/write heads mounted in sets that read all the corresponding tracks of all the surfaces on all the platters simultaneously. Because this arrangement provides a "cylinder" of tracks, one on top of each other, a common way to refer to a hard disk's physical makeup is in terms of these *cylinders*. However, as we'll see, the physical layout of a hard disk may or may not have anything to do with how the hard disk controller and your computer view the *logical* arrangement of the disk.

FACTORS AFFECTING HARD DISK PERFORMANCE

There are five major physical factors of the hard disk itself affecting how quickly a hard disk can write or read data. In addition, there are a number of other factors not related to the disk that can affect disk speed. These have to do with the computer itself or with DOS. They will be covered later in this book. For now, let's look at the physical factors of the hard disk. They are:

★Cylinder size and density

★Data transfer rate

★Sector interleaving

★Access time

★Average latency

Cylinder Size and Density

This is determined, in part, by the number of surfaces or platters in a hard disk. The more surfaces, the larger the cylinder, and the more data that can be read by the multiple heads in a given period of time. A hard disk with larger cylinders also can reduce the need for the read/write heads to move over the surface of the disk under some circumstances. If the information to be retrieved happens to be stored on several tracks within the same cylinder, it can be read without moving the read/write heads to a different track. This scheme is, in fact, put to work in some larger computer systems to improve I/O performance.

Cylinder density can also be increased by adding more sectors to each track. This is usually accomplished by changing to a different encoding method, which will be discussed shortly.

Data Transfer Rate

This is the rate at which data comes off the disk, usually about 5 megabits per second. With some computer systems, the data transfer rate is not a limiting factor, since information is read as fast as or faster than the CPU is able to handle it already.

However, personal computers are becoming faster all the time. The 10 MHz models, like the PS/2 Models 50 and 60, almost seem slow when compared to the 16 MHz to 25 MHz speed-demons based on the 80386 processor, like the Models 70 and 80. As such computers become more common, faster data transfer rates will be in demand.

Data transfer rate can be affected by rotation speed of the disk, bit density (sectors per track, determined by the encoding method used), and a factor called *sector interleaving*.

Sector Interleaving

At 3,600 rpms, each revolution of the disk takes about 1/60 second, but reading a full track of information generally takes longer. That is because the information on each track generally passes under the read/write head at a faster pace than the controller can receive, decode it, and pass it along to the computer system.

After reading sector 1, the controller must process that information and transmit it to the computer. However, since the next physical sector on the hard disk is written immediately following the first, the controller may not be ready to read that next sector.

One solution would be to have the read/write head *wait* until the disk made another entire revolution to bring the next physical sector into position. This would mean that it would require 17 revolutions to read an entire track.

More commonly, hard disk systems *alternate* or *interleave* the sectors on a track. The sector that the controller *logically* sees as sector 2 may in fact be the *fifth* sector on the track. It will read sector 1, process that information, then read sector 5, process that information, and read sectors 10 and 15 on a single revolution of the disk. Then, the controller will skip sectors 16 and 17, as well as sector 1 when the beginning of the track comes around again, and read the *second* sector on the disk—beginning the skipping process all over again. Instead of taking 17 revolutions to read a track, this process allows reading the entire track in only five revolutions.

The number of tracks that must be skipped to provide read reliability is called the *interleave* factor. The first IBM disk drives used an interleave factor of 6:1. Modern hard disks may use a factor of 4:1 or 3:1, or higher, depending on how fast they can process information.

For example, most 8088– and 8086–based computers can function well with a 4:1 interleave if they operate at the standard clock speed. A 3:1 setting is practical if the system is a clone with an 8 MHz "turbo" setting. If you have a PC-AT or PS/2 or other system with a 10 MHz clock speed, you may be able to use an interleave as high as 2:1. An 80386 system of some type is usually needed before you can dispense with interleaving altogether.

Setting an interleave factor that is too high can be as detrimental to performance as setting one that is too low. If a hard disk can't keep up with the information it is trying to read, it will have to wait for an entire revolution for that track to come around again—1/60 second, or almost 17 milliseconds. If this happens often enough, the consequences can be much more significant than the mere millisecond or two lost each revolution skipping sectors.

Since interleave factor is established when the disk is low-level formatted, to change the setting you'll need to perform this step again. Copy all the files from your hard disk to backup diskettes (make several copies if the information is especially critical). Then run the low-level formatting program supplied with your particular disk drive. One of the options included should be to specify an interleave factor.

Once the interleave factor has been set to its highest value for your particular computer system, the only ways to increase the transfer rate beyond 5 megabytes/second are to speed up the disk platter or to pack more information into each track to provide more sectors.

Access Time

Actually, the effective rate at which information is generally read affected most by the need to move the read/write head between tracks. Access time includes the amount of time it takes to move the read/write heads over the desired tracks (cylinders) to reach the specific track on the disk to be read. Once the heads have been placed at that track, they must settle down from the moving height to the height used for reading and writing. "Settling" time is normally included in the access time figures provided for a disk drive.

Average Latency

Once a head has finished seeking and settling, the disk drive controller must wait until the desired track spins the rest of the way around to the first sector before the read or write can actually take place. This nonproductive period is called *latency*. Since this period will be very short when only a few sectors remain before the start of the track, and much longer when the disk must spin around almost the entire distance, an average latency figure is given, corresponding to *half* the time needed for the drive to spin around. For hard disks that spin at 3,600 rpms, the average latency is 8.33 milliseconds.

These access speeds are commonly measured in terms of the average time needed to reach any given track on the disk. If the read/write head is located above track 1, it will obviously take less time to move from there to track 150 than to track 317. However, the track-to-track access time is generally given as the time needed to move from the edge of the disk to the center track, since the actual time needed will average out to this over many disk accesses. Access times can range from an average of 85 milliseconds (about 1/12 second, or five full revolutions of the hard disk!) to 28 milliseconds or less.

Since 85 milliseconds is three times as long as 28 milliseconds, the time needed to move from one track to another can have as great an impact on hard disk speed as the data transfer rate or interleave factor.

In providing high-performance hard disks for modern computers, manufacturers have attempted to make improvements in all three areas. Disk drives are built to operate with 1:1 interleave factors, and with even lower track-to-track access times.

Packing information more tightly within a track increases the number of 512–byte sectors that can be written to the track, and thus improves the data transfer time. However, it makes little sense to pack information closer together if the read/write heads are unable to read or write the information reliably, or if the controller is unable to process the data.

DISK CONTROLLERS AND INTERFACES

A device interface is a standardized way of communicating between two components, in this case the hard disk drive and the computer system. There are a number of standard and quasi-standard interfaces between hard disks (and other peripherals) and IBM PCs and compatible computers. The ST506/412 interface has been one of the most popular.

It was named after the Seagate Technologies 6-megabyte ST506 and its 12-megabyte successor, the ST412, which offer formatted capacities of five and ten megabytes respectively. It is what is called a *device-level* interface. In hard disks, such an interface links the controller and disk directly with a large collection of signal lines, each of which carries a separate value. Because the operation of the hard disk and the controller are so tightly linked, such an interface can be very efficient when the two are well matched. On the other hand, to upgrade the performance of one, you frequently have to replace both.

Given a few changes in the controller board to accommodate new logical disk sizes, any ST506/412-style drive can be controlled with any standard ST506–type controller. Such drives furnish the controller raw data bits containing both data pulses and timing pulses called *clock bits*. Data separator circuitry is built into the controller to sort out these two. Unless special encoding techniques are used, this type of interface is generally limited to data transfer rates of 5 megabytes per second.

Another device-level interface is the enhanced small device interface (EDSI), found in computers like the high-end IBM PS/2 models. This interface puts the data separator circuitry in the drive and not in the controller. While more expensive to implement, EDSI is potentially much faster than ST506, with the ability to run at 10 to 15 megabits per second.

There has been a trend in recent years to skip the device-level interface entirely, and put the controller circuitry right in the disk drive itself. The drive then connects to the computer with a *system-level* interface.

Unlike the device-level interface, where information is carried on dedicated lines, system-level interfaces convey information in logical terms. As a result, multiple devices (for example, more than one hard disk drive) can use the same connection in parallel fashion. More intelligence is required to decode requests from the computer (the drive has to decide that the request is for itself and not some other drive on the connection, for instance), so such system-level interfaces are termed *intelligent*. One well-known example is the SCSI (Small Computer System Interface; while there was a battle among proponents to refer to the SCSI acronym as "sexy," lack of true standardization has led to the more common reference of "scuzzy").

An SCSI device has circuitry on board that receives requests for information from the PC, and intelligently handles finding the data, retrieving it, decoding it, and passing it along to the computer on predefined data lines (ideally) common to all SCSI devices. Because the computer does not have to be concerned with the nuts and bolts of operating the peripheral, an SCSI can be a hard disk drive, a tape drive, an optical disk drive, or another peripheral. Such devices are intelligent, so the difference is transparent to the computer system. The SCSI interface has been applied to devices other than storage devices, such as printers and scanners. Unfortunately, manufacturers have had considerable flexibility in terms of what features they include or leave out of their SCSI interfaces while ostensibly still adhering to the "standard." As a result, there are SCSI interfaces and there are SCSI interfaces, and devices may or may not be compatible among computer systems implementing them.

DISK ENCODING METHODS

Controllers and interfaces can be built faster to accept information more quickly. However, the data transfer rate of a hard disk is necessarily limited by how tightly that information can be packed on the disk. That is, at a given rotational speed, more tightly packed information will be delivered to the read/write heads (and hence the controller) more quickly.

You might compare this to signs placed along the highway. You, the controller, need to be able to read the signs very quickly as you pass them. However, since you are limited to 55 miles per hour, no matter how fast you can read you can only absorb so much information if the signs (each holding 512 bytes of data) are placed 40 feet apart on the highway. But put the signs 20 feet apart and you will have doubled your ability to pick up information—assuming you can read that fast.

Faster controllers can always be built. A chief limitation on how much information can be put on the disk is how closely spaced data can be written and still read by the read/write head. To be read reliably, the bits can be spaced neither too widely apart nor too closely together. If the bits are too close together, the read/write head doesn't have time to read the bit before the disk surface has moved on to the next bit. If the bits are too far apart, the controller can make errors.

Why is this? Imagine that you are moving down that highway. Certain kinds of information will be placed on signs that are 20 feet apart. Other information will be conveyed by the absence of a sign. If there is a long string of signs, spaced 20 feet apart, you will have no problem reading them. If one or two signs in a row are absent, you'll also have little difficulty. You should even be able to estimate with fair accuracy whether two signs or one was missing. However, as the gap between signs grows, you'll tend to lose track of how many missing signs there are, probably because of small variations in the speed of your car. Was that eight or nine missing signs in a row? Ten, perhaps?

The hard disk operates in much the same way. Since zeros are marked by writing *nothing*, the accuracy with which the disk can measure how many zeros have been written is dependent on many factors, including the accuracy of the speed of the disk. Long strings of zeros present another problem: Since a zero is represented by an absence of a flux change, long periods with no change provide the disk head with an extended, constant signal strength. Even a small change in the strength, or amplitude, of the signal may be falsely interpreted as a flux reversal by the disk drive's detection circuitry.

In contrast, the drive has no trouble at all reading ones: if a flux change is present, then a 1 has been written. For clarity's sake, we'll refer to flux changes as *pulses*, and the lack of a flux change as a *pause*.

To help the disk drive better track the binary pulses and pauses, it is *encoded* first in a way that will minimize these potential errors.

One basic method of encoding is called *frequency modulation* (FM). With this method, an extra bit called a *clock bit* is recorded just before each data bit. When the disk drive reads back the information from the disk, the presence of the clock bit alerts the controller that a data bit follows. If a flux change is present between two clock bits, the controller interprets that change as a binary 1. If *no* flux change is present, a binary 0 is indicated. It's as if someone left you a marker on the highway indicating where a sign is supposed to *appear*. If you see the marker, but no sign, you know that a zero has been recorded.

Such a system is inherently very reliable, because long strings of binary 0's do not occur together. Pauses are always separated by a clock bit and two binary 1's are never placed too closely together, because at least one clock bit should always separates them. However, two pulses are needed to record each bit of data, so the FM encoding scheme means that only 50 percent of a disk can be used for data. To write five ones to a disk, you would need to record the bit-pattern 1111111111, and to write five zeros you would record 1010101010.

This scheme is called frequency modulation because the frequency of pulses for data bits is twice that for zeros. Under this method, the *run length* of pauses (no flux reversals) is zero. The maximum pause is 1, since the alternate clock bits guarantee at least one flux reversal every other pulse. It is convenient to refer to encoding methods by this ratio, called *run length limitation* (RLL). You might think of FM encoding as 0,1 RLL, since the run length of zeros is 0 and the run length of pauses is 1.

Modified frequency modulation (MFM) records binary 1's as a flux change, and 0's as the lack of a flux change within a given period. However, MFM encoding does *not* insert the redundant clock bits between data bits. Instead, an extra pulse (a binary 1) is inserted between consecutive binary 0's to "break" them up.

In other words, a 1 is always recorded as 01 (a pause followed by a pulse). An 0 is recorded as either 10 or 0. It will be written as 0 if there had just been a flux change recorded, or 10 if no flux change had been recorded. This scheme means that a minimum of one, but no more than three, pauses between flux changes can take place. Therefore, MFM can be considered as 1,3 RLL recording.

Because many fewer extra bits are used, MFM is capable of 50 percent higher recording densities than FM. This encoding method is the most common found on hard disks used in IBM PCs and compatibles today (and is used with floppy disks as well).

However, there are newer encoding methods. A system called 2,7 RLL is also used. As you might guess, this technique allows at least two pauses between successive pulses, and limits the number of these zeros that can appear in a row to seven. 2,7 RLL was first developed by IBM for its mainframes and then soon applied to a new breed of special hard disk controllers.

Simply, RLL systems convert data through an elaborate coding scheme that allows even more information to be recorded in one chunk. Each 8–bit byte received by the controller is translated into a new code pattern 16 bits long. However, only *half* of the possible patterns are used. The other half of the patterns consists of those codes that are most troublesome to record and to read, because they contain long strings of binary 0's. These patterns are never used. The remaining 16–bit code patterns allow from 2 to a maximum of 7 binary 0's between binary 1's. (2,9 RLL and other schemes also are used.)

Such a system requires twice as many bits to encode the data (16 bits instead of 8 for each 8–bit byte). However, since only the binary 1's cause flux changes, and they are always spaced at least three bits apart from each other, the information can be effectively recorded three times as densely. The net result is a recording scheme that is three times as dense as MFM, for 50 percent *more* information per track.

Instead of 17 or 18 sectors, each containing 512 bytes per track, RLL allows from 25 to 27 sectors. A 20-megabyte hard disk can be packed with 30 megabytes of information. Because the hard disk still *rotates* at the same speed, the *transfer rate*, or rate at which the data is read from the disk, increases proportionately. A typical 5-megabits-per-second rate with MFM encoding is increased by 50 percent to 7.5 M under RLL. You should also know that this higher speed can be too quick for some computers' system buses, particularly those found in 4.77 MHz PCs and XTs. As a result, the interleave factor may be especially critical, and, in fact, a higher interleave may be required when RLL controllers are used.

More complex encoding schemes have followed. These include *Enhanced Run Length Limited* (ERLL) and *Advanced Run Length Limited* (ARLL) (each manufacturer has tended to apply its own terminology to specific RLL enhancements). These schemes allow 33 or more sectors of 512 bytes, and a data transfer rate of 9 megabits per second.

All RLL-related encoding schemes require special, complex controllers to encode the data. These controllers don't work with every hard disk, as not all drives are able to handle the increased transfer rate. Controller manufacturers either supply a compatible disk drive or provide a list of tested, recommended models that will work. However, many users of hard disks can upgrade to higher capacity simply by purchasing a new controller for their existing drive. RLL encoding has been applied to hard disks using the ST506/412 interface, and thus can be adapted for a very wide range of devices.

Before a hard disk can be used by DOS, it must be *low-level formatted*, *partitioned*, and *high-level formatted*. The low-level format, often performed by the manufacturer, places basic information on the disk, and establishes the interleave factor. A utility program is usually provided with the hard disk to allow the user to reformat the disk to this level later. The process can take 20 minutes to several hours, depending on the capacity of the disk and the particular formatting program.

Partitioning, done with DOS's FDISK program, sets aside a portion of the disk for the operating systems you will be using. You may partition an entire disk for MS-DOS, or you may divide it between DOS and XENIX, or DOS and CP/M-86. Only rarely will you find a hard disk that has been partitioned for anything other than 100 percent MS-DOS or, perhaps, OS/2. In fact, with DOS 3.3 and later, you cannot separate the hard disk into partitions bootable by different operating systems. Partitioning will be discussed in more detail in Chapter Six.

SUMMARY

This chapter served as an introduction to hard disk technology. Some of the nuts and bolts may seem complicated, but you should find the information invaluable in understanding how your hard disk works with DOS. Now, it's time to go on and look at some simple DOS dommands.

5

First DOS Commands

INTRODUCTION

If you're already using a hard disk, you probably have a basic understanding of the simplest DOS commands. However, as this book is intended as a basic guide for all hard disk owners, particularly computing neophytes, we'll take some time to introduce some of the fundamental DOS functions. You can skim this section if you already understand commands like DIR and FORMAT. You should make sure you are familiar with what's contained here, as there have been some changes to these basic DOS commands with DOS 3.3 and DOS 4.0 that you might find useful.

THE DIR COMMAND

The DIR command is the first DOS tool that most users learn. It allows you to see what files are located on a disk. The information provided can include the file names, the size of each file in bytes, and the date on which the file was created or last modified. The syntax is as follows:

```
DIR d:\path\filespec
```

The **d:** represents the disk drive where the files are stored. You would substitute C: to see files on your hard disk (or perhaps D: if you have more than one hard disk). Drives A: and B: (if B: is present in your computer) are floppy disk drives, and may be either 5.25–inch 360K or 1.2-megabyte drives, or 3.5–inch 720K or 1.44–megabyte drives.

\path stands for the directory path to your file. The concepts of directories and subdirectories will be explained in Chapter 7. For now, you can ignore paths until the other aspects of the DIR command have been explained.

Filespec represents the name of the file or files you wish to look for with the DIR command. All these specifications, or *parameters*, are optional. If you simply type:

```
DIR
```

DOS will provide you with a list of all the non-hidden files stored on the currently logged disk drive. The chief difference between this DOS 4.0 directory display and one provided by earlier versions of DOS is that the *volume number* as well as *volume label* is shown at the top of the listing. The volume label is an eleven–character name that you may apply to the disk after formatting. This name does not necessarily have to be unique; you can name several hard disks or floppy disks with the same eleven characters.

On the other hand, the volume number is calculated by DOS using an internal algorithm and can't be easily changed. Odds are excellent that each disk you format will have a unique volume number. This provides DOS with a nearly foolproof way of differentiating between disks. Even if you made an exact mirror image copy of a disk, the duplicate would have a different volume number, allowing DOS to tell them apart. This is a long overdue and welcome addition to the operating system.

DOS tells you which is the currently "logged" drive by the prompt, which will look like one of these unless you change it to something else:

```
A>
B>
C>
```

If the prompt that is shown is C>, DOS will show you the files on drive C: when you type DIR on a line by itself. To log to a different disk drive, type its name:

```
A:
```

will log you over to A:.

When you type DIR followed by a file specification, DIR will only display those files that match that parameter. You may use the wild cards discussed in Chapter 3 to specify multiple files. A drive letter can preface the file specification to refer to a different disk drive:

DIR COMMAND.COM	Display directory entry for COMMAND.COM on current drive, if it exists.
DIR C:COMMAND.COM	Display directory entry for COMMAND.COM on drive C:. This syntax is valid even if you already happen to be logged onto drive C:.
DIR C:*.COM	Display all directory entries on drive C: ending with .COM extension.
DIR *.*	Display all files; this is the same as DIR alone.

Sometimes there will be so many files on a disk, even those meeting the file specification you enter, that the screen will fill and some entries will scroll off the top. The DIR command allows two *switches*, which are parameters prefaced by a slash. You may add /P, /W, or both, as you wish. The /P switch tells DOS to pause when the screen is full and then wait for you to press a key to continue. The /W switch asks DOS to display only the file names, arranged five columns wide on the screen. If you have a very long directory listing, you can use both switches to see a wide, paged display. Figures 5.1 and 5.2 are examples of directory displays using the /W and /P switches.

THE ERASE AND DEL COMMANDS

In many ways, the syntax of the ERASE and DEL commands is similar to that used for DIR. Instead of displaying the directory listings for the files you specify, ERASE and DEL will *remove* those files from your disk. Once you have erased a file in this way, it cannot be retrieved using DOS; you'll need to resort to one of the "unerase" utilities that are widely available.

ERASE, ERA, and DEL are exactly the same command. Note that there is no DELETE command; ERASE, ERA, and DEL are your only choices. The syntax is as follows on page 70:

Figure 5.1 Example of a directory with /W switch:

```
Volume in drive D is DRIVE D
Directory of D:\DOS
    .              ..             AC           NOTES          PHONE
DIR      $$$   ARCDOC   ARC   NOTES    BAK   PHONE    BAK   DW4       ASC
ARCE     COM   ASSIGN   COM   BACKUP   COM   BASIC    COM   BASICA    COM
BOOT     COM   CHKDSK   COM   COLOR    COM   COMMAND  COM   COMP      COM
DEBUG    COM   DIREDIT  COM   DISKCOMP COM   DISKCOPY COM   ECHO      COM
EDLIN    COM   FAKE123  COM   FDISK    COM   FORMAT   COM   GRAFTABL  COM
GRAPHICS COM   INOCULAT COM   INPUT    COM   KEYB     COM   LABEL     COM
LOCATE   COM   MAP      COM   MELT     COM   MODE     COM   MORE      COM
NOKEY    COM   NOPARITY COM   PRINT    COM   PRNTREDI COM   RECOVER   COM
RESTORE  COM   SELECT   COM   SK       COM   SKINST   COM   SKLOAD    COM
SYS      COM   TREE     COM   UNINNOC  COM   WAIT     COM   YESNO     COM
4201     CPI   5202     CPI   EGA      CPI   LCD      CPI   ARC       DOC
APPEND   EXE   ARC      EXE   ARCE     EXE   ATTRIB   EXE   FASTOPEN  EXE
FIND     EXE   JOIN     EXE   NLSFUNC  EXE   REPLACE  EXE   SCAN      EXE
SHARE    EXE   SORT     EXE   SPEEDUP  EXE   SUBST    EXE   SYSCHK    EXE
XCOPY    EXE   SKHLP    SKI   NST      MSG   BASIC    PIF   BASICA    PIF
ARC      TXT   MORTGAGE EXE
        82 File(s) 3039232 bytes free
```

```
Volume in drive D is DRIVE D
Directory of  D:\BATCHES

.               <DIR>         1-30-88    4:23p
..              <DIR>         1-30-88    4:23p
A        BAT        7         3-20-85   11:27a
ARCHIVE  BAT       61         2-05-88   12:19p
B        BAT        9         7-26-85   10:00a
BASIC    BAT       12         2-01-88   10:40a
C        BAT       22         2-17-86    3:12p
CD       ASC        3         5-21-87    2:52p
CHECK    BAT       13         2-29-84    5:13p
COM      BAT      199         3-17-88   12:02a
D        BAT        7         7-16-85    4:48p
DOS      BAT       11         7-24-87   10:20a
DS       BAT       18         1-31-88    1:22p
E        BAT       19        12-01-87   11:50a
ED       BAT       42         1-31-88    1:27p
FONESOR  BAT      123         3-19-88   11:37p
KDIR     BAT      194         9-26-85    1:53p
KILL     BAT      195         6-19-86    3:16p
LOCATER  BAT       69         2-19-85   12:08p
LOOK     BAT       10         3-08-84    3:17p
MOVE     BAT       47         2-24-88   10:09a
MSG      BAT      480         2-09-85    2:02p
NU       BAT       39         1-31-88    1:26p
Strike a key when ready . . .
OLDPATH  BAT       39        12-03-87   11:25a
RETURN   BAT       12         4-21-88    2:43p
TOP      BAT       10         2-22-85   11:52a
TRANS    BAT      335         9-24-84   10:55a
UP       BAT       10         3-22-85   11:13a
UPLOAD   BAT      191         1-31-88    1:30p
W        BAT      226         2-01-88    1:41p
WP       BAT       17         1-31-88    7:43p
X        BAT       73         2-01-88    2:07p
Z        BAT       37         3-24-88    2:37p
WINDOWS  BAT       30         3-31-88   11:16p
34 File(s)    3039232 bytes free
```

Figure 5.2 Example of a directory with /P switch:

```
ERA d:\path\filespec
DEL d:\path\filespec
```

As with DIR, the d: represents the disk drive where the files are stored; d: and \path\ are optional. If you do not enter either, DOS will substitute the current drive and directory. You must enter a file specification, which can include wild cards. However, if you type:

```
ERA *.*
DEL *.*
```

DOS will first ask you "Are you sure (Y/N)?" before erasing all the files. With DOS 3.3 and earlier versions, no such check is made for other wild card file specifications, such as:

```
ERA *.COM
```

With DOS 4.0, a /P parameter was introduced. This causes DOS to display each file name in turn and ask you if you wish to delete that file. The prompt includes the name of the file (including the full path name) and requires a Y or N response:

```
C>DEL *.DOC /P
C:\WP\LETTER.DOC, Delete (Y/N)?_
```

It's a good idea to pair ERASE or DEL commands with the comparable DIR command to first view a list of files you will be deleting. This is true even if you are using DOS 4.0 with the /P parameter. Users have been known to type Y when they mean N or to type Y out of habit without really realizing what file is being displayed. This precaution will provide you with a final check before doing (perhaps) irreparable damage. For example, you might type in the following:

```
DIR A:*.COM
```

```
ERASE A:*.COM
```

ERASE and DEL cannot be used to remove the system files, IBMBIO.COM and IBMDOS.COM (or their MS-DOS equivalents), from a disk. You *can* erase COMMAND.COM, although you shouldn't do this unless you know what you are doing. You might, for example, wish to erase the files from a bootable diskette in order to reuse that disk for something else. In that case, the command:

```
DEL *.*
```

would delete all the visible files. You can then treat the disk as a data diskette, although it will have less than the full 360K, 720K, 1.2 megabytes, or 1.44 megabytes of space; the rest is taken up by the invisible files. However, you could make the diskette bootable again at a later time by copying COMMAND.COM to it. The fastest way to erase *all* the files on a bootable disk is to reformat it.

When ERASE and DEL remove a file, they do not actually wipe out the file on the disk. The entry in the file allocation table (FAT) that reserved the sectors taken up by the file is changed. Then, those sectors are available for use by other files. Until another file actually claims them, the sectors remain unchanged on your disk. That's why various utility programs are able to successfully "unerase" a file. All that is necessary is to reallocate the sectors in the FAT.

Early versions of DOS always selected the most recently freed up disk sectors when writing a new file. That insured that the sectors that belonged to recently erased files would be used quickly, making it impossible to unerase those files. DOS now continues through the file allocation table, assigning the *oldest* available sectors first before going back to the beginning and starting over with newer sectors. This last-in-last-out scheme makes file recovery a bit easier. However, your best bet is not to erase files that you mean to have later on, if at all possible (an amazing feat of prescience), or to back up files that you might conceivably want for any reason in the future.

THE RENAME COMMAND

RENAME is another command that operates on files. In this case, it changes the name of a file to a new name that you specify. The syntax for RENAME (which can be abbreviated REN) is:

```
RENAME filespecification newname
REN filespecification newname
```

You would substitute for **filespecification** any file name, including wild cards, that defines the name of the file or files that you would like to rename. For **newname**, you would provide another file specification conforming to the new name(s) you would like to apply to the files. Wild cards may also be used here. You can include the drive specification where the original file(s) are stored, but cannot put a drive letter in front of the new name. That is because files can be renamed, but not moved in a single step with the RENAME command. That requires the COPY or XCOPY commands, to be discussed later.

DOS won't let you create two files with the same name, so in some cases, global characters used in RENAME will result in an error message:

```
Duplicate file name, or file not found.
```

As you might guess, you'll also see this message if you attempt to individually rename a file with the name of an existing file, or if DOS is unable to locate the file that you wish to rename. The various combinations will become clearer if we look at a few examples:

```
RENAME WILLIAMS.DOC WILLIAMS.LET
RENAME *.WK1 *.WKQ
RENAME DB??03??.DOC DB??03??.BAK
```

The first example would rename a file called WILLIAMS.DOC as WILLIAMS.LET, providing a new extension. Perhaps the wrong extension was applied when the document was first created. The second example would change all documents with a .WK1 extension (Lotus 1–2–3 worksheets) to .WKQ (Quattro worksheets). The third example would allow you to rename only the files beginning with DB and including 03 in the fifth and sixth positions. Using a file naming system where the first two characters stand for the author, and the fifth and sixth for the month, this would apply new extensions to all documents created for DB during 03 (March). You can see how RENAME can be used with your own system.

THE TYPE COMMAND

TYPE is another simple command that allows you to see the contents of text files. These files, also called ASCII files, contain only alphanumerics, punctuation, and other common symbols. Batch files, files like CONFIG.SYS, and files created by some word processors are all ASCII files. DOS file types will be discussed in more detail in Chapter 10. For now, all you need to know is that you cannot TYPE program files and other files containing control characters or other binary information. If you attempt to do this, you'll see a collection of odd characters, hear beeps from your computer's speaker, or even experience some strange behavior from your printer. Don't worry; nothing has been damaged. You've just seen what happens when a binary file is directed to one or more devices that weren't intended to receive it. (Turn off your printer, if necessary, to reset it.)

The syntax for TYPE is as follows:

```
TYPE filename
```

For **filename**, you may *not* use wild cards, since DOS will allow you to TYPE only one file at a time. To see how TYPE works, you may want to try and list a typical ASCII file. Your hard disk probably has an AUTOEXEC.BAT file that was installed by the person who configured your system. AUTOEXEC.BAT is simply a list of commands your computer should carry out each time the computer is turned on or rebooted. To see its contents, enter this command at the DOS prompt:

```
TYPE C:\AUTOEXEC.BAT
```

You may see something like this:

```
ECHO OFF
PATH C:\;C:\DOS
PROMPT $p$g
```

AUTOEXEC.BAT files can be very long, and will probably differ quite a bit from this example. We'll show you how to create a useful AUTOEXEC.BAT file in Chapter 10. If DOS provides a BAD COMMAND OR FILE NAME message, then your system does not have an AUTOEXEC.BAT file. You can create a sample ASCII file by typing the following lines at the DOS prompt. (Do not type in the characters within angle brackets; they indicate single keys to press.)

```
COPY CON:TEST.ASC<Return>
This is a sample ASCII file.<Return>
It contains no useful information.<Return>
<F6><Return>
```

Now, you may type in this command:

```
TYPE TEST.ASC
```

to see the text you have just typed in. COPY CON allows you to COPY text from the console device (the keyboard) to the file name you specify. We'll be using this tool more later in this book.

INTERNAL VS. EXTERNAL COMMANDS

The DIR, ERASE/DEL, RENAME, and TYPE commands provide you with an introduction to some of the simpler DOS commands. All of these are what are called *internal* commands, which are loaded into memory with DOS and are always available. Other commands in this book are *external* commands. These are separate files, and may end in .COM or .EXE extensions. Note that you don't have to type the extension to invoke any of these. When you type a command, DOS will attempt to find a file ending in .COM, .EXE, or .BAT (in that order) and run it.

Internal Commands

There are 23 internal commands supplied with DOS through Version 4.0. They are:

BREAK	DIR	VER
CHCP	ERASE	VERIFY
CHDIR	MKDIR (MD)	VOL
CLS	PATH	
COMMAND	PROMPT	
COMP	RENAME	
COPY	RMDIR (RD)	
CTTY	SET	
DATE	TIME	
DEL	TYPE	

There are nine additional commands that are used mostly within batch files that are also internal DOS commands:

@	IF
CALL	PAUSE
ECHO	REM
SHIFT	FOR..IN..DO
GOTO	

External Commands

The external commands can be used only if they are available to DOS as files on your disk. The 35 external commands for DOS through Version 4.0 are:

APPEND	ATTRIB	CHKDSK
ASSIGN	BACKUP	DISKCOPY

DISKCOMP	KEYBxx	SELECT
FASTOPEN	LABEL	SHARE
FDISK	MEM*	SHELLB*
FIND	MODE	SHELLC*
FILESYS*	MORE	SORT
FORMAT	NLSFUNC	SUBST
GRAFTABL	PRINT	SYS
GRAPHICS	RECOVER	TREE
IFSFUND*	REPLACE	XCOPY
JOIN	RESTORE	

* Special DOS 4.0 command.

There are several reasons why DOS has both internal and external commands. You'll notice that the internal commands are generally those that are used most often. Because DOS has them already in memory, they can be carried out quickly. The operating system does not need to locate a file called DIR.COM in order to show you a directory.

Second, because these are key commands, having them stored internally avoids a host of possible unpleasant situations. If important commands were stored externally, and you happened to boot from a disk without, say, DIR.COM on it, you'd not only be unable to get a disk directory, you'd have difficulty finding out that a missing DIR.COM was the problem.

Third, by keeping *only* the key commands in memory, DOS avoids becoming cumbersome and overly large. The memory requirements of the system are much lower than if all the commands had to be kept in memory all the time.

By having some commands as external files, DOS is much more open-ended: Programmers can create their own DOS commands to add capabilities. You may even replace a DOS command with one of your own. For example, if you don't like the way FORMAT.COM operates, you may rename it to something else and write your own program (called FORMAT.BAT) that works the way you want. Henceforth, when users type FORMAT, they'll access *your* program instead of the one supplied with DOS. You'll be shown how to do this later in the book.

In fact, this might be a good time to look at FORMAT and study how it works.

THE FORMAT COMMAND

Let's look at an external command, FORMAT. When your hard disk was created, it contained absolutely no information: The surfaces used to store your data were a barren plain of randomly oriented magnetic material. To use a hard disk or floppy disk, it must be encoded with information that DOS uses to find its way around the disk. This marking of the disk is done with the *FORMAT* command.

The FORMAT command is one of the first commands any user learns, because it allows creating the disks we use to boot our system, or on which we store data. FORMAT is an external command stored in the file FORMAT.COM or FORMAT.EXE (depending on the version of DOS). It is used to create both bootable disks and disks that contain nothing but files. For example, if you have a large hard disk you may have it partitioned into two logical drives: drive C:, which is the disk the system boots from, and drive D:, on which you may store nothing but files. Floppy disks may also be bootable, or *system* disks may be non-bootable data disks.

Hard disk users may think that they have no use for a bootable floppy, since their systems always starts up from the hard disk. However, it is still a good idea to have a floppy system disk available. Later on, when we show you how to modify and customize your hard disk, you'll discover there are a few errors you can make that will make your disk temporarily non-bootable. If that happens, you can pull out your bootable floppy, restart the system, and fix the error. We'll show you how to use format to make such a disk in this chapter.

Up until DOS 4.0, DOS was supplied on an ordinary bootable disk and a supplemental programs disk. With the latest version, DOS is furnished on two 720K 3.5–inch microdisks or five 360K 5.25–inch floppies. One of each set is labeled INSTALL, and is used to create bootable disks. None of these can't be used to simply start up the computer. So, you're advised to create your own standard bootable DOS 4.0 diskette once you've installed the system.

In addition to the system files, a disk also contains a directory, and a file allocation table (FAT) that tells DOS how each sector of the disk is set aside for use. The syntax for FORMAT is as follows:

```
FORMAT d: /switches
```

For d: you should substitute the drive letter of the disk you wish to format. If you are formatting a floppy disk, DOS will load the FORMAT program and ask you to insert a blank disk in the proper drive and press Enter when ready. Early versions of DOS allowed you to type FORMAT without any parameters to format a disk in the current drive. The latest releases require you to type a drive letter, so that you don't accidentally reformat a disk you don't mean to.

Additional safeguards are enacted to prevent unintentional formatting of the hard disk. Before DOS will proceed, it will first ask you to enter the hard disk's volume label. If you really mean to format a hard disk, and don't remember the label name, you may have to type DIR first to see what it is. Even after you have typed in the label, DOS will warn you that all information on the hard disk will be destroyed and ask for confirmation one last time.

You can see that since you usually boot from the hard disk and store most of your programs and data there, reformatting it is considered a major step. In fact, you'll rarely have to reformat a hard disk. You may want to do it every year or two, as some of the magnetic information can be damaged or become garbled with constant use. There are utility programs that can repair disk sectors that are damaged electrically but not physically. However, if you have backed up all your files, it may be just as simple to reformat the disk once in a while. The reformatting step also gives you the opportunity to lock out from use any sectors that may actually be physically damaged.

Once a disk has been formatted, the information it formerly contained cannot easily be retrieved. You may even want to remove the FORMAT command from your hard disk. This is sometimes done in organizations where some or most of the users are relatively unsophisticated with computers. The FORMAT command is instead stored on a floppy disk under the control of the system administrator, who may also format and supply floppy disks to the end users.

FORMAT has several options or *switches* that tell it to format a disk in slightly different ways. One of these is /S, which tells DOS to make a bootable, or system, disk. When this option is specified, DOS will leave room on the disk for the invisible system files (which must reside in a certain location), and then transfer the operating system files to the disk after formatting has been completed. This option works even for DOS 4.0, so you may use it to create a back-up boot disk in case your hard disk becomes damaged.

Another option is the /1 switch, which will force DOS to create a single-sided floppy disk, even though the disk drive may have double-sided capabilities. When the format command is issued, DOS checks to see which type of disk drive is in the target drive, and will produce a disk to match. If you want to make a single-sided floppy (say, for use with a very, very old PC that has only single-sided drives), you can use the /1 switch.

Another option along these lines is the /8 switch, which will make an 8–sector-per-track disk for use with DOS versions before 2.0. Again, you'll rarely need this option, since there are few, if any, systems operating under these stone-age conditions.

The /B switch allows creating an 8–sector/track floppy disk that has room for the system, but that does not contain the system files. This allows you to make a disk that users can turn into a system disk, but without your distributing the copyrighted operating system files themselves. Like /1 and /8, this command is really only needed if you want to make allowances for the tiny number of users of DOS versions earlier than 2.0 that you may encounter. From DOS 2.0 and up, the system files can be transferred to floppy disks even if the /B switch is not used.

The /V switch tells DOS to prompt you for a volume label of 11 characters or less when formatting is completed. Prior to DOS 3.0, this was the only way to apply a name to a disk short of using a utility program or DEBUG. More recently, the LABEL command lets you name a disk at any time. Even so, the /V switch is useful as a way to remind you to label disks at the most logical time: when they are formatted.

The /V switch works in two different ways with DOS 3.0 and with DOS 4.0. With the earlier versions, DOS will ask you to supply the 11–character label when formatting is done. If you do not use the /V switch, DOS won't bother to ask for a label.

However, with DOS 4.0, you will *always* be asked for a label once formatting has concluded, *unless* you use the /V switch to bypass this step. With DOS 4.0, the syntax for the switch is slightly different:

```
FORMAT /V:label
```

where /V: is followed by the 11–character label you wish to apply. DOS will check to see if the label is valid before carrying out the FORMAT step. If you enter illegal characters (those not allowed in a file name), the process will abort.

When using any of these switches, keep in mind that you may use several of them on the same line, as long as they are not mutually exclusive. For example, you may type this command:

```
FORMAT A: /S /V
```

However, the following command, an obvious contradiction, is illegal:

```
FORMAT A: /S /B
```

Later versions of DOS include switches to accommodate the new disk drive types introduced with computers like the PC/AT and PS/2 models. Both DOS 3.0 and DOS 4.0 have a provision for formatting a disk for less than the maximum capacity of the drive. This allows you to produce 360K formatted diskettes in a 1.2-megabyte disk drive, or 720K disks in a 1.44-megabyte drive. You'll occasionally need these to exchange software with machines that don't have the higher capacity drives.

The /4 switch will create a single- or double-sided 360K diskette in a 1.2-megabyte disk drive. This option was added with DOS 3.0. While DOS will automatically accommodate 720K and 1.44-megabyte 3.5–inch floppies, DOS 3.3 added the capability to specify the number of sectors per track and tracks per disk during formatting. The /N:xx switch will allow you to indicate the sectors per track, while the /T:xx switch lets you enter the number of tracks you want to format. While the intent of these options was admirable, most users have found the need to remember how many tracks and sectors their disks have to be a considerable inconvenience.

DOS 4.0 has alleviated the problem. You now need only to remember the *capacity* of the diskette you wish to format, and you don't have to be exact in your terminology. This magic is accomplished through the /F parameter, which greatly simplifies formatting a disk with less than the maximum capacity of a particular drive. The syntax is as follows:

```
FORMAT /F:size
```

where **size** can be entered in K (kilobytes) or M (megabytes), no matter what size disk is being produced. That is, a 1.2-megabyte disk can be referred to as 1200 or 1.2 and DOS will understand what you mean. Table 5.1 will clarify the possible combinations.

Table 5.1.

Disk	160K	180K	320K	360K	720K	1.2M	1.44M
Size (in.)	5.25	5.25	5.25	5.25	3.50	5.25	3.50
Sides	1	1	2	2	2	2	2
Sectors	8	9	8	9	9	15	18
Tracks	40	40	40	40	80	80	80
/F:							
Parameters	160	180	320	360	720	1200	1440
	160K	180K	320K	360K	720K	1200K	1440K
	160KB	180KB	320KB	360KB	720KB	1200KB	1440KB
						1.2	1.44
						1.2M	1.44M
						1.2MB	1.44MB

IBM has thoughtfully (finally) included a table of the legal FOR-MAT switch combinations in its DOS manual. These include those shown in Table 5.2

Table 5.2

Disk size	Switch parameters
160K/180K	/S, /V:label, /1, /8, /B, /4, /F:size
320K/360K	/S, /V:label, /1, /8, /B, /4, /F:size
720K/1.44M	/S, /V:label, /B, /F:size
1.2M	/S, /V:label, /B, /F:size
Hard disk	/S, /V:label, /B

The last specification may be somewhat surprising. FORMAT lets you create a hard disk that has *room* for the system files, but that does not contain them, by use of the /B switch. Why would you want to do that? *You* probably would not. But a hard disk manufacturer who provides a high level of service might want to prepare your hard disk for you—up to and including high-level formatting (which is what this step is called, to differentiate it from low-level formatting, discussed in the following chapter). If that manufacturer hadn't purchased a license from IBM or Microsoft to distribute DOS with the hard disk, it would be illegal to sell it to you after formatting with the /S switch. Instead, just as in the days when most PCs were booted from floppies, the disk can be formatted, but space left for you to transfer the system files on your own. You might think this is a bit esoteric, but it does demonstrate how flexibly DOS can be used to meet the needs of a wide variety of situations.

SUMMARY

This chapter looked at some of the first DOS commands, including DIR, ERASE, RENAME, and TYPE. You learned more about the differences between internal and external commands, and began working with the FORMAT command.

With hard disks, FORMAT has some special uses. We'll get into those in the next chapter when we begin learning how to set up and configure a hard disk.

6

Setting Up Your Hard Disk

INTRODUCTION

Most of this chapter will deal with installing DOS on a hard disk for the first time. We'll assume that the basic physical formatting of the hard disk has been performed by the maker of the hard disk, or by the store that installs the hard disk in your computer. This is by far the most frequent scenario. You'll need only to divide your hard disk up into *partitions* and *logical drives* and to format it for use by DOS.

In some cases, your hard disk will already be formatted for DOS, but will contain an earlier version than the one you wish to use. So, first we'll look at how you can use the SYS command to transfer an updated copy of DOS to a hard disk in such cases.

THE SYS COMMAND

To use this command you must boot a copy of the DOS you wish to install with a floppy disk. This, of course, means that you must have a bootable disk in a format compatible with your drive A:. If you have, for example, a PS/2 equipped with an external 5.25–inch drive, you must still have a 3.5–inch version of DOS to install it on your hard disk. If you have purchased the wrong version, try to find another user with both types of drives who *can* boot your disk. Once that computer has brought the new version of DOS up, a bootable disk in your format can be produced using FORMAT with the /S parameter.

You must also have the SYS.COM program available on your disk. The syntax for the command is as follows:

```
[path\drive:]SYS d:
```

where the optional **path\drive**: designation indicates the path to the location of SYS.COM, and d: is the drive you wish to install DOS onto. The target drive specification is *not* optional. SYS will not install the DOS files on the current drive. DOS 4.0 changed the operation of SYS somewhat by allowing the user to specify an optional source and drive; otherwise DOS will use the current default drive to find the SYS command. The change was made to allow using SYS with networked disk drives.

For SYS to work properly, the DOS files should reside on the source disk (that is, it should be a bootable disk), and the destination disk should have room on it for the DOS files. A disk that is formatted but entirely empty, or one that has been formatted with the /B or /S switches, will leave enough room to transfer the system files.

You may run into some exceptions. IBM versions of DOS may not allow you to transfer system files to disks already containing Microsoft versions of the operating systems. That's because with some older versions of DOS, the Microsoft invisible files have a different name from the IBM equivalents.

DOS will confirm that the operation has taken place successfully by displaying the message **System transferred**. You'll need to copy other DOS files to the disk, set up a subdirectory hierarchy (Chapter 8 has some tips), and take care of other chores.

If SYS does not work, you may have to format or reformat the hard disk. That's a simple task, but can lead to errors if you are not careful.

FORMATTING A HARD DISK

Let's look at the procedure for formatting a hard disk in more detail since, as we've seen, some special considerations apply. One of the most important, which we'll repeat, is that *you rarely need to format a hard disk, and certainly don't want to do so accidentally.*

Until fairly recently it was common to reformat a hard disk once a year or so simply to reestablish the electrical markings on the disk that define the track and sector structure. Many users also found it convenient to reformat while copying all the files back to a clean disk to produce an efficiently organized, nonfragmented file structure. Today there are a number of utility programs which can handle both chores for you without the need to reformat the disk. Steve Gibson's SpinRite utility, for example, will repair disk sectors as necessary automatically. There are a number of other utilities that will locate fragmented files and recopy them to contiguous sectors for you.

DOS has included ever-more stringent safeguards with each new release to prevent inadvertent formatting of the hard disk, up to and including requiring the user to enter the volume or label name of the disk before proceeding with the format.

Hard disks are actually formatted in two separate procedures. The first is the low-level format, often called the physical format. This step puts the basic information on the disk, and also allows identifying and locking out bad sectors. Low-level formatting is *not* a DOS function, and is generally performed by the manufacturer of the hard disk. Most also provide the low-level format program in case you need to do this step again at some later time.

The first task that users of hard disks are likely to get involved with that does involve DOS is *partitioning*. This step is carried out somewhat differently in DOS 3.2 and earlier versions, DOS 3.3, and DOS 4.0.

A *partition* is a logical area on a hard disk set aside for use by a given operating system. You may have DOS partitions on your disk, as well as those set up for other operating systems such as XENIX. One partition can be marked as active. This is the partition that is used to boot up your computer when the power is turned on, which for most of us is a DOS partition. Once the system has booted, you can use a utility program like FDISK to change to another partition. FDISK is also used to create and delete partitions, to mark them as active, and to create logical disk drives within a disk partition.

That is, if you have a hard disk with 44 megabytes of storage, you can divide it into two 22–megabyte partitions called drive C: and drive D:. Or, you might want to divide the second partition into two smaller 11–megabyte drives, D: and E:. With DOS 4.0 you have even more options, since a single partition can be larger than 32 megabytes if you wish.

Let's look at the partitioning procedure, and explore why at least one of the described scenarios might not be a very good idea for you. Some of the following information applies to DOS 3.3 and DOS 4.0, so you should read the following section even if you don't have a version of DOS earlier than 3.3.

USING FDISK WITH DOS 3.2 AND EARLIER VERSIONS

With the type of partitioning introduced with DOS 2.0 and carried through DOS 3.2, sections of the disk are set aside, or partitioned, for one or more operating systems. As mentioned, all of the disk is usually allocated to DOS, although you may want to set aside more than one partition to allow XENIX or some other alternate OS. Partitioning is done with the program FDISK. When it is run, you'll see a list of options like the following:

```
Current Fixed Disk Drive: 1

Choose one of the following:
1. Create DOS Partition
2. Change Active Partition
3. Delete DOS Partition
4. Display Partition Date
5. Select Next Fixed Disk Drive

Enter Choice:_
```

You would choose menu item 1 to create a DOS partition. You might see a message like, **DOS partition already created,** which means that DOS has already been allowed for. In such cases, if you are unable to get a directory of the hard disk (you would have booted from a floppy containing DOS, or from another hard disk on your computer), all you probably need to do is perform a high-level format with the FORMAT command. If you have only one hard disk and it doesn't boot, but FDISK indicates that a partition has already been created, you still must use the FORMAT command. Use the /S parameter to transfer the DOS system files to the hard disk when formatting is completed.

If FDISK won't recognize your hard disk at all, you probably need to perform the low-level formatting step. Locate the utility disk that came with your computer or hard disk. There will be a program with a name like HFORMAT or something similar to perform the physical format for you.

Otherwise, you can go ahead and partition the disk by choosing option 1. The program will show you a screen like this one:

```
Create DOS Partition
Current Fixed Disk Drive: 1
Do you wish to use the entire fixed disk for DOS
(Y/N)?_
```

By typing Y, you will set aside the entire disk for one operating system, DOS. Next, FDISK will ask you to insert a DOS disk in drive A: and press a key. You can then perform the high-level format by typing:

```
Format C: /S /V
```

This formats the hard disk as a master disk, much as DOS-bootable floppy disks were produced as described in the last chapter. As with the creation of all master disks, DOS will copy the boot sector information and the DOS invisible files, IBMBIO.COM and IBMDOS.COM, over to your hard disk. You can reboot your computer now, and DOS will load from the hard disk.

While DOS 3.2 and earlier versions' FDISK allow you to divide the hard disk into one to four partitions, only one can be active at a given time. Even if a partition is not bootable, you can still access it if you boot from a floppy disk or from the active partition, and then use FDISK to change the active partition before rebooting.

FDISK also allows you to select and partition a second hard disk, delete a DOS partition, or see your disk's partition data.

PARTITIONING UNDER DOS 3.3

For DOS 3.3, FDISK was considerably enhanced, with the addition of support for multiple DOS partitions. However, only one bootable partition can be created per disk. If you want to run both DOS and, say, XENIX or OS/2, you'll need to boot the second or third operating system from a floppy disk.

With more and more users having two or more hard disks in their computer, it's necessary to differentiate between different *physical* hard disks and different *logical* hard disks. For example, your computer might contain two separate 32–megabyte disks mounted in different bays. If each were divided into only one partition, and each were fully devoted to DOS, your computer would see them as drive C: and drive D:. This is a different condition than if you had a single hard disk that happened to be divided into two logical disks called C: and D:.

The reason this is important is that with DOS 3.3 and later versions the hard disk that can be booted can be divided into something called a *primary* partition as well as an *extended* partition. The primary partition is the bootable one. A non-bootable disk (your second or third hard disk, say) can be divided only into an extended DOS partition.

The primary DOS partition is similar to the DOS partitions created with previous versions of DOS, and can be no larger than 32M under DOS 3.3. The non-bootable extended DOS partition can be as large as the drive itself, even if that is larger than 32 megabytes. However, DOS 3.3 still won't allow you to have a logi-

cal (or physical) drive specification larger than 32 megabytes.
FDISK requires you to divide the partition into multiple logical
drives, which can each be not larger than 32M (or smaller than
one cylinder).

The opening menu of FDISK (DOS 3.3 and later) looks like this:

```
Current Fixed Disk Drive: 1
Choose one of the following:
1. Create DOS Partition
2. Change Active Partition
3. Delete DOS Partition
4. Display Partition Date
5. Select Next Fixed Disk Drive
Enter Choice:_
```

Choosing menu option 1 brings up a screen display like this:

```
Create DOS Partition
Current Fixed Disk Drive: 1


1. Create Primary DOS partition
2. Create Extended DOS partition
3. Create logical DOS drive(s) in the Extended
DOS partition


Enter choice: [ ]
Press ESC to return to FDISK Options.
```

FDISK will show you how much space is left in a drive for creating an extended partition, or within a partition for creating a logical DOS drive. You can choose to divide up the hard disk as you
wish within these limits. A 32–megabyte hard disk could be
divided into five or six logical drives, each with five megabytes or
less of capacity.

In one sense, this might be a good plan. You could divide up files
according to application and store each of them on a separate logi-

cal hard disk. As we'll discover in the next chapter, DOS has a better way, though: the hierarchical directory structure.

There is another drawback to having too many (small) logical drives. DOS does not allocate disk storage in terms of individual sectors. Instead, it uses a larger unit of measurement called the *cluster*. With smaller-capacity floppy disks, a cluster is 512 bytes (in this case, a single sector). Higher capacity flexible disks can use a two-sector or 1,024–byte cluster. With hard disks, the cluster size chosen depends on the capacity of the particular disk.

Hard disks smaller than about 16 megabytes use a cluster size of 8,192–bytes, or 16 sectors. Larger disks use a 2,048–byte (four-sector) cluster size. DOS is unable to allocate disk storage space to a file in anything smaller than a single cluster for that disk. So, if you have a one-byte file, DOS will set aside 8,192 bytes for it with a 10–megabyte hard disk, and only 2,048 bytes with a 20–megabyte drive. Clearly, much less space will be wasted with a smaller cluster size.

You might think that you will store few files that small on your disk, so cluster size isn't a major concern. In truth, you might be surprised to discover that so many of the files you will be using regularly, particularly batch files, are fairly small and are stored inefficiently with a large cluster size.

But there's more to it than that. Almost without exception, *all* the files you store on your disk will require some odd number of disk sectors to hold all their information. Some of them will require a certain number of clusters, plus a little more. Others will almost fill the clusters allocated to them. On the average, the final cluster of each file will be only half used. So, if you have 8,192–byte clusters, an *average* of 4K will be wasted per file. With 2,048–byte clusters, only 1K will be wasted per file. Multiply those numbers by the 700 to 1000 files that an average hard disk will contain and you'll see the difference a megabyte or more of wasted space can mean.

There are two sides to everything, of course. Larger clusters are more efficient with large files, since DOS can read larger chunks of information at one time. If your applications involve only large files, you might find it desirable to set aside a small logical disk for them.

So you can see that dividing a 44–megabyte hard disk into 32– and 12–megabyte primary and extended partitions would give you one large 2,048–byte cluster disk, and one smaller 8,192–byte cluster disk. In this case, a pair of 22–megabyte logical drives makes more sense.

That's about all you need to know to partition a hard disk under DOS 3.3. You may be interested to know, however, that partitions created by DOS 3.3 will be compatible with OS/2 from a file standpoint. Should you need to run both DOS 3.3 and OS/2 from a single computer, you can install either as the primary operating system, and then boot from the other as required, using a bootable floppy disk. Each will be able to access files on disks created by the other. That's not always true with DOS 4.0, as we'll see shortly.

USING FDISK WITH DOS 4.0

The ballgame changed considerably when DOS 4.0 was introduced. A basic part of the upgrade was a new installable file system that allowed single logical disk drives larger than 32 megabytes. How this was accomplished will be discussed in more detail later in this book. For now, we just want to get you up and running. First, let's look at the opening menu for FDISK version 4.00:

```
IBM DOS Version 4.0
Fixed Disk Setup Program
(C) Copyright IBM Corp. 1983, 1988


FDISK Options


Current fixed disk drive:1

Choose one of the following:

1.    Create DOS Partition or Logical DOS Drive
2.    Set active partition
3.    Delete DOS Partition or Logical DOS Drive
```

```
4.   Display partition information
5.   Select next fixed disk drive

Enter choice:[ ]


Press Esc to exit FDISK
```

This menu looks something like that of FDISK for DOS 3.3. You'll note that option 4 offers a display of partition information, instead of just partition date, while options 1 and 3 mention creating or deleting partitions as well as logical drives. You'll see option 5 only if your system happens to have more than one hard disk.

Creating a Primary DOS Partition

If you choose option 1, you'll be shown a submenu listing another set of options. That menu will look something like this:

```
Create DOS Partition or Logical DOS Drive

Current fixed disk drive:1

1. Create Primary DOS Partition
2. Create Extended DOS Partition
3. Create Logical DOS Drive(s) in the Extended DOS Partition

Enter choice:[ ]
```

As in DOS 3.3, the primary DOS partition is the bootable partition, and cannot be divided into more than one logical drive. If you wish to have more than one logical drive you must divide your disk into both primary and extended DOS partitions. Submenu option 3 will let you create those logical drives.

However, things get interesting at this point. DOS 4.0 will allow you to create a primary DOS partition that is larger than 32 megabytes. The extended DOS partition can also be larger than 32 megabytes (as was possible with DOS 3.3), but the logical drives there may *also* be larger than 32 megabytes. For the first time, you may create DOS logical drives of almost any size.

There is an "odd" limitation on the size parameter, however: FDISK will allow you to create a disk partition of 33 megabytes, and one of 31 megabytes. It won't let you create one that is exactly 32 megabytes. If you select 32 megabytes from the previous menu, FDISK will accept it, but substitute a value of 31 megabytes when the program actually partitions the disk. It appears that the 32-megabyte barrier has not only been removed, it has been *ignored*.

However, you may not want to create a disk partition larger than 32 megabytes in any case. *This is important.* If you *do* create a drive that is larger than 32 megabytes, another DOS or OS/2 system you happen to boot up with will be unable to recognize that drive. You will still be able to boot up your computer with a floppy disk containing another operating system, such as DOS 3.3 or OS/2. But neither will be able to access that drive. If you have only a single hard disk, and that disk has been partitioned as a 32–megabyte-plus drive, DOS 3.3 or OS/2 will function as if you had no hard disk at all. So, if you need to maintain compatibility with other operating systems, *don't* take advantage of this new feature. Use only smaller partitions.

Of course, since OS/2 has an installable file system, it is entirely probable that a future release will also contain changes along these lines. In fact, it is inevitable. However, at this writing, the only way to insure compatibility between OS/2 and DOS 4.0 files is by sticking to 32–megabyte and smaller logical drive sizes.

When you create your primary DOS partition, the first thing you'll see will be yet another menu, which looks like this:

```
            Create Primary DOS Partition

Current fixed disk drive: 1

Do you wish to use the maximum available size for a Primary
DOS Partition and make the partition active (Y/N).....? [Y]

Press Esc to return to FDISK options.
```

Y is the default value, and will cause DOS to set aside the largest available space as your primary DOS partition. If you reply N, DOS will tell you how much space is available on the hard disk, and report the maximum available for the primary partition. You can enter the amount you wish to use either in megabytes or as percentages. With a 60-megabyte disk, you could enter *30* or *50%* to set aside half of it as the primary partition. (The percent sign is the indicator to DOS that you are entering a percentage and not a megabyte amount.)

The primary partition must be made active by choosing option 2 from the *main* FDISK menu, so it can be used to boot your computer from the hard disk.

Creating an Extended DOS Partition

If you have another hard disk, or if you do not set aside your full hard disk as the primary partition, you'll be returned to the previous menu and given the opportunity to create an extended DOS partition. The next menu you'll see will look like this:

```
            Create Extended DOS Partition

Current fixed disk drive:1

Partition Status  Type   Size in Mbytes  Percentage of Disk Used

C:1         A      PRI DOS     30                   50%

Total disk space is 60 Mbytes (1 Mbyte = 1048576 bytes)
Maximum space available for partition is 30 Mbytes (50%)

Enter partition size in Mbytes or percent of disk space (%) to
create an Extended DOS Partition..................[30]

Press Esc to return to FDISK Options
```

The first column shows the drive letter and the number assigned to a given DOS partition. The A indicates that the parti-

tion is active, while Type shows that is the primary DOS partition. The Size and Percentage columns are self-explanatory. As
with creating a primary partition, you may enter the size of the
extended partition(s) in megabytes or percentages. Repeat until
you have created all the partitions you want on all the drives you
want.

Each time an extended DOS partition is created, FDISK will
show you a menu that will allow you to create logical drives within
the partition. That menu looks like this:

```
Create Logical DOS Drive(s) in the Extended DOS Partition

No logical drives defined

Total Extended DOS Partition size is 30 Mbytes (1 MByte = 104857  bytes)
Maximum space available for logical drive is 30 Mbytes (50%)

Enter logical drive size in Mbytes or percent of disk space (%)...[ ]

Press Esc to return to FDISK options.
```

Deleting DOS Partitions or Logical Drives

You have several other choices from the main FDISK menu.
These allow you to delete the primary DOS partition, an extended
DOS partition, or any of the logical drives you have created in the
extended partition(s). Be careful: Deleting any partition will in
effect erase all the data in that partition from your hard disk.

FDISK will help you avoid the most obvious blunders. It will
warn you that deleting a primary partition will destroy all the
data. It will prevent you from deleting the primary DOS partition
while an extended partition exists. Similarly, you must first delete
the logical drives within an extended partition before you can
delete the partition. In summary, the procedure for deleting a
primary partition would be something like this:

1. First delete all the logical drives in any extended partitions
on that physical disk drive.

2. Next delete all the extended DOS partitions.

3. Finally, delete the primary DOS partition.

When you begin this process, by deleting logical drives, FDISK will show you a listing of all the drives in the extended partition. The listing will look like this:

Drv	Volume Label	Mbytes	System	Usage
D:	WP	15	FAT12	25%
E:	DATA	30	FAT16	50%
F:	PROGRAMS	15	FAT12	25%

FDISK will tell you the total size of the extended partition, and ask you which drive to delete (by drive specification, D:, E:, etc.) as well as the volume label (to make very sure you want to delete it). FDISK will ask you one final time if you want to delete the logical drive (to make very, very sure) before erasing it. If you happen to want to delete only one of the logical drives in a partition, FDISK will rename the remaining logical drives to take up the gap. For example, if you removed E:, then F: would be renamed as E:.

FDISK can also be used to display the existing partition information, showing you the size and percentages of the primary and extended partitions for each drive in your system. Choose option 4 from the main FDISK menu to use this feature. A submenu within the Display Partition Information module will show you information about each of the logical drives in an extended partition.

USING MORE THAN ONE OPERATING SYSTEM

Earlier in this chapter we pointed out that at this writing it is necessary to limit your disk volumes to 32 megabytes or less in order to ensure that any other operating systems you may boot from the floppy drive will be able to access your hard disk.

You should also know that Microsoft has provided its software developers with instructions for implementing a *dual boot* capability on some hard disks. This feature allows installing two operating systems, such as OS/2 and MS-DOS, on the same hard disk. A built-in program asks the user on boot-up which OS to use or, if no reply is given, to boot up one of them as the default.

While some enterprising software company may provide an automated system for installing dual boot in the future, the do-it-yourself approach is probably beyond the capabilities of most of the readers of this book.

For example, the OS invisible files for both OS/2 and DOS have the same names, IBMDOS.COM and IBMBIO.COM, even though OS/2 can't run .COM files. Since the boot-up files must reside in the root directory and since two files can't have the same name, you can see that the problems start early. The dual-boot facility involves things like changing the names of these files, and then using DEBUG to find and replace every occurrence of the names in the boot software. This is not an easy task.

If you *are* up to patching COMMAND.COM, there have been articles in publications like *PC TECH Journal* that will get you started. Don't expect to find step-by-step instructions. You'll need to understand most of what you're doing.

SUMMARY

In this chapter, we have covered the basics of setting up your hard disk with the FDISK command. We looked at the differences between FDISK in DOS 3.2 and earlier, DOS 3.3, and DOS 4.0. Those of you who do not have DOS 4.0 can skip ahead to Chapter 8, Where you'll find a discussion of hierarchical subdirectories.

DOS 4.0 users will want to continue on with Chapter 7, which will explain some of the ins and outs of installing DOS using SELECT.

7

Using SELECT to Install DOS 4.0

INTRODUCTION

Until DOS 4.0 was introduced, installing DOS on hard disk could be particularly confusing for the new user. First it was necessary to boot the computer using a floppy disk with the version of DOS one wished to install. Then, the system files could be installed on the hard disk using the SYS command. Or, if the hard disk was new and unused (or if the owner wanted to start from scratch), the FORMAT command with the /S parameter could be put to work.

Yet, that was only the start. The rest of the DOS files had to be copied over manually, preferably into an appropriate subdirectory. Nearly every user in the world eventually decided to use C:\DOS as the home for DOS files, but an alarming number had to figure this out the hard way. Then each user had to figure out how to interface the printer with DOS, install a disk caching program, or perform some other tasks that seem routine for the experienced DOS veteran but might be confusing for the neophyte.

DOS 4.0 introduced a revamped setup program, SELECT.EXE, which, since it was invoked automatically when the INSTALL disk was booted, became the default means of installing DOS on disk. Previously, SELECT was a more limited utility used to choose country information for your keyboard. If you had no need to change to a different country code page, you probably never had occasion to use SELECT. In fact, prior to DOS 3.3, SELECT worked only with floppy disks, and not hard disks.

Now SELECT has evolved into a more versatile setup program that will indeed help the neophyte install DOS 4.0 more easily. This chapter will explain how it works, and how to bypass it, if necessary.

BYPASSING SELECT WITH FORMAT AND SYS

If you are installing DOS 4.0 for the first time, you will have only the IBM-supplied diskettes. One of these will be labeled "IN-STALL." Boot that diskette, allowing the program to automatically load the SELECT program. Immediately press F3 to EXIT SELECT and go to the DOS prompt. From there, you may install DOS 4.0 using SYS or FORMAT with the /S option, as described in the last chapter.

You can use this method to make bootable disks of another format if your computer is equipped with disk drives of several sizes. You can also install DOS 4.0 on your hard disk in this way.

You must make sure that you copy all the DOS 4.0 files to your hard disk, replacing any of those from an earlier version, if you happened to update with SYS. If you try to use FORMAT, CHKDSK, or another DOS external command from one version of DOS with a different version, you'll be shown an error message. It's up to you to properly update these files if you elect to bypass SELECT.

STARTING UP SELECT

To install DOS using SELECT, insert the INSTALL disk in drive A: and boot your computer. You'll be shown the IBM DOS SELECT screen. If you are using 3.5–inch diskettes, you may press Enter. If you have booted from 5.25–inch disks, remove the INSTALL disk and insert the one labeled SELECT.

As the program progresses, you'll be asked to supply information, and to move from one selection to another. As with most programs, the cursor keys will move the cursor in the direction of the arrow printed on them. You can also move from one selection on a screen to the next using the TAB key. The Enter key will take you to the next step, while Escape will allow you to "back up" and return to a previous screen, which also nullifies the entries you have made on the current page.

Three function keys can also be used within SELECT. The F1 key displays on-line HELP, which you can page through using the PgUp and PgDn keys. As previously noted, the F3 key will EXIT the SELECT utility and return you to the DOS prompt. The F9 key will let you see the special key assignments of SELECT while using the HELP facility.

The various steps of the SELECT process include choosing a drive and DOS location, and entering information used to build customized AUTOEXEC.BAT and CONFIG.SYS files (both these files will be explained in detail later in this book).

Note: SELECT is very forgiving. You may choose the options you want in the order listed below, but will still have a chance to review them and make changes before the actual installation is done.

1. After some explanatory screens, SELECT will ask you if you want:
   A. minimum DOS function; maximum program workspace.
   B. balanced DOS functions and program workspace.
   C. maximum DOS function; minimum program workspace.

   Don't be alarmed. The choice you're being asked to make here is not as complicated as it appears. When SELECT installs DOS, it creates certain default files for you that can enable or disable optional DOS functions, such as the ability to print graphics screens by pressing the Control-Prt Scr key. These extra functions all take up extra memory from the 640K basic memory you probably have in your computer. The more of them you add, the less memory you have available for applications programs. Some of these require a lot of memory to run, while others, such as spreadsheets, function better with more memory.

With minimum DOS functions, SELECT will not add any extra features; with the maximum, it will add things like ANSI.SYS support and GRAPHICS support. However, you can always add these at another time. We'll show you what to do later in this book. For now you may safely choose either the minimum DOS functions for balanced DOS functions if you wish.

2. SELECT will next ask if you wish to use the predefined COUNTRY code for your computer. For most of you, the program will choose the U.S.A. as the default value, and you may accept it.

3. Select installation drive. SELECT will ask you whether you want to install DOS 4.0 on your hard disk or one of the floppy disk drives. To install on the hard disk, choose option 1.

4. Next, SELECT will ask you to specify the location for DOS. A directory called C:\DOS is the default. You may press Enter to accept that name, or type in a name of your choice.

5. SELECT will ask you to specify the number of printers you have, and what type. A list of different IBM printers is presented; you may also choose Other Parallel Printer and Other Serial Printer if you have some other manufacturer's model. Up to seven different printers can be specified, including the printer port each is connected to (LPT1, LPT2, LPT3 and COM1, COM2, COM3, and COM4).

6. After that, if your hard disk already contains DOS files, you will be asked if you wish to update all the DOS files on the fixed disk, or just copy non-system files to the directory you have selected.

7. Finally, SELECT will ask you if you wish to accept the default values entered by the program for DOS functions, or to make changes of your own. If you decide to review the list, you'll find that the choices include:

Code page switching
Extended Display support
GRAFTABL support
GRAPHICS Print Screen support
DOS SHELL
RAM disk

As noted, you can always add any of these to your system later, so if you don't understand the options now, don't worry about it. They will be explained later in this book.

Finally, when you are satisfied with the options, you can go ahead and proceed with the installation. SELECT takes care of copying the necessary files automatically. It will also create files called AUTOEXEC.400 and CONFIG.400, which you may rename as AUTOEXEC.BAT and CONFIG.SYS. The .400 extension is used to keep the new files from overwriting any existing AUTOEXEC.BAT or CONFIG.SYS file you may have on a hard disk being updated. If you have no such files (say, because the disk has just been formatted), you may rename the files SELECT creates. You may also examine them and incorporate their commands in your own start-up files.

Both AUTOEXEC.BAT and CONFIG.SYS will be addressed in more detail later.

SUMMARY

In this chapter we learned how to install DOS 4.0 on a hard disk, using the SELECT command. We also looked at how to bypass SELECT entirely, in case you are a more advanced user, or need simply to update a disk that already has DOS installed on it. Each of the steps in the SELECT utility were covered in some detail. If you understood everything except how to choose a subdirectory for your DOS files, your questions will be answered in the next chapter. There, we'll look at one of the basic tools of the hard disk user: hierarchical directory structures.

CHAPTER

8

Hierarchical Directories

INTRODUCTION

Learning DOS is something of a circular procedure: It's much easier to understand if you already know how it works. Many of the topics in this book form a foundation for others that are presented later. In some cases, though, you really need to understand something that is explained later to get a good grasp of the present topic. Yet, it's impossible to explain *everything* first.

The concept of subdirectories is one of those essential topics that are absolutely necessary for hard disk users to understand. To understand how subdirectories work, you need to know something of how a hard disk operates, and a few simple DOS commands. However, knowing about subdirectories also helps you to understand how the hard disk works and how to better use those simple commands.

So, now is as good a time as any to jump into the subject of *hierarchical* directories. If you weren't familiar with subdirectories before, some of the things discussed earlier in the book may become clearer now.

AN ORGANIZATION SCHEME

Uncle Scrooge liked to keep all his money in a big vault where he could see at a glance the extent of his fortune. The rest of us are happier that banks allot us individual accounts so we can keep things separated. A hard disk drive represents riches of another sort: vast quantities of storage space, resembling in some ways Scrooge's money vault. While it might provide some with a sense of power to type DIR and watch as seven or eight hundred files scroll past on the screen, most of us would soon tire of the lack of organization.

One solution might be the sort of file naming scheme discussed in Chapter 3. We could then limit the number of files displayed by DIR only to those matching a given file specification. However, you would be unable to view files conveniently without stopping to think of the desired combination of characters. You also might still have hundreds of files meeting the specification, or might even run out of characters to use to properly differentiate files with some schemes. Those who didn't want to implement a detailed file naming plan would be out of luck.

For once, floppy disk users seem to have an advantage: They can simply store files on separate disks. These can be clearly labeled and filed on the desktop in a suitable container. When you want a letter written by David Busch in 1988, it's a simple matter to retrieve the floppy disk labeled BUSCH LETTERS 1988 and look for the one you want. Of course, with 360K disks, a given type of file may fill up the available space quickly. It would be necessary to create BUSCH LETTERS 1988–A, BUSCH LETTERS 1988–B, etc. to accommodate a very active person.

Not surprisingly, a hard disk can provide the same capability as a floppy disk, with some important advantages. The hard disk can be divided into separate, logical "floppies" that can store individual sets of files. Unlike a floppy disk, each of the logical floppies can be of any size we need, up to the capacity of the hard disk itself. And, there is no need to swap disks in and out of the computer to use the logical disk we want; they can all reside on the hard disk at one time.

These imaginary floppy disks are in fact provided in the form of DOS's *hierarchical directory structure*. The hard disk is the cabinet that you keep your set of "floppies" in. Individual disks can be grouped by dividers (subdirectories in the cabinet), further differentiated by labels (further subdirectories), and marked by individual file names. DOS 3.3 and later versions even allow you to have several different cabinets, the DOS partitions and volumes. Adding another hard disk lets you expand to include *more* cabinets.

The label on the outside of the drawer corresponds to the main or *root* directory of your hard disk. Assume for a moment that a certain hard disk computer is used only for storing customer order information for a mail-order company. That label might be OR-DERS: underneath that would be a listing of the various folders within the drawer, broken down by some convenient classification, such as quarters of the year. So, the major folder headings might be 1QUARTER, 2QUARTER, 3QUARTER, and 4QUARTER. These headings would correspond to the major subdirectories listed in your root directory.

On the front of each folder might be further classifications. On the 1QUARTER folder there may be a label listing PAID ORDERS and BACKORDERS. (Be assured that no mail order company actually uses this organization, which is simplified for the sake of the example.) Because all the classifications are nested one inside another in an arrangement that can be charted to look something like a tree, hierarchical directories are said to be *tree-structured*. Translated from a file cabinet to a computer, our directory structure might look something like this:

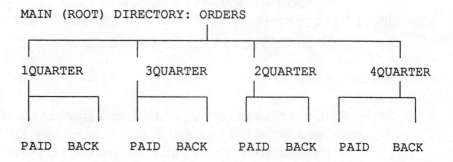

```
MAIN (ROOT) DIRECTORY: ORDERS

   1QUARTER        3QUARTER        2QUARTER        4QUARTER


  PAID   BACK    PAID   BACK    PAID   BACK    PAID    BACK
```

Nested within each directory may be one or more subdirectories containing files or other subdirectories. For example, in addition to the subdirectories like PAID or BACK, the 3QUARTER subdirectory may contain files of its own that pertain to the entire quarter, such as sales reports. The PAID subdirectory could include paid invoices as well as reports on payments, statements, aged listings, etc.

When you are logged into the root directory, the contents of the directories below are invisible to you. DIR will reveal only the names of the files in the root directory, plus the names of the subdirectories themselves.Subdirectories are always shown with the indication <DIR> in the size column:

```
Volume in drive C is ORDERS
Volume Serial Number is 2611-1DF8
Directory of  C:\

COMMAND   COM         37637 06-17-89 12:00p
CONFIG    SYS           427 08-19-89 10:55a
AUTOEXEC  BAT          2194 08-19-89 10:38a
2QUARTER       <DIR>         10-15-89  9:02a
4QUARTER       <DIR>         10-15-89  9:03a
3QUARTER       <DIR>         10-15-89  9:04a
1QUARTER       <DIR>         10-15-89  9:04a
```

You are looking only at the root directory and its files, representing a tree that looks something like this:

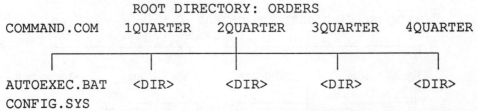

```
          ROOT DIRECTORY: ORDERS
COMMAND.COM    1QUARTER    2QUARTER    3QUARTER    4QUARTER
   ┌───────────────┬───────────┬───────────────┬───────────┐
   │               │           │               │           │
AUTOEXEC.BAT    <DIR>       <DIR>         <DIR>          <DIR>
CONFIG.SYS
```

A subdirectory is nothing more than a special type of file that contains a list of the files within that subdirectory. DIR will display the subdirectory's file name, but you can't erase or move the file with conventional DOS commands. Special commands for creating and removing files will be introduced shortly.

There are other differences between subdirectories and conventional files. When you type

```
DIR filename
```

DOS shows you whether or not that file exists in the specified directory.

```
DIR C:\COMMAND.COM
```

would produce a display like this:

```
Volume in drive C is ORDERS
Volume Serial Number is 2611-1DF8
Directory of  C:\

COMMAND   COM       37637 06-17-89 12:00p
```

However, when you type

```
DIR directory name
```

DOS will display the file names of the files *within* that subdirectory. For example, DIR 3QUARTER would generate a screen display like this:

```
Volume in drive C is ORDERS
Volume Serial Number is 2611-1DF8
Directory of C:\3QUARTER
.              <DIR>        10-15-89  9:02a
..             <DIR>         9-14-89  8:00a
PAID           <DIR>        10-15-89  9:08a
BACK           <DIR>        10-15-89  9:08a
```

The subdirectory hierarchy forms a *path* leading from the root down through the directories to the particular file that you want to access. To view the contents of a subdirectory, you must include in the DIR command the names of all the *parent* directories above that subdirectory to provide DOS with the proper path to that directory. The subdirectory names are separated with a backslash, and the root directory is referred to simply with a backslash. Either of these two commands could be used to produce a listing of the files in the top directory of your hard disk:

```
DIR C:\
DIR \
```

The first version would work even if you happened to be logged onto another disk or another directory in drive C:. The second version would only provide a directory of C:\ if you happened to be already logged onto drive C:. If you were logged onto drive A:, the command would produce a listing of the root directory of that drive instead.

The correct path will provide you with a list of the files in any directory you want. For example:

```
DIR C:\2QUARTER
DIR \2QUARTER
```

would provide a directory of C:\2QUARTER, with the same limitations as the previous example. You would be shown a list of the files as well as subdirectories in that particular directory, which is one level down from the root directory, \.

You can access directories several levels below by typing out the proper path to those files. To see all the backorder files from the first quarter pertaining to SMITH, type:

```
DIR C:\1QUARTER\BACK\SMITH\*.*
```

MOVING THROUGH DIRECTORIES: THE CHDIR COMMAND

To change the active directory from the root directory to one of the subdirectories, you may use the CHDIR command, commonly abbreviated CD. (Abbreviations, such as REN for RENAME and ERA for ERASE, must be those built into DOS.) Go back to the root directory ORDERS (what you think of as the directory name of the root is actually the *volume* name or label applied by DOS after formatting, or by using the LABEL command). If you were to type CD 4QUARTER, and then DIR, you would see the following:

```
Volume in drive C is ORDERS
Volume Serial Number is 2611-1DF8
Directory of C:\4QUARTER
.               <DIR>         10-15-89   9:02a
..              <DIR>          9-14-89   8:00a
PAID            <DIR>         10-15-89   9:11a
BACK            <DIR>         10-15-89   9:12a
```

Subdirectory names have the same restrictions as other file names: eight characters plus an optional three-character extension. Most users don't apply the extension, but you may otherwise have to abbreviate to fit the name you wish into the eight-character limitation.

The single dot entry represents the current directory. Typing

```
DIR .
```

is the same as simply typing DIR alone. The double dot represents the next directory level up, or the parent directory. Within a given directory, you may see the files in the directory *above* by typing

```
DIR ..
```

at the DOS prompt. Other DOS commands also make use of these abbreviations: You may erase the files in the current directory by typing one of the following:

```
ERASE  .
DEL  .
```

It is possible to jump from one subdirectory to another in great leaps by typing the CD command and the correct path name. If you happened to be in subdirectory C:\3QUARTER\PAID, and wanted to go back up the tree and down again to check on back-orders in the second quarter of the year, you could type

```
CD\2QUARTER\BACK
```

to get there in one jump.

CREATING A SUBDIRECTORY: THE MKDIR COMMAND

Subdirectories are created with the MKDIR or MD command. You may type

```
MD directory name
```

to create a directory below the parent directory you are in. If the current directory was C:\3QUARTER and you wanted a new directory called C:\3QUARTER\LETTERS to store correspon-dence, you could type:

```
MD  LETTERS
```

From the root directory, it would have been simpler to type in:

```
MD  \3QUARTER\LETTERS
```

If a directory already exists by that name, or the name you have chosen is invalid, DOS will helpfully remind you.

REMOVING A SUBDIRECTORY: THE RMDIR COMMAND

Directory names cannot be erased by normal DEL or ERASE commands. You must *first* erase all the files in that directory (ERASE C:\3QUARTER\LETTERS, for example, will delete all the files, but *not* the subdirectories or *their* files in subdirectory C:\3QUARTER\LETTERS). Then use the RMDIR or RD command:

```
RD C:\3QUARTER\LETTERS
```

THE TREE COMMAND

The DOS TREE command will allow you to display the structure of all the directories in a hard disk system. It includes an /F option that will in addition show the files in those subdirectories. The examples that follow show typical output for TREE, both with and without the /F switch. The command works identically for both DOS 4.0 and earlier versions. However, with DOS 4.0, a graphic representation of the tree structure is made by connecting subdirectories with lines (and by connecting files and subdirectories with lines if the /F switch is used). The examples shown below represent the earlier, non-graphic display style.

Output of TREE command:

```
DIRECTORY PATH LISTING FOR VOLUME DRIVE D
Path: \BATCH
Sub-directories:   None
Path: \DOS
Sub-directories:   None
Path: \DW4
Sub-directories:   None
Path: \FINDER
Sub-directories:   None
Path: \KEYWORKS
Sub-directories:   None
Path: \QUATTRO
Sub-directories:   FILES
```

```
Path: \QUATTRO\FILES
Sub-directories:   None
Path: \SYS
Sub-directories:   None
```

TREE Command with the /F switch:

```
DIRECTORY PATH LISTING FOR VOLUME DRIVE D
Files:             AUTO     .BAT
                   COMMAND  .COM
Path: \BATCH
Sub-directories:   None
Files:             A           .BAT
                   ARCHIVE  .BAT
                   AUTOEXEC.BAT
                   B           .BAT
                   BASIC    .BAT
                   BATCHES  .BAT
                   CHECK    .BAT
                   COM      .BAT
                   ED       .BAT
                   EDRIVE   .ASC
                   KILL     .BAT
                   LOCATER  .BAT
                   MOVE     .BAT
                   MSG      .BAT
                   NU       .BAT
                   PURGE    .BAT
                   X        .BAT
                   Z        .BAT
Path: \DOS
Sub-directories:   None

Files:             ASSIGN   .COM
                   BACKUP   .COM
                   BASIC    .COM
                   BASICA   .COM
```

```
BOOT     .COM
MEM      .EXE
COMP     .COM
DEBUG    .COM
DISKCOMP .COM
DISKCOPY .COM
EDLIN    .COM
FDISK    .COM
FORMAT   .COM
GRAFTABL .COM
GRAPHICS .COM
KEYB     .COM
LABEL    .COM
LOCATE   .COM
MODE     .COM
MORE     .COM
PRINT    .COM
RECOVER  .COM
RESTORE  .COM
SELECT   .COM
SYS      .COM
TREE     .COM
4201     .CPI
5202     .CPI
EGA      .CPI
LCD      .CPI
ATTRIB   .EXE
FASTOPEN .EXE
FIND     .EXE
JOIN     .EXE
NLSFUNC  .EXE
REPLACE  .EXE
SCAN     .EXE
SHARE    .EXE
SORT     .EXE
XCOPY    .EXE
```

```
Path: \DW4
Sub-directories:   None
Files:             DW4A0100.HP1
                   DW4A0100.PG1
                   DW4A0100.PG2
                   DW4A0100.PG3
                   DW4A0100.PG4
                   DW4PG   .COM
                   DW4VCAPC.COM
                   PROFILE .PRF
                   USENGL  .DIC
                   USENGL  .SUP
Path: \FINDER
Sub-directories:   None
Files:             WF      .EXE
                   WFBG    .SYN
                   WFINSTAL.EXE
Path: \KEYWORKS
Sub-directories:   None
Files:             KWHELP
                   KWCONFIG
                   KEYWORKS.EXE
                   DEFAULT .KW
Path: \QUATTRO
Sub-directories:   FILES
Files:             123     .ALT
                   123     .RSC
                   CLASS   .PRN
                   CONFIG  .BGI
                   DRV0    .BGI
                   DRV1    .BGI
                   DRV2    .BGI
                   DRV3    .BGI
                   DRV4    .BGI
                   DRV5    .BGI
```

```
                             EURO     .CHR
                             LOADPROG.EXE
                             Q        .EXE
                             Q1       .OVL
                             Q123     .DEF
                             Q2       .OVL
                             Q3       .OVL
                             Q4       .OVL
                             QM123    .DEF
                             QUATTRO  .DEF
                             QUATTRO  .HLP
                             QUATTRO  .RSC
Path: \QUATTRO\FILES
Sub-directories:  None
Files:                       BILLS    .WKQ
                             ACCT     .WKZ
                             CONTRIB  .WKZ
                             DEPOSITS.WKZ
                             DRAW87   .WKZ
                             EXPENSE  .WKZ
                             FINANCE  .WKZ
Path: \SYS
Sub-directories:  None
Files:                       ANSI     .SYS
                             COUNTRY  .SYS
                             DISPLAY  .SYS
                             DRIVER   .SYS
                             KEYBOARD.SYS
                             PRINTER  .SYS
                             VDISK    .SYS
                             RAMQUEST.SYS
                             RQDISK   .SYS
                             RQEMM    .SYS
                             IBMCACHE.SYS
                             CONFIG   .SYS
```

DIVIDING UP YOUR HARD DISK

Designing your hard disk directory structure has a lot in common with organizing any sort of information management system. Unless you have a logical structure, particular files will be difficult or impossible to locate. You should take some time to figure out a system that will work efficiently for you.

The first thing to decide, if you are using DOS 3.3 or later, is how many volumes to divide your hard disk(s) into. As noted in Chapter 6, DOS 3.3's FDISK command introduced the ability to create a primary and extended DOS partition on a single disk. The extended partition can be further divided into individual volumes, each no larger than 32 megabytes (with DOS 3.3). With DOS 4.0, we gained the ability to make these volumes larger than 32 megabytes.

If you have an IBM PS/2 Model 60 or 80 equipped with a 44–megabyte hard disk, you might want to divide the disk into two logical volumes, drives C: and D:. The size of each volume is set by FDISK. DOS uses disks that are larger than about 16 megabytes in a more efficient way than it does smaller disks. As explained at greater length in Chapter 6, because of this, you may not want to divide your 44–megabyte disk into one large 32–megabyte volume and one smaller 12–megabyte volume. Instead, two 22–megabyte volumes or a 28–megabyte and 16–megabyte partitioning scheme may make more sense.

With DOS 4.0, you may choose to have a single, very large hard disk, or several volumes of a size you select. Having one large hard disk means that you don't have to remember whether a given file is stored on drive C: or drive D: or drive E:. On the down side, such a large disk may be more unwieldy to manage. Having several volumes lends itself to dividing up files in a logical, easy-to-remember way.

You might, for example, choose to store all your applications programs on the second volume, drive D: while data files are located on drive C:. There are two main reasons to do this.

First, most of the manipulation of files that you do will be of the data files used by your programs. If these are stored on drive C:, you'll already be logged onto that drive when the computer boots, and ready to do your housekeeping. File maintenance will be easier with all the files located on a single disk volume.

Second, applications programs are generally copied over to the hard disk and remain there, unchanged until replaced by an updated version. Keeping all your software on a single hard disk volume allows storing those files in the most efficient way, with all the sectors in consecutive order or *contiguous*. DOS can find and read them much faster than if the sectors of your programs were scattered all over the disk.

Of course, when you first load your hard disk with software, if the disk was blank DOS will automatically place the files contiguously, whether they are stored on drive C: or drive E: or some other drive. With continuous use, as files are erased and replaced, the available free sectors inevitably become scattered. Any *new* software you copied to the hard disk might be stored in fragmented form. This new software would include the updates to your current programs. If the new files happened to be longer than the old, DOS would have to find some empty sectors elsewhere on the disk for them. The result: DOS will take longer to load your software.

If you keep only software on a given volume, less fragmentation will result, because files are not copied and erased so frequently. You can quickly back up your software erase that volume and copy it back once a year or so if you wish to eliminate any small amount of fragmentation that creeps in. As mentioned earlier, there are various utility programs that you can purchase that will eliminate fragmentation. However, why pay extra money for a utility that you may not need to use if you plan your hard disk usage carefully?

ANOTHER SCHEME

Here's another possible hard disk partitioning scheme. Some of us may find that we need to use *both* DOS and another operating system, such as XENIX or OS/2. DOS versions later than 3.2 don't allow you to have more than one bootable DOS partition (barring the dual-boot scheme discussed in Chapter 6). Even so, you may use many of the same files with both OS/2 and DOS. The only stickler is that you can boot only one or the other from your hard disk. The other must be booted from a floppy disk.

A well-thought-out DOS partitioning scheme can simplify this situation considerably. Set aside drive C:, which is the bootable partition, for the operating system you use most often. All the boot-up files as well as external commands would be located on that disk. A second, non-bootable volume can be designated for the alternate operating system. You can store all the operating system files, including external commands, on that disk.

You would boot the second operating system from a floppy disk. However, that disk would contain *only* the files necessary to start the boot-up process. In the case of DOS, these would include the DOS invisible files, COMMAND.COM, CONFIG.SYS, and AUTOEXEC.BAT. A SHELL command in the CONFIG.SYS file would tell the floppy-based system to look for COMMAND.COM on the hard disk.

AUTOEXEC.BAT and CONFIG.SYS are special files, to be explained later in this book, that contain lists of commands the operating system uses to configure itself and run programs when the computer is first booted. You can include commands in AUTOEXEC.BAT that will transfer control over to an equivalent command file on drive D: to finish the boot-up process. It would also tell DOS to look for COMMAND.COM thereafter on drive D: Another command would tell DOS to look for its external commands and other files on drive D: Once the computer has booted, you can remove the floppy disk and run just as if you had booted from the hard disk.

DESIGNING A SUBDIRECTORY STRUCTURE

The next step is to design the subdirectory structure itself. Many people find it convenient to store *only* the minimum files necessary to boot the hard disk in the root directory. These would include AUTOEXEC.BAT, COMMAND.COM, and CONFIG.SYS (all these are explained in more detail later). Then, the root directory's subdirectories would be created, based on the particular applications of the user. Here is a typical directory structure, based on the assumption that the user has only one hard disk or one hard disk volume, on which are stored both programs and data:

```
ROOT
Subdirectories:
BATCH
DOS
LOTUS
Subdirectories:
 WKS-ACCT
WKS-TAX
DRIVERS
GRAPHICS
COMM
WP
Subdirectories:
LETTERS
86
87
88
MEMOS
REPORTS
PROPOSALS
STYLEFMT
UTILITY
Subdirectories
SIDEKICK
OUTLINE
DOS
```

Note that we don't really have two subdirectories named DOS; one is called C:\DOS, while the other is C:\UTILITY\DOS. Their full path names are different, and DOS would never get them confused.

NAMING FILES

To help make finding and manipulating files in subdirectories easier, it might be useful to review a few of the file naming conventions discussed in Chapter 3. A file's true name includes its drive specifier (A:, B:, C:, etc.) as well as the *full* path name. That's why you can have two files on line at one time with the same name if they are in different drives or directories. Both might be called TEST.DOC, but, on closer examination, the full file names may be A:TEST.DOC and C:\WP\TEST.DOC.

The reason why you don't always have to type the full file name is that DOS accepts certain values as *defaults* when they are not otherwise specified. For example, when you are logged onto A:, that drive specifier becomes the default. Should you type DIR JONES.DOC, DOS will assume you mean DIR A:JONES.DOC. Similarly, when logged onto a hard disk subdirectory, DOS will assign that directory's name path name as the default.

Thus, when logged onto C:\3QUARTER, you may type DIR JONES.DOC in order to see if C:\3QUARTER\JONES.DOC is there. If the file desired happened to be called C:\3QUARTER\LETTERS\SMITH.LTR and you were in subdirectory C:\3QUARTER, it would be necessary to type only DIR SMITH.LTR; DOS would add the C:\3QUARTER automatically as the default.

If no file specification is typed after a subdirectory name, DOS assumes that you are specifying *all* the files in that subdirectory. So, you need type only DIR LETTERS, and not DIR LETTERS*.*, to view the contents of subdirectory LETTERS. Similarly, to ERASE an entire subdirectory, you may type ERASE LETTERS instead of ERASE LETTERS*.*. DOS will even ask you "Are you sure (Y/N)" exactly as if you had typed ERASE *.*.

Further, to COPY from one subdirectory to another or to another disk, you may specify a subdirectory name:

```
COPY LETTERS B:
COPY LETTERS ..
COPY LETTERS ARCHIVE
COPY LETTERS C:\MISC\FILES
```

The first example would copy all the files in subdirectory LET-TERS to B:, while the second would copy all the files in that subdirectory to the next highest, or parent, directory. The third example would copy the files to another subdirectory at the same level (that is, within the same parent directory) called ARCHIVE. The last example would copy all the files to a subdirectory called C:\MISC\FILES.

THE ENVIRONMENT AND THE PATH COMMAND

Starting with version 2.0 of MS-DOS and PC-DOS, the operating system automatically begins searching through the Path specified in something called the system *environment* when looking for files ending in the .COM, .EXE, and .BAT extensions. The environment is a special area of memory reserved for storing information that can be accessed by DOS, various programs, and even simple files that you write yourself. The environment will be discussed in more detail in Chapter 11.

This area of memory is not complex to understand or use at all, since the information stored there is in the form of variables and definitions. From the DOS prompt type SET to see the current environment variables that have been defined. You may see something along these lines:

```
COMSPEC=C:\COMMAND.COM
PROMPT=$n$g
```

These values were set for you automatically by DOS when you booted up. However, simply by typing SET and a variable name and value you may redefine the environment variable. (Try typing "SET PROMPT Hello There!" Your system prompt will change from C> (or A>, etc.) to Hello There! Now, type SET alone on a line once more to see how the environment variable has been changed.

To return your prompt to normal, just type PROMPT on a line by itself. Then type SET to see that the environment variable has been returned to its default.

There is one important environment variable that is useful to hard disk users, PATH. This variable provides a listing of the disk drives and subdirectories that should be searched for system files (the .COM, .EXE, and .BAT files previously mentioned) if the file is not found in the current directory. You may string them together in the order to be searched, separated by semicolons. From the command line, type:

```
SET PATH=C:\;A:\
```

Then type SET to see your new environment variable. Actually, in the case of the variables with predefined functions, SET is optional. DOS doesn't allow using PATH, or PROMPT, or COMSPEC variables for any other purpose, so you may type them alone without using SET.

```
PATH=C:\;A:\
```

would produce exactly the same results: causing DOS to search, first, the current directory for a system file, then C:\ and A:\. This is a powerful capability, because it allows us to store frequently used files in subdirectories of our choosing on the hard disk, and still have DOS find them no matter *what* subdirectory we happen to be using at the moment. For that reason, many users like to copy all their DOS files (the external commands like FORMAT.COM and utilities) to a subdirectory called DOS. By keeping them separate, it is easy to update a hard disk to a new version of DOS, simply by using the SYS command and then copying all the other programs over to the DOS subdirectory.

You may also elect to keep batch files separate in a BATCH subdirectory, and other programs in their own directories. A simple PATH command will tell DOS exactly where to look:

```
PATH=C:\;C:\DOS;C:\BATCH
```

It is not a good idea to have a PATH command that includes too many subdirectories. If a file does not reside in any of the listed directories, because it does not exist at all, or you made a typo when you typed the name, or it resides in some other directory, DOS can waste a lot of time hunting through a long list of subdirectories specified by PATH.

For example, if your PATH command looked like this:

```
PATH=C:\;C:\DOS\UTILS;C:\BATCH;C:\DOS\CMDS
```

each time DOS looked for a file, it would search through all the paths listed, in that order. Checking C:\ wouldn't take long. However, to view the next subdirectory in the path, DOS would first check the root directory of C: for a subdirectory file called DOS. It would read that file, looking for one called UTILS. Then DOS would read the UTILS file to look for the program being searched for. Because DOS treats subdirectories as files, it isn't possible to go directly to C:\DOS\UTILS. Each of the "parent" files in turn has to be read.

This is a very good reason for keeping your PATH short, and your subdirectories nested only a few levels deep. Also keep in mind that DOS allows the PATH command to be no more than 128 characters long.

Most put the PATH command in their AUTOEXEC.BAT file so the environment is set properly as soon as they boot the computer.

In Chapter 10, we'll explore ways of tailoring your system through tools like the AUTOEXEC.BAT file, and present a sample file you can use as a model in configuring your own system.

THE APPEND COMMAND

APPEND is a parallel command to PATH, introduced with DOS 3.3. It tells DOS to search in the listed directories for *data* files regardless of extension. Just as PATH provides DOS with a list of directories to search for .COM, .EXE, and .BAT files, APPEND provides DOS with a list to search for any file not in the current directory, regardless of extension.

APPEND is a memory-resident utility (it becomes an internal command once it has been loaded; DOS no longer needs to load it from disk each time you call it). It has the syntax:

```
APPEND d:path /X /E
```

As in the PATH command, **d:path** can include a series of directory and path names, separated by semicolons. The optional switches increase the flexibility of the command. The /X switch tells DOS to search the paths specified by APPEND for the DOS executable files (just like the PATH command). If /E is specified, the APPEND path is stored in the environment variable "APPEND", where it can be changed or viewed with the SET command. Without /E, the APPEND path is stored internally and is not available for changes or batch file access by the end user.

APPEND on a line by itself will display a list of the appended paths, once it has been loaded for the first time in a session. You can cancel the APPEND paths with this syntax:

```
APPEND ;
```

APPEND requires about 4K of memory, or more, depending on the length of the path. The /X and /E parameters can only be invoked the first time following bootup that APPEND is used.

Advanced users take note (the rest of you will understand this paragraph better after reading Chapter 11): Any path specified by APPEND is passed along to any secondary command processors located after the initial copy of COMMAND.COM. Changes made to the APPEND path by the secondary command processor are passed back to the parent copy on EXIT, but only if APPEND had previously been loaded. In other words, you cannot load APPEND for the first time from a second command processor and expect the changes in the path to be passed back to the original command processor.

XCOPY, BACKUP and RESTORE should not be used while an APPEND path is in effect.

With DOS 4.0, several changes were made to APPEND. You can now turn the /X option on or off at will (previously, it could only be switched on.) The syntax for this is:

```
APPEND /X:ON
APPEND /X
```

to turn the feature on and

```
APPEND /X:OFF
```

to turn it off again, so DOS will no longer search the APPEND path for executable files.

You may also turn off APPEND's ability to search for files in the APPEND path that already have a path specified in the command line. Again, previously you could turn APPEND on but not off without rebooting. The correct syntax is:

```
APPEND /PATH:ON
APPEND /PATH:OFF
```

When the OFF option is invoked, DOS will not use the APPEND path to search for files if a path is already indicated. This saves some time. It also means that if a data file is not found in the subdirectory indicated by the path statement, your application program will have an error to handle; no additional searching will take place. Obviously, turning APPEND off in this case should be done only if you are fairly certain that DOS will be able to find the file in the path indicated, or that if it does not, it wouldn't have found it in the APPEND path anyway. Otherwise, you are gaining a small bit of speed, at the expense of losing APPEND's advantages.

SUMMARY

This chapter has provided an introduction to hierarchical directories, which are a basic concept for understanding how hard disks work. We learned some ways that a hard disk can be divided into logical volumes, and further allocated into subdirectories.

The PATH command, which allows DOS to find specific executable files, also was explained. Now you know enough to explore a few DOS commands that are of particular interest to hard disk users.

DOS Directory Structures and the FAT

INTRODUCTION

In the last chapter, we looked at how DOS keeps track of files through a hierarchical directory structure. To use your hard disk, you really need to understand the concept of directories and sub-directories. This chapter delves in a little more detail into the way DOS stores files on your hard disk. None of the information here is essential to use a hard disk, and may be a bit too technical for your taste. Feel free to skip to the next section of the book, which is devoted to explaining the key DOS commands and features.

Those of you who want a not-too-technical explanation of a highly technical topic may enjoy this chapter, which explores the DOS directory and tells you just how DOS 4.0 was able to crash through the 32-megabyte barrier.

THE DOS DIRECTORY

During formatting, DOS creates a directory and file allocation table (FAT). This directory, which is initially empty, is referred to as the *root directory*. Other directories can be created at a later date and placed into the root directory, as *files*. These, known as subdirectories, were discussed in detail in Chapter 8.

The root directory is, quite literally, a table of contents of a disk. With a floppy disk, you may be quite limited as to how long that table may be. Single-sided 5.25–inch diskettes can have no more than 64 entries in the root directory, while double-sided 320K, 360K, and 720K disks may have up to 112 entries. High capacity diskettes (either the 1.2M 5.25–inch or 1.44M

3.5-inch disks) can contain 224. This limitation applies *only* to the root directory of floppy disks. Subdirectories, since they are stored as files, may contain any number of entries. Their files can grow to accept a virtually unlimited number of file names.

However, the data displayed by the DIR command are not all the information that DOS stores about the file. You are shown only the information that would have meaning to an end user. As you know, by typing DIR at the command line, you'll see a typical directory entry that looks something like this:

```
TEST DOC 4959 5-07-89 12:00p
```

This information is stored as a 32-byte entry in your DOS directory. These bytes represent the file name and file name extension, the length of the file in bytes, the date on which it was created, and the time at which it was created. The last two of these are encoded to allow them to be stored in two bytes each.

In addition to this information, DOS manages to cram into those 32 bytes data about the type of file, the file's *attribute*, and a pointer that determines how the directory entry relates to the FAT.

There are six possible file attributes stored in the directory entry. Several of these are switch-like attributes: they have only two states, on or off. For example, the read-only attribute is stored as a single bit in the directory entry of a file. If the bit is a 1, then that file may be loaded into memory, but may not be written from memory back to disk. In effect, you can see the contents of the file, but may not replace it with an altered version. Nor can you erase a file that is marked as read-only. If the file's read-only attribute bit is a zero, you may read as well as write to the file.

Files also have an *archive* bit. This bit is given a value of 1 every time the file is written to disk. So, a file that you have just created as well as one that has just been updated will have an archive bit set. This bit is reset to 0 when the file is copied using XCOPY or BACKUP. In effect, the archive bit is used as a flag to tell DOS whether or not a file has been backed up since it was last changed.

The ATTRIB command, explained later in this book, can be used to set or reset the archive and read-only bits of your DOS files.

Files may be marked as *system* files. IBMDOS.COM is a system file, and is marked as such in its directory entry. Normally, you won't see such files during operations.

The rest of the directory entry is used to store the disk's volume label, and to mark a subdirectory (which DOS treats as a special type of file). Also found in the directory is the pointer to the appropriate location in the file allocation table for that file.

THE FILE ALLOCATION TABLE

Note that the directory entry doesn't tell DOS where to find a file. Instead, it provides the *starting cluster number* for that file, the first portion of your disk allocated to the file by the FAT. DOS uses the FAT to maintain information about every sector on your disk, and to track which sectors on which tracks are used to store the data that are associated with each file. In other words, the FAT sets aside or *allocates* all the sectors of the disk.

The layout of the FAT entries aren't important to you as a user of DOS, so we won't go into them here. There are, however, several things you need to know about how the FAT operates.

One of these, discussed briefly earlier in this book, is how that FAT allocates disk sectors. A bit of review might be in order, even if you already understand DOS's FAT scheme fairly well.

Each unit of disk space is assigned a unique number. With earlier versions of DOS, this number was a three-digit hexadecimal number or 12 binary digits. As such, the number range that could be represented was 0 to FFF in hex or 0 to 1111111111 in binary. Those both translate as 0 to 4,095 in decimal notation.

In other words, DOS was able to keep track of only 4096 different disk allocation units, or *clusters*, with a 12–bit number. (In truth, only 4,078 were available; some of the numbers were reserved by DOS for its own use). Since each DOS sector holds 512 bytes, some quick arithmetic will show you that no more than about 2 megabytes of disk storage can be allocated under such a scheme.

With floppy disks, that method is adequate. While there are some specialized disk formats that provide more than 2 megabytes of storage, the largest amount we have to contend with on a practical basis is the 1.44 megabytes provided by the high-density 3.5–inch microdisk. In fact, single-sector cluster sizes are used by DOS with single-sided diskettes—the 160K and 180K variety that no one uses any more, as well as 1.2M 5.25–inch high capacity disks. Other diskette formats use 1,024–byte, two-sector clusters.

Hard disks demand a different allocation method. Instead of assigning one of these valuable numbers to a single sector, DOS uses them to refer to a group of sectors. This makes sense, since most files consist of more than one sector's worth of data; in fact, the majority will have four or more sectors full of information. By making a cluster represent 16 sectors, or 8,192 bytes of data, DOS was able to refer to 16 x 8,192 or 32 megabytes of disk storage space, still using only a 12–bit number.

However, as we've seen, the larger cluster size is not without problems of its own. Such large clusters are not particularly efficient users of disk space, particularly when the operator has many small files.

With DOS 3.0, the FAT was changed to allow both 12–bit and 16–bit representations of cluster ID numbers. This had one unpleasant result. If you happen to boot your computer from a floppy disk containing DOS 2.x, and then try to read a hard disk that has been formatted under DOS 3.x or 4.0 using the 16–bit FAT, DOS 2.x will refuse to recognize it as a DOS disk.

However, on the plus side, a scheme whereby hard disks smaller than about 16 megabytes were formatted using 8,192–byte clusters and those larger than 16 megabytes with 2,048–byte clusters was introduced with DOS 3.0.

The 16–bit number FFFF in hex or 1111111111111111 in binary could represent numbers in the range 0 to 65,535.. That's 512 megabytes using 8,192–byte clusters and 128 megabytes even when the smaller 2,048–byte clusters are used. However, to retain compatibility with earlier versions of DOS, versions through DOS 3.30 still limited DOS logical disk drives to 32 megabytes or smaller. Compaq did introduce a version called DOS 3.31 that had an offbeat FAT scheme and larger disk volumes, but it never caught on.

With DOS 4.0, the full potential of the 16–bit FAT was realized. Several utility programs, including IFSFUNC.EXE and FILESYS.EXE, had to be introduced to take care of the new file system. In addition, changes were made to SHARE.EXE to support the larger disk volumes. CHKDSK was also changed to tell you what size clusters were used on your disk, as well as the number of allocation units still available. If you're fond of peeking at your disk sectors with tools like DEBUG, you'll notice that FORMAT now leaves a telltale marker in the boot sector of both floppy disks and hard disks marking them as FAT12 or FAT16.

The downside of the new system is the previously discussed incompatibility with earlier versions of DOS. If you do format a hard disk larger than 32 megabytes, you'll be unable to access it with earlier versions of DOS, or, at this writing, with the current version of OS/2. As always, you decide what your needs are, and make your choice.

HOW DOS FINDS A FILE'S SECTORS

The FAT entries on your hard disk for a particular file make up a chain of individual clusters, linked by pointers within each cluster. You might visualize the system as a series of notes left for you by a friend as he or she moves from one party to another on a particularly busy night. You arrive at the first party, only to find your friend has left. A note left for you provides the address of the next soiree. If it's a particularly swinging neighborhood, the parties may be next door to each other. Or, they might be scattered across town.

Similarly, DOS knows where to find the *first* cluster in a file's chain of clusters from the figure stored in the directory entry. That initial cluster in the FAT either contains a number representing the *next* cluster in the chain, or else indicates that it is the *last* cluster in the file. So, the chain of clusters which make up a file can easily be scattered all over your disk. DOS finds the address for the next cluster at the last one it read.

Such fragmentation is not a particularly efficient way of using your disk drive, since the drive must hunt back and forth across the platter surfaces to find all the clusters in a file. But it does allow the hard disk to use *all* the good clusters on a disk.

Sometimes a cluster can become orphaned. This usually takes place when a program opens a file but never closes it. Perhaps you shut off your computer or rebooted it while the program was operating. Since the orphaned file's directory entry is never completed, DOS doesn't know how to find that first cluster, which may be, nevertheless, already allocated to the file. DOS's CHKDSK program, discussed in more detail later in this book, can help you find and fix these orphaned clusters.

FINDING UNUSED SECTORS

In allocating space for a write request, DOS searches through the FAT until it finds a vacant cluster. DOS marks each cluster in the FAT to show its current status. A cluster marked with a 0 is free and available to be allocated to a file. Other numbers are used to mark that cluster as bad and unusable by DOS under any circumstances (these reserved numbers are part of the reason why DOS has fewer than the full number of FAT entries available to assign to clusters).

The remaining numbers provide the pointer that indicates the next cluster used by a file. There are some reserved numbers that are used to indicate the end of a file. DOS will pass over all these allocated clusters in searching for a free cluster. Versions of DOS prior to 3.x used a *first fit* algorithm. That is, when a new file is created, or sectors are added to an existing file, DOS begins looking for vacant space at the beginning of the FAT. DOS 3.x introduced a *next fit* algorithm, whereby DOS begins looking at the point at which it last began searching the FAT.

The net effect of this change is to cause DOS to use the oldest freed-up sectors first. The most recently freed-up sectors remain untouched, allowing you to restore erased files with software such as the Norton Utilities more successfully. Under the old scheme, unerasing files was most useful only if the chore could be carried out before any new files were written to the disk.

Once DOS locates a vacant cluster, it writes the data to that cluster and marks it used in the FAT. If more data than one cluster-ful are to be written, DOS will continue through the FAT until it finds the next available cluster. It will continue in this manner until all the information has been written to the file.

The space-management requirements for fixed disks dictate that the size of the FAT be variable on demand. With double-sided floppy disks, clusters are created on the lowest track number of disk side 1 first, and then the next disk plane (side 2) is addressed. This minimizes the amount of thrashing around that the disk head has to do to load or save a disk.

That's about all you need to know to understand FATs and the disk directory. Unless you intend to go mucking around with disk sectors (a very dangerous procedure for hard disk users), other details are superfluous.

SUMMARY

This chapter has been a brief discussion of how DOS tracks directory entries and notes the location of allocated sectors with the FAT. It should help you understand just how DOS 4.0 crashed through the 32–megabyte barrier. At this point, we've finished with our theoretical journey through the basics of DOS, and are ready to attack some of the more practical aspects of using DOS commands.

PART

Using
DOS
Features

10

Batch Files

INTRODUCTION

In a way, the hard disk has helped bring the batch file to full maturity as a tool for the personal computer user. Back in the bad old days, computers used floppy disks for more than backup and the transferring of programs and data. We actually booted our systems from floppies and ran programs with them.

Things are relative, of course. The author started in microcomputing in 1977 with a *cassette*-based computer and spent a year patiently waiting six to twelve minutes every time a program was loaded from tape. Several hours' work could be lost because a lightning storm crept up and caused a split-second power outage before a program could be saved. In those terms, even a simple floppy disk system seemed like a miracle of efficiency and power.

Batch files existed in those days under different names, and their use was extended to the first IBM PCs in 1981. Still, you would lose the ability to use a favorite batch file when you swapped disks; it wasn't until the hard disk that batching commands really began to take off.

With any floppy-based system, carrying out any decent sized series of tasks required much disk swapping and juggling. It was almost easier to carry out a series of commands manually, since you were stuck with the manual task of inserting and removing disks anyway.

Today, the average user's hard disk contains *all* the programs that user is likely to run, as well as *all* the data files that go with them. That makes it simple to tie all of them together with batch files. This chapter will explain what a batch file is, outline all the special DOS commands that are used in batch files, and provide you with some tips for writing your own.

BATCHES OF COMMANDS

A batch file is nothing more than a batch of commands that DOS carries out one at a time. The ability to type up a list of the commands to carry out, store that list in a file, and then tell DOS to carry out that batch simply by typing the file name is extremely valuable. After all, many of the things we do with hard disks require carrying out a number of steps in a predictable order.

Each time a particular word processing program is run, it may be necessary to first log over to drive C: (in case you were logged to another drive), change to the word processing subdirectory, load a memory-resident dictionary or thesaurus program, and then type a command that activates the WP software. Of course, when you leave the program, you'll want to exit the WP subdirectory.

Rather than type all these commands in each time such a series of operations is carried out, you can create a batch file to do them for you. A sample file, WP.BAT, might look like this:

```
ECHO OFF
C:
CD\ WP
C:\UTIL\THESAURUS
WORDRITE C:\WP A:
CD \
```

Note that some word processing programs, such as the fictitious one used in the example above, allow putting one or more *parameters* on the command line, providing information that is passed along to the program. This may include the names of subdirectories where the WP program files are stored, and/or the name of the disk drive or subdirectory where text files are to be stored. Some allow passing along the name of a configuration file to be used to set up a customized profile, as well as specifying alternate paths for program files and temporary files. Activating a program like this is almost impossible without an appropriate batch file.

With WP.BAT stored in our C:\BATCH subdirectory, and an appropriate PATH command activated (more on PATH later) to point to that subdirectory, we can simply type WP when logged onto any drive or directory to start up the word processing program.

WP.BAT has become, for all intents and purposes, a new DOS command available for instant access. It is possible to incorporate other series of commands into batch files to custom-design your own DOS commands. For example, if you wanted to see the directories of all the disks in your system in turn, you could create a batch file, called DIRS.BAT, with the following lines:

```
ECHO OFF           ECHO OFF
DIR A:       or    DIR A: /P
DIR B:             DIR B: /W
DIR C:             DIR C:\WP\*.TXT
                   DIR C:\WP\MEMO*.TXT
```

As you can see, the new command, summoned by typing DIRS, can be tailored quite precisely to your own particular needs. Batch files can be even more flexible because they can include not only the same commands that you type from DOS, but some additional, lesser-known commands that make up a simple batch file language. These are in most cases not different from "regular" DOS commands, but don't have many applications outside batch files. You may, for example, type:

```
ECHO Hello there!
```

from the DOS command line, and the operating system will obediently display "Hello there!" on the screen. That's not particularly useful.

There are only a few batch file commands. They are often called *subcommands*, since they are used in most cases within batch files. However, they are all full-fledged DOS commands that can be used in many powerful ways. We'll look at each of them, including the new ones introduced with DOS 3.3, in this chapter.

THE ECHO COMMAND

This command has three forms:

```
ECHO message
ECHO ON [or OFF]
ECHO
```

The first use displays **message**, which follows the command on the line to the screen. Unlike PRINT in BASIC, no quotation marks are needed. For example:

```
ECHO Please insert a new diskette in drive A:
```

ECHO OFF will turn off the display of batch file commands as the commands are carried out. ECHO ON will turn on the display of the commands. When printed on a line by itself, ECHO will display the current ECHO status (either ON or OFF).

For example, compare these two batch files and their respective screen output.

Example 1
```
ECHO OFF
DIR A:*.DOC
ECHO Insert Disk
PAUSE
```

Example 2
```
DIR A:*.DOC
ECHO Insert Disk
PAUSE
```

Output of Example 1

```
ECHO OFF

Volume in drive A has no label
Directory of  A:\

MEMOS     DOC     11264     8-31-89  11:34a
LETTERS   DOC     27648     9-24-89  10:36a
2 File(s)   11112782 bytes free
Insert Disk
Strike a key when ready . . .
```

Output of Example 2

```
ECHO DIR A:*.DOC
Volume in drive A has no label
Directory of  A:\

MEMOS     DOC     11264     8-31-89  11:34a
LETTERS   DOC     27648     9-24-89  10:36a
2 File(s)     146432 bytes free
ECHO Insert Disk
Insert Disk
PAUSE
Strike a key when ready . . .
```

These examples differ only in the presence of ECHO OFF as the
first line in the first batch file. ECHO OFF is usually the first line
in batch files. It is inserted to reduce the confusion and clutter on
the screen while the batch file operates. The key exception is in
the case of specialized files using the PROMPT command to pass
certain keystrokes to the ANSI.SYS device driver. Then, ECHO
must be ON for ANSI.SYS to recognize the special codes (examples illustrating this will follow later on).

Note: With DOS 3.3 or DOS 4.0 you may also suppress
ECHOing of a command to the screen by putting an *at* (@) as the

first character on a line. With earlier versions of DOS, the initial line, ECHO OFF, had to be displayed, because ECHO was still on at that point. Now, you may suppress even that display:

```
@ECHO OFF
```

would produce *no* screen output.

In earlier releases of DOS, it was possible to print a blank line in a batch file by including ECHO, followed by two or more spaces. (ECHO alone returns the ECHO status, remember.) That non-documented feature became a non-feature with DOS 3.0 and later versions. A semi-blank line can be incorporated by putting nothing but a period after the ECHO statement. A completely blank line can be inserted by telling DOS to print an invisible character such as ASCII 255. To enter that character (or any non-keyboard character), hold down the Alt key while typing the character's code on the numeric keypad (*not* the row of numbers at the top of the keyboard).

The ECHO command is an excellent way of highlighting one of the chief problems with batch files: They are a bit *slow*. That's because of the way DOS carries out the list of commands they contain.

You might think that DOS would read the entire file into memory and then carry out the commands one at a time. That would make sense, except that DOS can't really do two things at once in the command mode, which is what it would have to do if it kept a list of commands in memory while carrying them out. Instead, it opens the batch file, reads the first command, closes the file, stores a pointer that tells it where it was in the batch file, then carries out the command if it can.

The command may be to load another entire program, or simply a DOS command like FORMAT or COPY. When DOS has finished with the command or program, it looks to see if a batch file is currently being processed and, if so, reopens the file, moves to the line indicated by the pointer it saved, and then loads the next command.

DOS is fairly dumb in this regard. In fact, you may run a batch file stored on a floppy disk, remove the disk while DOS is busy doing something else, and substitute a different one. If the new disk also contains a batch file with the correct name, DOS will obediently open what it thinks is the same file when it is ready. This procedure isn't recommended unless you know what you are doing.

However, all this opening and closing of a file takes some time. As a result, ECHOing a series of lines to the screen can be fairly slow, particularly with old 4.77 MHz PCs and XT systems. The worst case of all is with a floppy disk-based 8088 computer. You may run out of patience before the batch file runs out of lines to display.

A better practice, in such cases, would be to TYPE a file containing the message you wish to display. DOS can carry that out as a single command.

THE CLS COMMAND

This command simply clears the CRT screen so you can start with a fresh display. Like the other batch commands, it also works from the DOS command line. You may type it in whenever your screen gets cluttered and you want to start with a blank screen.

THE PAUSE COMMAND

This command will cause the batch file to suspend execution until the user presses a key. The pause can be used to allow the operator to change her mind, insert a disk, or do some other task. For example:

```
ECHO Press Control-C to Abort Batch File Now
PAUSE
ECHO Insert Volume 2 Disk In Drive A:
PAUSE
```

THE GOTO COMMAND

Like GOTO in BASIC, this command sends control of the batch file to a different line. However, since line numbers are not used, a *label* is used instead. Labels must start with a colon, and are used only by DOS to find the relevant portion of the batch file. Everything else on a label line is ignored. This batch file shows examples of GOTO and labels:

```
ECHO OFF
GOTO DIRECTORY
ECHO This line is never called.
:DIRECTORY
DIR A:
GOTO END
ECHO This line is never called, either.
:END Anything else on this line is ignored.
CLS
```

THE REM COMMAND

This command allows inserting remarks in your batch files. Anything after REM on a line is ignored:

```
REM This line will be ignored by DOS if ECHO is
OFF.
REM If ECHO is ON, DOS will display the line.
: This is also a remark, masquerading as a label.
: DOS will not display this remark even if ECHO
is ON.
```

As you can see, labels can also double as remarks and, in fact, generally provide a less cluttered appearance in the batch file. As a bonus, labels don't ECHO to the screen even when ECHO is ON. In this book, we will use labels instead of REMs for those reasons.

THE IF COMMAND

This is a "crippled" version of IF as used in BASIC and other languages. IF may test *only* for three conditions:

★Whether one string equals another

★Whether a file by a given name exists

★What the current ERRORLEVEL is

In the first case, the strings must match in case (upper- or lowercase) to be considered identical. You may follow IF with NOT to test for "not equal," as the <, , and <> string comparisons of BASIC are not allowed in batch files. For example:

```
IF "AAA" == "aaa" ECHO They are the same case!
IF "AAA" == "AAA" ECHO They are the same case!
```

In this example, only the second line would cause the message to be ECHOed to the screen. Note that a double equals sign must be used. This convention is borrowed from languages which, unlike BASIC, make the proper distinction between equals used to *assign* values, and equals used to express equivalence. If this isn't clear, consider the following examples:

```
A=B
IF A==B GOTO END
```

In the first case, A will *always* equal B after the line is run, because the value of A is assigned to B by that line. In the second case, no such assignment takes place. Instead, the line merely checks to see if the two are equal and, if so, performs some other task. Variables are assigned in batch files using the single equals sign. These are variables stored in the DOS *environment* and will be discussed in more detail in Chapter 11.

For now, just remember that for comparisons, the double equals sign is required:

```
IF "Hello There"=="Hello There" GOTO END
IF NOT "Hello There"=="Hi" GOTO END
IF Notice No Quotes==Notice No Quotes GOTO END
```

Quotation marks are not required for string comparisons in batch files, but there is a reason for using them that will be explained shortly.

IF can check to see if a file already exists within a given directory or disk. This is useful as a means to keep from over-writing files used by batch routines. You can also use this as a sort of "flag," by creating and erasing dummy files with certain names depending on a status you want to convey to the batch file:

```
IF EXIST A:DATABASE.DOC GOTO DONOTERASE
IF EXIST A:FLAG.$$$ GOTO END
```

ERRORLEVEL is a code set by DOS when certain errors occur during the execution of a command such as XCOPY. IF can also check for the ERRORLEVEL status within a batch file. However, only a limited number of DOS commands actually set the ERROR-LEVEL, so this test has limited utility. Some public domain utilities with names like INPUT.COM or ASK.COM translate key presses into ERRORLEVELS that you can interpret in your batch files. The Bantam book *DOS Power Tools* includes one such utility, while my own *Hard Disk Solutions* incorporates two versions. *this book has one simple version in chapter 21.

THE FOR COMMAND

This subcommand is the closest thing batch file language has to the FOR...NEXT loop of BASIC. A variable, designated by double percent signs, is sequentially assigned a value, and then the operation specified after DO is carried out.

The syntax of the command is:

```
FOR variable IN (set) DO command
```

This will become clearer if you examine the following example:

```
FOR %%a IN (*.*) DO ERASE %%a
```

Each time through the loop, variable %%a will be assigned a different file name represented by *.*, whereupon that file will be erased. This particularly example is a diabolical perversion of the ERASE *.* command, since, in this case, DOS will *not* ask "Are you sure (Y/N)?"

You may separate items within the parentheses by spaces to include many different specifications for the set:

```
FOR %%a IN (C:\WP\*.DOC C:\ARC\MEM*.*) DO COPY A:
```

Note that **set** does not have to be a list of file names. You can also incorporate a list of commands, as in the following example:

```
FOR %%a IN (COPY ERASE) DO %%a A:*.DOC
```

This line would first COPY all the files ending with the .DOC extension on drive A: to the current drive and directory, and then erase them.

USING REPLACEABLE PARAMETERS IN BATCH FILES

The previous examples should have piqued your interest in exactly what replaceable parameters are. This book has taken the somewhat unorthodox approach of leaving a discussion of replaceable parameters in batch files for last. Most explanations bring this aspect in too early, when those new to batch files may still be easily confused. At this point, you are familiar with nearly all the special subcommands that can be used in batch files. However, the concept of parameters is a key one.

When you type in the root name of a batch file, you may follow on the same command line with a series of additional parameters, separated by spaces. You may type in as many as you can fit on a command line. However, DOS is only equipped to handle 10 of them at one time, numbered %0 to %9.

When you press Return and the batch file commences, DOS assigns the name of the batch file to the parameter %0, which you might think of as a variable similar to those used in BASIC. A line such as:

```
ECHO %0
```

would echo the name of the batch file to the screen. Similarly, the next nine parameters you typed on the command line would be assigned to %1 to %9. If you wanted to erase a series of files with a batch file called KILL.BAT, the file itself could look like this:

```
ECHO OFF
: [*] KILL.BAT [*]
ERASE %1
ERASE %2
ERASE %3
ERASE %4
ERASE %5
ERASE %6
ERASE %7
ERASE %9
```

You could then use KILL.BAT by typing the following line:

```
KILL OLD.BAK MCI.ASC MEMOS.* C:\WP\*.BAK
```

In this case, %1 would be assigned the value OLD.BAK, while %2 would become MCI.ASC, and so forth. Since only four parameters have been typed, %5 through %9 would have null values and no files would be erased. You can use these replace-

able parameters in many ways just as you would variables in a
BASIC program:

```
ECHO OFF
IF %1==HELP GOTO HELP
IF %1=="" GOTO HELP
IF %2==END GOTO END
ERASE *.*
:HELP
ECHO You need help, friend.
:END
```

Note that a problem would occur if the user happened to start
this particular batch file without entering any parameters. In the
third line, *nothing* would be substituted for %1, and nothing does
not equal the null string (" ") so no match would take place. To
avoid this problem, we can put the parameter inside quotes, too:

```
IF "%1%"=="" GOTO HELP
```

Then, if no parameter is entered, " " will equal " ". The double
quotes were used around the parameter just to make what is
going on clear. However, any single character can match on both
sides of the equals signs:

```
IF X%1==X GOTO HELP
```

In this case, if nothing is entered as a parameter, then X will equal
X and the label HELP will be accessed.

THE SHIFT COMMAND

This is the final batch file subcommand, saved until now because
it is of use only with replaceable parameters. SHIFT causes each
parameter typed in on the command line to move over one place
to the left towards %1. So, %2 becomes %1, %3 becomes %2, and
so forth. %0 always keeps its identity as the batch file name.

SHIFT has two effects. First, it allows typing more than 9 parameters on a command line. You could type 18 or so short parameters, have the batch file operate with nine of them, and then shift over (invoking SHIFT nine times) and work on the next nine.

In practice, only the second effect of SHIFT is of use: that of sequentially moving each of the parameters over to become %1 in turn. Our example KILL.BAT above could be made much more effective as follows:

```
ECHO OFF
: [*] KILL.BAT [*]
:ERASE
ERASE %1
SHIFT
IF NOT "%1"=="" GOTO ERASE
```

Now, we could type as many file names as could fit on a command line, and the batch file will move each one in turn to parameter %1, and erase it.

Replaceable parameters can call labels, if necessary:

```
ECHO OFF
IF NOT "%1"=="" GOTO %1
:HELP
ECHO Help is on the way.
GOTO END
:ERASE
ERASE *.*
GOTO END
:DIR
DIR A:
GOTO END
:END
```

In this example, you could type the label name on the command line when summoning the batch file. If no label name was typed as a parameter, HELP would be shown. However, if a name that did *not* correspond to a label was entered, the LABEL NOT FOUND error message would result. For this reason, the user must be very familiar with the input expected for a batch file so that an allowable label is supplied.

Note that in this example, the *case* of the parameter as typed from the DOS command line does not matter, since DOS automatically converts to uppercase for you in interpreting the parameter as a label name. So you could type "help" or "HELP" or even "HeLp" as a parameter. The value of %1 would be considered as if it were HELP in any case, and thus direct control to the proper label.

This is *not* true within the batch file. You must include tests for all possible combinations of upper- and lowercase characters if you want to be perfectly safe:

```
ECHO OFF
IF  "%1"=="YES"  GOTO  ROUTINE
IF  "%1"=="yes"  GOTO  ROUTINE
IF  "%1"=="Yes"  GOTO  ROUTINE
IF  "%1"=="YEs"  GOTO  ROUTINE
IF  "%1"=="yES"  GOTO  ROUTINE
IF  "%1"=="yeS"  GOTO  ROUTINE
IF  "%1"=="yEs"  GOTO  ROUTINE
GOTO  END
:ROUTINE
ECHO Whew, you said yes.
:END
```

THE CALL AND COMMAND COMMANDS

DOS 3.3 introduced the CALL command, which allows a batch file to call another batch file. Users of earlier versions of DOS can accomplish exactly the same thing with the COMMAND command.

Ordinarily, all of the commands in a batch file will be carried out by DOS's command processor, COMMAND.COM. The command processor is loaded into memory when DOS is booted and ordinarily remains there, unless some of the memory it occupies is needed by an application program. So, when we start up another program with a batch file, the command processor will remember our "place" in the batch file while the second program or process is underway. When we exit the program, DOS can return to where we left off to carry out the next command in the batch file.

However, COMMAND.COM can only process one batch file at a time. If we attempt to call one batch file from another, DOS will "abandon" the first and begin to process the new batch file. When the second is finished, control will *not* return to the first batch file. This effectively precludes using one batch file as a "subroutine" for another.

DOS users of versions 2.0 to 3.2 could get around this limitation by including the COMMAND command in their batch files. This command is an internal DOS command that causes DOS to load *another* copy of COMMAND.COM into memory and to pass control to it. That new copy can be used to carry out any commands desired. Then the user may return to the original copy of COMMAND.COM by typing EXIT.

COMMAND has other features of less interest to those who are programming with batch files. For example, following the COMMAND command with a /P switch will make the new processor permanent. An /E switch is available to set the size of the DOS environment. (The next chapter will cover the environment in detail.)

For DOS 4.0 and later, COMMAND also provides for the /MSG option, which causes DOS to load in system messages and retain the text. This option can only be used if the command processor has been made permanent with the /P switch.

We are most interested in the /C switch, which allows passing a DOS command line string to the new copy of COMMAND.COM. That string will be carried out, and then DOS will automatically return control to the previous version. For example, this line inserted in your batch file:

```
COMMAND /C DELETER %2
```

will load a new copy of COMMAND.COM, and tell it to run the batch file DELETER.BAT. The replaceable parameter %2 from your batch file will be passed along to DELETER.BAT as its *first* parameter (%1). When that batch file is finished, your original batch file will take up where it left off.

CALL is a new command, introduced in DOS 3.3, that effectively does the same thing, with much simpler syntax. You need only put CALL in your batch file, followed by the drive and path name of the batch file to be run. The chief difference between CALL and COMMAND is that CALL is intended for accessing other batch files, while COMMAND can actually be used to carry out *any* DOS command you wish.

AUTOEXEC.BAT

The AUTOEXEC.BAT file is a special batch file that is called by DOS when your system boots. It can contain a list of commands you want DOS to carry out on power up. These can include loading special utility programs, such as SIDEKICK, setting your PATH, and other functions.

The best way to see all the things an AUTOEXEC.BAT file can do is to look at one line by line. An atypical AUTOEXEC.BAT file might look like the one that follows. After much soul-searching, we decided to present you with the latest version of the author's real-life AUTOEXEC.BAT file. This one incorporates a number of special features, many of them beyond the scope of this book. However, we thought you'd find it interesting to see how complex, and perhaps convoluted, an advanced DOS user's AUTOEXEC.BAT file can get. Each line is numbered and annotated to explain what is happening.

```
1.   @echo off
2.   cls
3.   Echo Y | c:\UTILS\syschk 46412,40183,21423 A:>NUL
4.   if errorlevel 32 goto stop
5.   if errorlevel 16 goto stop
```

```
6.    if errorlevel 2 goto stop
7.    c:\utils\locate 1,1
8.    echo SYSTEM CHECK PASSED
9.    path c:\batch;c:\dos;c:\utils;c:\
10.   echo on
11.   prompt $e[32m
12.   prompt $e[s$e[2;53H$p$e[1;53H$t$h$h$h$h$h$h$d$e[u$n$g
13.   @echo off
14.   cls
15.   locate 1,20
16.   echo   SETTING MOUSE DRIVER
17.   c:\UTILS\msmouse /p>nul
18.   c:\UTILS\popup>nul
19.   c:\utils\fast 00>Nul
20.   locate 1,53
21.   echo ADJUSTING KEYBOARD SPEED
22.   if exist c:\dos\dw4.asc Erase c:\dos\dw4.asc>nul
23.   SUBST e: c:\COMM>NUL
24.   locate 2,1
25.   Echo SETTING COMSPEC
26.   set comspec=c:\command.com
27.   locate 10,10
28.   c:\UTILS\NOPARITY
29.   cls
30.   cd \keyworks
31.   keyworks /e c:\keyworks\DEFAULT.KW NUL
32.   cd \utils
33.   skc
34.   CD \
35.   :BYPASS
36.   erase c:\file
37.   cls
38.   echo
39.   echo
40.   echo
41.   echo                        Enter choice:
42.   echo               1.)     Dial MCI Mail
43.   echo               2.)     Load DisplayWrite 4
44.   echo               3.)     Load PC-Talk
45.   echo               4.)     Dial BBS
                         5.)     Go to DOS
```

```
46.   echo
47.   echo
48.   type c:\ASCII\cr.asc | DATEFILE.BAT
49.   type c:\ASCII\cr.asc | time>file2.bat
50.   CALL FILE
51.   erase file.bat
52.   erase file2.bat
53.   ECHO AT S0=0>COM1:
54.   :INPUT
55.   ECHO <alt-7><alt-7><alt-7>
56.   INPUT
57.   IF ERRORLEVEL 49 IF NOT ERRORLEVEL 50 GOTO 1
58.   IF ERRORLEVEL 50 IF NOT ERRORLEVEL 51 GOTO 2
59.   IF ERRORLEVEL 51 IF NOT ERRORLEVEL 52 GOTO 3
60.   IF ERRORLEVEL 52 IF NOT ERRORLEVEL 53 GOTO 4
61.   IF ERRORLEVEL 53 IF NOT ERRORLEVEL 54 GOTO 5
62.   GOTO INPUT
63.   :1
64.   cls
65.   locate 10,10
66.   ECHO ==== Calling MCI Mail ====
67.   c:
68.   cd \comm
69.   ECHO AT S0=0>COM1:
70.   c:\KEYWORKS\KEYWORKS /S
71.   COMM s2
72.   CD \
73.   ECHO AT S0=0>COM1:
74.   c:\KEYWORKS\KEYWORKS /R
75.   :2
76.   cls
77.   locate 10,10
78.   ECHO ==== Loading DW4 ====
79.   w
80.   :3
81.   com
82.   :4
83.   c:
84.   cd \comm
85.   ECHO AT S0=0>COM1
```

```
86.   c:\KEYWORKS\KEYWORKS /S
87.   COMM S6
88.   cd \
89.   c:\KEYWORKS\KEYWORKS /R
90.   GOTO :2
91.   :5
92.   cls
93.   goto end
94.   :stop
95.   ECHO   SYSTEM CHECK FAILED!
96.   :END
```

Checking for Computer Viruses

Lines 1–8 are the beginning of the AUTOEXEC.BAT file. First ECHO is switched off and the screen is cleared. Then, a utility program called SYSCHK.COM that looks for a primitive form of computer virus is called in line 3. SYSCHK will calculate a checking value for each of the three DOS files, and compare those values with the numbers entered on the command line at the same time. If the numbers *don't* check out, then SYSCHK loads a value into ERRORLEVEL of either 32, 16, or 2. Lines 4–6 check to see if any of those ERRORLEVELS were produced, then the AUTOEXEC.BAT file branches to a label called :STOP and processing ceases. At this point, the author will panic, then, probably, discover that a new version of DOS has been loaded on the hard disk and he forgot to update the SYSCHK values in the file.

If ERRORLEVEL reports a 0 value, control of the batch file drops down to line 7. Here, a public domain utility called LO-CATE.COM is used to move the screen cursor to row 1, column 1. Then, line 8 ECHOs the message SYSTEM CHECK PASSED to the screen.

Customizing the System PATH, Screen Display, and Mouse

Line 9 sets the PATH for this system, using the guidelines discussed in Chapter 8.

Lines 10–11 turn ECHO on, so the following two lines will work, then change the default DOS screen color combination to green characters on a black background, more or less duplicating the effect of a green-screen monochrome monitor.

Line 12 redefines the system prompt, in order to print the date and time and currently logged directory in the upper right hand corner of the screen.

Lines 13–16 turn ECHO back on, clear the screen, locate the cursor at column 20 of row 1, then print a message to screen that the mouse driver is being loaded. Messages of this sort will help you debug an AUTOEXEC.BAT file, as well as let you know of the progress your file is making.

Lines 17–18 load mouse driver programs.

Lines 19–21 speed up the extended keyboard of the PS/2 Model 60, using a utility program. Note that in this example as well as others in the file, the >NUL trick is used to redirect the output of the utility or command to the NUL device. This prevents the output from being echoed to the screen. Redirection will be discussed in detail in the next chapter.

A Trick for Your Applications Programs

Line 22 checks for the existence of C:\DOS\DW4.ASC. This is a dummy file that is created by the batch file that loads the DisplayWrite 4 word processing program, and then erases it when the program is terminated. Other programs and batch files can check for the existence of this dummy file and determine whether they are being run under DOS, or under DisplayWrite 4's DOS Commands mode. The action the files take can be different in each case.

For example, our COM.BAT file will print the EXIT command to return to DW4 if it was running under DW4's DOS Commands. If not, it will load our specialized MENU program instead.

However, this whole house of cards only works if DW4.ASC is always absent during DOS mode. If DW4 is exited in other than the normal way, the file won't be erased properly. So, this line erases it the next time the computer is booted, just in case.

Custom Drive/Directory

The author likes to upload and download all telecommunicated files to a fictitious disk drive, drive E:, which can be created with the SUBST command (explained in Chapter 17). Line 23 will create that drive, using the subdirectory C:\COMM as the directory to substitute.

Line 26 tells DOS where to find COMMAND.COM. This line is in here because at times, during experimental work, it is desirable to tell DOS to use a different COMMAND.COM.

Putting Some Utilities to Work

Lines 28–33 load several utilities that are put to work each time DOS is booted. NOPARITY turns off parity checking, useful for writers who would rather not lose an entire document to a tiny memory error. Those working with spreadsheets a lot would be better off allowing parity checking to continue. There is no easy way for *them* to locate a tiny error in their spreadsheets otherwise.

KEYWORKS and SIDEKICK are loaded next.

A Menu of Choices

The :BYPASS label is included in the AUTOEXEC.BAT file to allow easy bypassing of all the preceding commands when adding a new feature to the file. A GOTO BYPASS line is placed at the beginning of the AUTOEXEC.BAT file, and then the new feature to be tested is placed immediately after the BYPASS label. When the new feature is working satisfactorily, it can be relocated to some other portion of the file, or the BYPASS label moved to follow it.

Lines 35 and 47–51 are used with some batch file utilities that check an ASCII file for appointments on the current date, and then display them to the screen after the menu.

The boot-up menu itself is displayed by lines 37–46. As noted earlier in this chapter, it would be quicker to have DOS TYPE a file instead of ECHOing a series of lines for such a long display— except that with a 10 MHz 286 computer, there really isn't much difference in speed.

Line 52 simply tells a connected autoanswer modem not to answer the phone. The computer is plugged into a multiline phone system so the modem can be used with any line punched in by the user, for telecommunications as well as for SIDEKICK autodialing. However, we don't want the computer to *answer* any of those lines, hence this command.

Waiting for Input

Line 54 signals that the setup portion of the batch file is finished, by beeping three times (ECHOing Alt-7 will produce a beep). Lines 53–61 loop through a series of commands that examine user keyboard input, and branch to an appropriate subroutine if one of the number keys from 1 to 5 is pressed. The author's own INPUT.COM program (presented later in this book) is used to accept and filter these keypresses, producing an appropriate ERRORLEVEL which is checked by lines 56–61.

Each of the sections starting with line 62 marked with labels :1 through :5 perform the tasks associated with their menu entries. There aren't a lot of things to say about them beyond that.

SUMMARY

We're not done with batch files by any means. However, this chapter will serve as your introduction to this useful tool. Now, let's look at how you can get even more from batch files with another DOS feature, the little-understood environment.

CHAPTER

Using the DOS Environment

INTRODUCTION

The DOS environment has been with us a long time—since DOS 2.0 was introduced. However, it has remained as an *undocumented* and unused feature for an extended period of time. One reason for this neglect is that because it was an unheralded feature, most DOS users didn't understand the environment and therefore didn't bother to use it. Others felt that it was primarily of interest to serious programmers. We'll soon see that this is far from true. In fact, the environment is one of the most useful aspects of DOS in terms of utility to those who write their own batch files, or wish to pass information of one sort or another between programs.

While the environment may seem daunting, it is actually quite elegant in its simplicity. The DOS environment is nothing more than a special area of memory called the *master environment block*. DOS sets aside the MEB to store variables and the values that have been assigned to them. Unlike other areas of memory, the MEB can be easily accessed and modified by the user from the DOS command line, or from within batch files.

The concept of variables has already been covered in the discussion of batch files in Chapter 10. You'll remember that batch files can handle ten variables or replaceable parameters. These variables are indicated by a percent sign: %0, %1, %2, etc.

The environment variables are similar in concept. However, we can type information that we wish to store in the variable simply by using the SET command, an equals sign, and the string we wish to assign to the variable.

Environment variables are stored in the following form:

variable=value

where the variable is a name defined by you using the SET command, or by DOS as one of its reserved variables. The value is the string that can be assigned using SET.

Type the following command to see how SET works:

```
SET NAME=ISHMAEL
```

Press Return. DOS will indicate that nothing has happened. However, you can view the MEB's contents to see that your new variable has, in fact, been stored there by typing:

```
SET
```

all by itself on a line. DOS will then display all the variables and definitions currently in the MEB. Don't be surprised to find your environment is far from empty. There are certain reserved variables defined by DOS with special meanings of their own. Several of them will be familiar to you: PATH and PROMPT, for example. Another that DOS defines is COMSPEC, which indicates the name of the command processor you are using.

DOS will create COMSPEC and PATH variables for you by default if you do not indicate them. The usual place for the user to define these is in the AUTOEXEC.BAT file. If you have not redefined the system PROMPT, then the variable PROMPT will not appear in the MEB.

Because they have been reserved for a special purpose, you don't need to type SET to redefine PATH, PROMPT, or COMSPEC. You can simply type the variable and its new definition at the DOS prompt, or embed it in your batch file:

```
PROMPT=Ready Master!
PATH=C:\;c:\DOS
```

However, you could also use the SET command if you wished for these:

```
SET PROMPT=Ready Master!
SET PATH=C:\;c:\DOS
```

Entire groups of environment variables may be defined if you wish. For example, you could enter the following commands from the DOS PROMPT, or through the same lines included in a batch file:

```
SET DRIVE=C:
SET MOUSE=YES
SET PASSWORD=GORBACHEV
PROMPT Ready Master!
PATH C:\;C:\BATCHES
COMSPEC D:\
```

From the DOS prompt, you could then type SET on a line by itself, and see a list of the current environment variables and their values:

```
DRIVE=C:
MOUSE=YES
PASSWORD=GORBACHEV
PROMPT=Ready Master!
PATH=C:\;C:\BATCHES
COMSPEC=D:\
```

You are limited to a total of 127 characters in defining a given environment string, whether that string was entered from the DOS command line or from a batch file. However, this allowance can only be fully used if you are defining one of the preset DOS environment variables, such as PATH. That is because SET and the mandatory space that follows it are included in the count. So, in defining your own variables you will be limited to 123 characters.

You might think this is not much of a limitation. After all, what variable would need to be that long? Consider, though, that a single variable can contain several separate values, separated by semicolons. For example, you might wish to create a variable that contains a list of several file names where files to be displayed by a batch file are stored.

```
SET LIST=INTRO;FILE1;FILE2;FILE3;FILE4;FILE5
```

Your batch file might look like this:

```
echo off
cls
for %%a in (%list%) do type %%a.ASC
```

First note that to *access* an environment variable from within a batch file, we must precede and follow the variable with percent signs, to let DOS know we are referring to an environment variable. This particular batch file would first display INTRO.ASC, followed by FILE1.ASC, FILE2.ASC, FILE3.ASC, etc. What use is this? Why not simply have the batch file *type* each of the files in turn through conventional type commands?

While that would work, what if you wished to have a batch file sometimes display FILE1, FILE2, FILE3 and other times display ALTFILE1, ALTFILE2, ALTFILE3, etc. Or, what if you wanted to display the files in reverse order? All you would need to do would be to reset the environment variable LIST to include the file names you wanted, in the proper order. Your chief limitation would be that the list of names would have to be 123 characters or less. You could have duplicate lines and similar variable names to display more files, though.

You can also define a list of authorized users of your computer system. You might store these names in a variable, USERS, lodged in the MEB where few would think to look for it. A simple command in your AUTOEXEC.BAT file would SET the USERS variable:

```
SET USERS=JONES;SMITH;WHITE;KASCZLWSKI
```

Your batch files that load certain programs could then check USERS to see if a valid name has been entered as a variable parameter accompanying the batch file. For example, you might have a batch file called UNLOCK.BAT, typed like this:

```
UNLOCK SMITH
```

The file itself could include these lines:

```
:CHECK
FOR %%a IN (%USERS%) DO IF "%1"=="%%a" GOTO ACCESS
:INVALID
ECHO    ==================================
ECHO    = UNAUTHORIZED ACCESS ATTEMPTED =
ECHO    ==================================
GOTO END
:ACCESS
ECHO Greetings, %1!
ECHO Software now being loaded....
cd c:\secret
WP
:END
```

This example was only shown for illustrative purposes. Such a security system would, in fact, be fairly easy to circumvent. However, you probably get the idea of how environment variables can be used in a batch file from these examples.

You can *delete* an environment variable by typing

```
SET variable=
```

with *nothing* following the equals sign. This would allow you to reset the variable, totally removing it from the environment.

To *add* to an environment variable, simply repeat it, followed by the new value:

```
SET USERS=USERS;Hogan
```

This will take the current value of USERS and add the name Hogan to it. If you put this line within a batch file, you must place percent signs around the variable on the right of the equals sign: One application for this feature would be to add to your PATH, either on a permanent or temporary basis. Look at the following batch file:

```
echo off
set oldpath=%path%
path=%path%;D:\
```

In this case, a new environment variable, **oldpath**, has been defined to store our current PATH setting temporarily. Then, PATH is redefined to include the current PATH, followed by D:\. If you wanted D:\ to have *first* priority in the new PATH, you could place it first:

```
path=D:\;%path%
```

Any time you wished to return to the original PATH setting you would need only to invoke from a batch file this line:

```
path=%oldpath%
```

Note that you can't perform these changes from the DOS command line. Try typing these lines from the DOS prompt:

```
set oldpath=%path%
```

```
set oldpath2=path
```

Then type SET to see what happened. You'll see that an environment variable called oldpath has been created with the value "%path," and a variable called oldpath2 has the value "path." Neither has been assigned the value of your current PATH. Keep this in mind when assigning and redefining environment variables: Your best bet is to create a batch file to perform the task for you.

ENVIRONMENT LIMITATIONS

Ointments always seem to have flies. Just when you are becoming excited about the power of the DOS environment, we are forced to make you aware of some of its limitations.

One serious drawback is that the master environment block is actually created at boot-up time, and is difficult for the user to change. What happens is that each program or process that you run receives a *copy* of the environment used by the program that launched it.

For example, DOS loads COMMAND.COM to process our DOS commands. COMMAND.COM receives a copy of the MEB. That is well and good, since we generally will run one program at a time and return to that copy of COMMAND.COM before running the next. However, as you have learned, some batch files and many softwares call a secondary command processor, which is a copy of the first. For example, compilers like Turbo Basic and word processing programs like DisplayWrite 4 have a DOS commands task. The capability of using DOS commands from within these programs is actually accomplished by loading a second copy of COMMAND.COM (available memory permitting, remember). Your BASIC programs can also load another copy of COMMAND.COM through the SHELL command.

If you have DOS 4.0 and want to see how each use of the COMMAND command affects memory, type COMMAND, and then use the MEM command with the /PROGRAMS option. You'll see COMMAND listed twice in the list as the second DOS command processor and its environment are stored in memory. Type COM-

MAND again, and repeat the MEM command. There you'll see *another* copy of COMMAND loaded in the program list. Note that you'll have to type EXIT several times to get out of these new command processor copies.

Since the new command processor receives a copy of the old COMMAND.COM's environment, everything works the same—until you make some change to the new environment. When you return to the original copy of COMMAND.COM, the changes you made are lost. There are complex ways of getting around this. One way would be to use the SET command and redirect its output to a file; then, on return, use the contents of that file to reset the current environment to the values reflected therein. Whew.

One case where this will definitely affect you, however, is in using batch files with a second command processor, as discussed in the last chapter. Since COMMAND.COM is a program like any other, it receives a copy of the environment, and this copy is what you work with when executing your batch files. The same copy of COMMAND.COM is generally used to run the batch files and other programs you might want to pass values to through variables. So, these will all be using the same copy of the environment, or will receive a copy of that same environment when they run.

However, DOS allows loading a second copy of COMMAND.COM. This is done to allow batch files to call other batch files during their execution. You'll recall that DOS 3.3 introduced a CALL command which does allow one batch file to call another, if sufficient memory is available. As explained earlier, exactly the same thing can be accomplished with earlier versions of DOS using the COMMAND command.

COMMAND /C command

The /C tells DOS to carry out the command specified, and then return automatically to the original copy of COMMAND.COM. Of course, **command** can be anything, such as DOS commands like DIR, programs, or other batch files.

COMMAND.COM must be available to DOS, either on your hard disk or a floppy. Invoking a second copy of COMMAND.COM does require an extra 3,000 bytes or so of memory (and each additional copy you load does the same), so you may want to avoid nesting too many levels of COMMAND.COM with your batch files. Given these constraints, there is no reason why batch files can't call other batch files which call other batch files still.

The big limitation of this method is that since the second copy of COMMAND.COM is using a copy of the first batch file's environment, any changes the second batch file makes to the environment will be lost on return. A partial solution is to create *files* to be used as indicators, or "flags" that can be tested with IF EXIST.

The other major limitation of the environment is the limitation on its size. DOS 2.0 has an environment block limited to 160 bytes; and since a minimum of 29 characters are taken up by the PATH and COMSPEC variables, a maximum of 131 are available for the user.

DOS 3.0 has a number of bugs that limit its usefulness with environment variables. However, DOS 3.1 and later versions fix those problems and provide an easy way of expanding the environment. That method is the SHELL command, to be included in your CONFIG.SYS file. (CONFIG.SYS is explained in the next chapter.) Syntax is as follows:

```
SHELL=COMMAND.COM /P /E:size
```

The /P switch tells DOS to load AUTOEXEC.BAT automatically. If you leave it off, AUTOEXEC.BAT will *not* be loaded at all, which might be useful only in some security system where you wanted to fool intruders into thinking that AUTOEXEC.BAT had some function, when it didn't.

The /E switch tells DOS what size environment you would like to set. With DOS 3.1, this must be shown as the number of 16–byte blocks you would like to set aside. That is, if you set the value to 16, your environment would be 256 bytes (16 x 16). A maximum of 992 bytes (62 blocks) can be allocated.

With DOS 3.2 and later versions, things improve considerably. The size of the environment can be set to from 160 bytes to 32,767 by entering the actual number of bytes you would like. Even the most elaborate programming is unlikely to exceed that limitation easily.

Those with DOS 3.2 or later can also change the size of the new environment with the COMMAND command, by appending the /E:xxxx switch to it. Replace the **xxxx** with the size of the environment desired, from 127 bytes to 32,767:

```
COMMAND /e:2000
```

This would create an environment with 2,000 bytes reserved for your environment variables.

SUMMARY

We've covered a great deal of territory in this chapter. The DOS environment, along with its limitations, has been explained, and several examples of uses have been provided. In the next chapter, we'll look at the new DOS 4.0 shell, and see how you can use it to save time.

12

Introducing the DOS 4.0 Shell

INTRODUCTION

A *shell* is a layer wrapped around a central core, usually with some protective purpose. In the case of an egg shell or a sea shell, the purpose may be to protect the living creature inside the shell. In the computer world, shells are usually created to protect the folks on the outside. A DOS shell is an additional layer of programming that stands between us and the operating system. When a shell is in place, we don't have to enter cryptic DOS commands (unless we want to). Instead, we can choose what we want to do from the shell's menus, and rely on its programming to translate our desires into valid commands DOS understands.

Shells are by no means a new phenomenon. Operating systems like UNIX have long been available with a variety of shells, each with different features, commands, and utilities. DOS itself can be spruced up with dozens of commercially available shell programs that streamline the command line and help users avoid syntax errors. Shells often come as part of a package that provides other features, such as multitasking or windowing. Microsoft Windows is probably the best-known shell-type program for DOS.

It happens to be a graphics-based shell, using icons and other symbols and graphics in addition to text.

DOS 4.0 is supplied with a simple DOS shell of its own, which will operate with a graphics mode as well as a text mode. You can use the shell to perform many functions, load programs, and manage your files. If you have a mouse, you can "point" to functions you wish to carry out in a natural and intuitive way. The DOS shell may not be for everyone, but new users in particular will find it simple to learn.

WHO NEEDS THE DOS SHELL?

The debate between DOS shell menus and command-line oriented interfaces boils down to the difference between easy-to-learn and easy-to-use. A menu system like that found in the DOS shell is easy to learn. The descriptions on the menu usually provide a good idea of what each choice does. Users can select a particular task or class of tasks and move on to the next menu, if necessary, to further classify what they want to do from the available options. However, this movement from layer to layer, while easy to learn, becomes difficult and cumbersome to use very quickly. Would you enjoy using Lotus 1-2-3 if every time you wanted to name a range it was necessary to activate the main menu, select RANGE from one menu, wait for the next and select NAME, then access a third and choose CREATE? It would be sheer torture, even if a mouse or other pointing device could be used to scroll among the menu choices.

If you are a Lotus user, you'll know that Lotus does not force you to undergo such contortions. You may, if you are a new user, view each layer of menus and read the descriptions. However, if you are familiar with the program, you can type in /RNC as a single command and quickly reach the point you want.

Of course, Lotus has the best of both worlds, providing both a menu and command line interface. DOS's command prompt, on the other hand, can handle only properly typed commands and their parameters. For the new user, this can be frightening or intimidating. One must literally learn all the syntax and commands to perform any of the tasks associated with them.

Yet, command lines are quite easy to use once you have learned DOS. Complex tasks like the following can be carried out with a single line:

```
XCOPY C:\WP\*.LET A: /M /P
```

This has several benefits. The end users can learn enough of DOS's commands to work comfortably with the system for everyday work. However, they can also do repetitive tasks easily without the need to learn complex syntax that is only really needed to set up the utility.

So, have DOS your own way. Click-and-point with a mouse or the cursor keys, or work with the DOS command line. Version 4.0 will allow you to do both.

INSTALLING THE DOS SHELL

The SELECT program will set up a batch file called DOS-SHELL.BAT that will configure the shell for you. If you're the sort of user who wants or needs to use the shell, you're probably best off going this route. A typical batch file might look something like this:

```
@ECHO OFF
C:
CD\DOS
SHELLB DOSSHELL
IF ERRORLEVEL 255 GOTO END
:COMMON
SHELLC/MOS:PCIBMDRV.MOS/TRAN/COLOR/DOS/MENU/MUL/SND/MEU:SHELL.MEU
 /CLR:SHELL.CLR/PROMPT/MAINT/EXIT/SWAP/DATE
:END
BREAK=ON
```

The various functions of this batch file are too complex for the typical DOS shell user to be much concerned with. Basically, the file tests to make sure that it is operating on a system that will accept the graphics-based shell. Then it installs the shell, using the previously defined default values, shell menu lists, color combinations, and features the end user has chosen through SELECT.

If the DOSSHELL command is embedded in your AUTOEXEC.BAT file as the last statement, it will load automatically when your system is booted. Depending on whether you have a graphics display card and a color monitor, the shell will be displayed either in monochrome or color and with text-only menus or menus that contain graphics elements. The cursor will appear as a tilted arrow if you have both a mouse installed and a graphics system.

If you have no interest in learning how to modify the DOS shell program, skip to the next section instead of reading the material that follows.

CUSTOMIZING THE DOS SHELL

Your chief tool for customizing the shell will be to make modifications in the command line in your batch file. This section will tell you what each of the options does, with suggestions for changes. If you have less than 360K of memory, you may not be able to install all of these.

Start-Up Options

The first group of options are start-up options.

/MENU This tells the shell to begin with the Start Programs menu. If you leave it off, the shell will begin with the File System menu, if that has been activated.

/DATE When activated, the date is displayed on the screen by the DOS shell.

/MEU:menu This tells DOS the name of the Main Group menu. The default is SHELL.MEU. However, those with net-

works can use this option to customize the menus for individual users on the network.

/CLR:name   This tells DOS the name of the file containing the color setup information to be used with this copy of the shell. SHELL.CLR is the default.

Performance Options

/MUL   This allows multiple directory and file buffers for the File System.

/TRAN   When this is activated, the DOS shell can operate in transient mode. In such a configuration, the shell does not remain in memory, but is loaded from disk each time. This frees up your system's memory, and should be used by those with hard disks. Those with floppy disk systems can leave this option off, forcing resident mode, in which the shell stays permanently in RAM.

/SWAP   When this option is activated, the system will save the file system directory and file data to a disk file while activating a program from a group or from the shell command prompt. This is intended primarily for hard disk systems, which have sufficient extra disk storage to allow swapping data in and out of memory. It will improve performance on such systems, since the File System doesn't have to search for all this information on individual directories.

Restricting User Functions

This group allows you to limit some of the functions the user has access to.

/DOS This needs to be activated to allow access to the shell File System. You may leave it off to set up systems for users who need to perform a set of tasks from the Main Group or various subgroup menus but shouldn't get involved with file maintenance.

/PROMPT This option allows maintenance to the DOS shell command prompt. Again, it may be deleted to set up specialized, limited-function systems.

/EXIT You can use this to Exit the shell and go to the DOS prompt. Like the last two options, you may wish to delete this in order to restrict the end user to the predefined shell programs and utilities.

/MAINT Without this option, the user will be unable to change, add, or delete programs from the groups.

/COLOR This activates the Change Color menu, so the end user may modify the colors the shell is presented in.

Choosing Text or Graphics Mode

/TEXT This starts up the shell in text mode.

/C01 This starts up the shell for use in systems with graphics adapters capable of supporting high-resolution, sixteen-color 640 x 350 pixel displays.

/C02 This starts the shell for use with systems that support two-color graphics with 640 x 480 pixel displays.

/C03 This starts the shell for systems with sixteen-color graphics and 640 x 480 pixel displays.

/B:nKB This sets aside an amount of memory to be used for buffers by the File System. Replace n with the number of kilobytes of memory to be used. This option can help save memory with systems using resident mode.

Hardware Options

/MOS:driver This option tells the shell which mouse driver to use. If you want to add mouse capabilities later, or change to a different mouse, include this option. Substitute for **driver** the name and path to the driver you wish to activate. You may use one of the three mouse drivers supplied with DOS 4.0.

If you elect to use another mouse driver, remove this option from the start-up file, and include an appropriate statement in your CONFIG.SYS file to load the mouse driver you do want to use.

/COM2 Use this to set up the shell to use serial mouse installed on the COM2 port instead of the COM1 port.

/LF Use this to set up the mouse for use by left-handers.

/SND This activates sound. You may wish to leave it off if you work in an environment where beeping sounds from your computer are objectionable. For example, those who work with the public over the telephone may find that the beeps are more distracting to the caller than the key-clicks caused by typing.

QUICK GUIDE TO THE SHELL MENU TREE

As with all menu-oriented programs, the DOS shell consists of a series of menus, organized in tree fashion somewhat reminiscent of the DOS hierarchical directory structure. The main menu,

Start Programs has three sections: Program, Group, and Exit. These are *pull-down* menus. When you access any of them, they will each have submenus of their own.

The Start Programs screen looks something like Figure 12.1

Moving among Menu Items

You may perform a number of actions from this menu. The cursor will start at the *action bar*, which is the line near the top of the screen where the Program, Group, and Exit menus are located. One of these will be highlighted. You may move the highlighting from one to the other with the left and right cursor keys. If you have a mouse, you may move the cursor directly to one of the three.

To activate any of the three pull-down menus on the action bar:

1. Move the highlighting to the menu with the cursor keys and press Enter.

2. Or, type the key letter associated with that menu. The key letter is underlined: **P**rogram, **G**roup, or **E**xit.

3. Or, move the cursor to the menu with the mouse and click the left mouse button.

```
04-02-89              Start Program      4:12 pm
Program    Group    Exit                 F1=Help
                Main Group
     To Select an item, use the up and down arrows.
     To start a program or display a new group, Press Enter.


Command Prompt
File System
Change Colors
DOS Utilities
F10 = Activities              Shift-F9 = Command Prompt
```

Figure 12.1

The highlighted line will then drop down to the first item on the pull-down menu. You may move the highlighting with the up and down arrow keys or by moving the cursor with the mouse. Cursor key movement will cycle continuously throughout the choices within a menu; when you reach the bottom using the down arrow key, another press will take you back to the top. To *select* one of the submenu items, either press Enter, or click on the left mouse button. To *exit* a submenu, press Escape.

One of the items in the Main Group menu will also be highlighted. You may move to the Main Group by pressing F10. Pressing F10 a second time will move the cursor back to the action bar. Within the Main Group, you may change the highlighting with the cursor up and down arrow keys or the mouse as before.

This may be confusing at first. Just think of the Start Programs screen as three menus offering a choice of actions. The Program submenu will allow you to perform some action with the program highlighted in the Main Group below. The Group submenu will let you add, delete, or change programs from the Main Group. The Exit menu will allow you to leave the DOS shell and return to the DOS prompt.

The Main Group may be thought of as a list of programs you may start. These can include your own programs (after you have added them to the Main Group) as well as some special DOS functions and utilities.

Let's look at these functions one at a time.

Function Keys and Special Key Definitions

At the Start Programs screen, there are several operations associated with function keys.

F1   Pressing the F1 function key will provide you with a series of help screens. You may page through the help screens using the PgUp and PgDn keys.

Shift-F9   This will take you to the DOS command prompt. You may return to the shell by typing EXIT.

F10 This key moves the cursor to the action bar if it is located in the Main Group, or to the Main Group if it is located in the action bar.

Similarly, at the HELP screen; function keys allow relevant operations.

Esc To leave HELP, press the Escape key.

F1 Instructions on using HELP appear when F1 is pressed.

F11 This provides an index to available help screens.

F9 This lists special key definitions.

USING THE PROGRAM SUBMENU

First, select the program menu from the action bar. If the cursor is located in the Main Group, press F10 to move it back to the action bar, then activate the Program menu with the mouse or keyboard.

The pull-down menu looks like Figure 12.2.

If you have a graphics-based shell, some of these choices may be dimmed or blurred to indicate they are not appropriate right now. If your shell is text-based, the underlined key letter will be replaced by an asterisk.

```
Start

Add...
Change...
Delete...
```

Figure 12.2

As with all DOS shell menus, you may choose an item by typing its key letter, moving the highlighting with the cursor keys, and pressing Enter, or by moving the highlighting with the mouse and clicking the mouse button.

Start If you select this menu option, the item in the Main Group displayed lower on the screen will be started. If the item is a program, DOS will attempt to load it using the specifications you supplied when the program was added to the Main Group. If the item is one of the four default Main Group selections (Command Prompt, File System, Change Colors, or DOS Utilities), DOS will move to the appropriate submenu for that selection. You can tell when another menu follows a given menu option, because a series of dots are used to end that selection. We'll discuss each of the default Main Group options later in this chapter.

Add This selection allows you to add a program to the Main Group. The next screen you are shown is an entry form that allows you to type in information about the program that you wish to add to the Main Group. (Figure 12.3)

You must enter a *title* for the program you wish to add. This will appear in the Main Group listing, and may be up to 40 characters long. Possible titles would include DisplayWrite 4, Lotus 1-2-3, or another applications program name. Note that a right angle bracket > is used to mark the right side of the entry field. As you

```
                    Add Program
          Required
               Title . . . . [                    >
               Commands . . [                    >
          Optional
               Help text . . [                       >
               Password . . [            ]
```

Figure 12.3

enter text, this bracket will move over to allow additional characters. When you approach the limit to the number of characters that can be entered, the bracket will change to a square right bracket and stop moving. Other entry fields in the shell conform to this practice, as well.

Next, type in the commands you want DOS to use to start up the particular program. These might be a command line entry like this one used to start DisplayWrite 4:

```
c:\dw4\DW4PG c:\dw4\PROFILE.PRF,c:\DW4,c:\DW4,c:\DW4,C
```

If your program requires several lines of commands (say, changing from one subdirectory to another), you may press F4 to indicate each new line. However, it might be simpler just to incorporate all of these into a batch file, and list the batch file name under **commands** instead.

There are a number of optional program start-up commands that will allow you to provide the user with instructional panels, data entry fields, and other information when they start up the program. There are nearly a dozen and a half of these, providing you with a mini-programming language that is more complex and versatile than batch file programming. You can, in effect, set up your own shells to insulate neophytes from difficult program start-up commands, yet allow flexibility in starting the program. Several chapters could be written on this topic, which is beyond the scope of this book.

You can also enter some HELP text, which the user can call up by pressing the F1 key. Up to 478 characters may be included.

A **password** may be typed, up to eight characters long. This will prevent anyone from using the program who does not know the access password. Both HELP and the password are optional.

When you have finished, press F2 to save your entries. The program you have defined will now appear on the Main Group.

CHANGE   You may change any of the program start-up information, through a menu similar to that shown in Figure 12.1. The functions are exactly the same, except that you are working with a program that has already been installed.

DELETE   You may remove a program from the Main Group with this menu.

COPY   This option lets you copy a program (and its start-up information) to another group.

USING THE GROUP SUBMENU

Selecting the Group submenu produces a display like that shown in Figure 12.4.

The first three of these functions are similar to those found in the Program submenu, except that instead of working with programs in the Main Group, you are actually creating or manipulating new *subgroups* below the main group.

For example, if your Main Group listing gets too long, you may wish to move some of the programs to subgroups. These subgroups can be organized by function. All word processing programs and utilities can be placed in one subgroup. All spreadsheet programs and utilities can be moved to another. Then, you would select the appropriate subgroup name from the Main Group and choose the actual program you wish to run from the desired subgroup. Several levels of subgroups can be created (something like a directory tree). However, for simplicity's sake, you'll want to keep this tree as easy to use as possible.

The Add Group screen looks like Figure 12.5.

        Add...
        Change...
        Delete...
        Reorder...

Figure 12.4

```
                    Add Group
        Required
             Title . . . . [                >
             Filename . . [      ]
        Optional
             Help text . . [                >
             Password . . [       ]

        Esc=Cancel  F1=Help  F2=Save
```

Figure 12.5

It works similarly to the Add Program screen, except that instead of *commands*, you list a file name for the group. The title may be up to 37 characters long, including blank spaces. The file name may be up to eight characters long.

The Group submenu will also allow you to *change* the specifications of the subgroups you have added, *delete* any of the subgroups, or *reorder* how they appear in the Main Group.

ADDING PROGRAMS TO A SUBGROUP

You may add programs to a subgroup by copying them from one group to another. You may also add programs to the subgroup using the Program submenu exactly as you did when adding programs to the Main Group.

First, move to the subgroup by highlighting its name on the Main Group and either pressing Enter or clicking the mouse button. Subgroups can be differentiated from programs in the Main Group by the elipsis (...) that follows their names. DOS will tell you if the subgroup is currently empty.

Next you'll see an action bar just like that found on the main screen. You may use the Program submenu here in the same way to add programs. To leave the subgroup, press Escape.

You may also add predefined subgroups to the Main Group. As DOS 4.0 becomes more popular, some software developers may supply their own subgroup menus along with their packages, much as many programs come with a .PIF (program information file) that can be used with Microsoft Windows and similar user interfaces. If the predefined subgroup menu conforms to IBM standards, it will have a .MEU extension.

To add such a subgroup to your Main Group, you simply copy the new .MEU file to the subdirectory on your disk where the DOS shell programs are stored. Then, access the Add option from the Group submenu. Use whatever title you want for the new menu, but enter the file name, excluding the .MEU extension, of the new menu. You may add HELP information or a password if you wish. Press F2 to store the new setup. That's all there is to it.

USING THE EXIT SUBMENU

From the Exit menu, you can either exit the DOS shell or resume the Start Programs menu. Unlike the Command Prompt option of the Main Group, or the Shift-F9 shortcut to the DOS prompt, you cannot return to the shell by typing EXIT. You have in effect completely unloaded the shell from memory, and must reload it to return to the Start Programs menu. You would choose the Exit option when you are through using the shell, and want to run some other program.

SUMMARY

This chapter has been an introduction to the DOS shell, covering how to set it up, move from one menu to another on the Start Programs screen, and start, add, delete, change, and copy programs. This chapter also dealt with creating new screen subgroups, and copying programs between them. The next chapter will cover the file system and other options found on the Main Group menu.

13

The DOS 4.0 Shell File System and Utilities

INTRODUCTION

The last chapter served to introduce the DOS shell, the basic features of the Start Program menu, and use of both the action bar and Main Group. Now, we need to get a little deeper into the options on the Main Group, including the File System and various utilities that are available to you. We'll start off with the four simpler options before getting into the multiple features of the File System.

MAIN GROUP COMMAND PROMPT OPTION

When you select this option, you are taken to the DOS prompt. A message on the screen advises you to type EXIT and press Enter when ready to return to the shell.

This option (as well as the Shift-F9 shortcut) loads a second copy of the command processor COMMAND.COM. You may use this additional copy of DOS to perform any DOS function, just as if you had loaded DOS conventionally. However, when you type EXIT, you will restart the shell, and return to the screen where you left off. You may have to use Escape to back out of help screens or other displays before the shell will allow you to use Shift-F9 to activate the DOS command prompt.

MAIN GROUP CHANGE COLORS OPTION

This option lets you choose from among a preselected group of color combinations for display of the DOS shell. The right and left cursor arrow keys will show you the various color combinations that can be chosen. When you have decided, press Enter. If you wish to leave the colors the way they were, press Escape.

MAIN GROUP DOS UTILITIES OPTION

This option will take you to a submenu that looks like the one shown in Figure 13.1.

Note that the Start Program title and action bar remain on the screen. The Main Group title is replaced with the DOS Utilities... heading and a new list of programs. Within this submenu, you

```
04-02-89             Start Program          4:20 pm
Program    Group     Exit                   F1=Help
                     DOS Utilities...
     To Select an item, use the up and down arrows.
  To start a program or display a new group, Press Enter.

Set Date and Time
Disk Copy
Disk Compare
Backup Fixed Disk
Restore Fixed Disk
Format

F10=Actions     Esc=Cancel        Shift+F9=Command Prompt
```

Figure 13.1

may still use the action bar much as you did from the Main Group, or from a subgroup that you have created.

In fact, the DOS Utilities subgroup is a subgroup exactly like those you create yourself, except that it has been set up already for you. The commands and prompts needed to operate the DOS utilities shown were entered by the shell programmers.

However, you may *add, change,* or *delete* programs from this menu just as you may from any subgroup. If you want to put CHKDSK on this DOS subgroup you may. It is possible to install any of the DOS functions you care to use, or other utility programs, in this subgroup.

Each of the DOS utilities in the group operates much like its counterpart at the DOS prompt, except that you are prompted to enter needed parameters. The Set Date and Time utility, for example, features an area for you to enter the date and time. If you add DOS functions of your own, you'll want to study the shell programming language to see how to include these features in your additions.

We won't duplicate discussions of how and why to use the DISKCOPY, DISKCOMP, BACKUP, RESTORE, and FORMAT commands here. For more information, use the HELP key in the DOS shell, or consult the relevant sections of this book.

INTRODUCING THE DOS SHELL FILE SYSTEM

The File System is one of the most complex parts of the DOS shell, but is also very easy to use once you learn how it works. The File System will allow you to view files and directories, copy files, create subdirectories, and do many of the hard disk and file maintenance tasks that are required.

To move to the File System, select File System from the Main Group. You'll see a new screen that looks like Figure 13.2. This menu looks different from the Start Program menu. There is still a title bar at the top with the title, date, and time (if the latter two are activated with your system). However, the action bar includes three unfamiliar options in addition to Exit. These are File, Options, and Arrange. They will be discussed shortly.

```
04-02-89              File System              4:35 pm
File  Options    Arrange   Exit                F1=Help
A    B   C_____
C:_____


Directory Tree  More: V |              *.*    More: V
C:\
|--DOS                       IBMBIO   .COM  30,831 03-01-88
                              IBMDOS   .COM  37,012 03-01-88
                             COMMAND .COM  39,812 03-01-88
                               CONFIG  .SYS     160 08-03-88
                             AUTOEXEC.BAT     183 08-03-88
F10=Actions         Shift+F9=Command Prompt
```

Figure 13.2

The line below that displays the various disk drives available in your system. If you have a graphics-based system, disk drive icons will be shown instead, and you'll see a message "Control+Letter Changes Drive." You may use that command to change the logged drive, or simply click on the icon with the mouse. The drive that is currently logged will be highlighted.

Next comes a line that shows the currently logged drive and path. Two windows underneath are shown side by side. The left window lists the current directory tree. It shows the subdirectories beneath the currently logged directory, and those parallel to it. Lines are used to link the directories to show the parent-child relationship. The right window displays the file names of the files in the current directory. To perform various File System functions with those files, you must select or deselect those you wish to work with or not work with.

SELECTING FILES

To select a file from the file name window, use the tab key to move to the file list, and then use the arrow keys to move the highlighting to the file you want to select. Then press the space bar. If you are using Text mode, a symbol will be placed on the line next to the file. In graphics mode, the icon representing the file (shown on the same line as the file name) will be highlighted.

If you have a mouse, you may also select a file by moving the cursor to the file's symbol and clicking the mouse button. A file may be deselected by moving the cursor to the symbol and clicking again, or by pressing the space bar. You may select all the files in the current directory, or deselect all that you have chosen, by using the Select All or Deselect All option from the File submenu described below.

In graphics mode, you will see a scroll bar displayed on the screen. The bar consists of two solid upward- and downward-pointing arrows, two double up and down arrows, and a slider box. The solid arrows are used to move up or down one line. Move the mouse cursor to the solid arrows and click. The highlighting will move up or down one line, depending on which arrow you selected.

The double arrow symbols will move up or down a page (table 13.1). You may drag the slider box up or down to scroll line by line more rapidly.

If you use a mouse in text mode, you may position the mouse pointer over the up and down arrow symbols, and press the mouse button to scroll through the file name list.

THE FILE SUBMENU

The submenu is selected in the usual way with your keyboard or mouse. You'll see a new pop up menu that looks like Figure 13.3.

You'll notice that most of these end with ellipses, and have associated menus or data input screens of their own. We'll examine each of these one at a time.

The Open (start) option This lets you run one of the files from the current directory listing. You'll be shown a screen asking you to enter any start-up options. When the program you start is finished, you'll be asked to press Enter to return to the DOS shell.

General
Esc   Cancel
Enter   Process the data
Pg Up/Pg Dn   Scroll information display
F1   HELP
F10   Switch to and from action bar
Shift+F9   Change to shell command prompt

Special
F4   Create Separator between startup commands.
F9   In View Files, switch from ASCII to hex.

In HELP
F9   View key assignments.
F11   Show HELP Index
Alt+F1   Show HELP Index

In File System
Tab   Switch to other panel
F3   Return to Start Programs
Spacebar   Select or deselect file or option

In Start Programs:
F2   Save information
F3   Exit DOS shell

Table 13.3   Shell Key Assignments

The Open option lets you run programs that aren't already listed on one of the Groups. You can also run a program from the File System by positioning the mouse pointer on it and double-clicking, or by selecting it from the file name list and pressing Enter. Only executable files may be run this way, obviously.

```
Open (start)...
Print...
Associate...

Move...
Copy...
Delete...
Rename...
Change Attribute...
View

Create directory...
Select all
Deselect all
```

Figure 13.3

The Print option   This lets you PRINT a file using the DOS PRINT command. This is a good way to get a quick copy of ASCII files on your disk.

The Associate option   This lets you tie a file together with the program that uses it. For example, you may have a group of word processing files or spreadsheet files. You may associate each of these with the word processing program or spreadsheet program that created them. Then, when you select that type of file, the program is loaded first. This function works by file *extension*, not by specific files. You may thus associate all .WKQ files with your Quattro spreadsheet, and all your .DOC files with your Display-Write 4 program, just by running the Associate option once.

The Move, Copy, Delete, and Rename options   These allow you to perform different functions with the files you have selected. You may move them from one subdirectory to another, copy them, remove them from the disk, or give them new names. As you summon each of these options, you'll be shown a data entry screen to input the necessary information. If you try to copy files so they overwrite existing files, or generate some other error, the shell provides you with options to resolve the problem. The functions are otherwise similar to those found at the DOS prompt, with the exception of MOVE which, of course, is not an ordinary DOS command at all.

The Change Attribute option   This lets you change the attributes of a file or group of files. You may alter the archive attribute and read-only attribute (just as you may with ATTRIB). However, you can also make a file hidden, or unhide a hidden file. This is a new function for DOS, although utility programs have been available for a long time that perform this chore.

When you select the option, you'll be asked if you want to work with the marked files one at a time, or all together. If you choose to work with them one at a time, you can apply different combinations of attributes to each. If you work with all at once, the combination you choose will apply to all of them.

For each file or group of files, you're shown a list that includes:

Read-Only Attribute
Hidden Attribute
Archive

Move highlighting to the attribute you want to change and press the space bar or click the mouse button. A symbol will appear next to the attribute to show it has been selected. You can then move the highlighting and select another attribute. Clicking on or pressing the space bar when an attribute that has been selected is highlighted will deselect that change. You may choose any combination of the three.

The View option   You may use this to view ASCII files or hexadecimal files (such as those used by programmers). As you view the selected file, you may scroll through it with the PgUp and PgDn keys. You can toggle between an ASCII display and hex representation with the F9 key. When finished viewing, press Escape to return to the File System.

The Create Directory option   This works like MKDIR at the DOS command line.

The Select All and Deselect All options   These allow you to select all the files in the current directory, or deselect them quickly.

THE OPTIONS SUBMENU

This menu provides a group of functions that allow you to alter how the files are displayed in the File System. You can also make changes in the DOS shell to tailor it more closely to your preferences. The Options submenu looks like Figure 13.4. Two of the three options have submenus of their own, shown in Figures 13.5 and 13.6.

Display options   This allows you to change the order in which files are displayed in the File System. You may specify all files (the default) or just enter the file specification of the files you want displayed in this way. In a graphics-based shell, *buttons* will appear next to each of the options. Clicking next to the option will cause its button to have a dark spot in the center, showing it has been selected. In text mode, a symbol appears. You may choose to

```
Display Options
File Options
Show Information


Enter      Esc=Cancel    F1=Help
```

Figure 13.4   Options Submenu

```
Name:*.*

Sort by:
Name
Extension
Date
Size
Disk Order

Enter      Esc=Cancel    F1=Help
```

Figure 13.5   Display options submenu

have the directory sorted alphabetically by file name or extension, or sorted numerically by the date last modified or by size. You can also return the directory display to the order the files appear on the disk.

File options   These allow you to tell the shell how you want it to perform certain functions. "Confirm on delete" requires the shell to ask you before erasing a file; otherwise it will just go ahead and remove it. "Confirm on replace" will force the shell to ask for an okay before copying a file over one with the same name. The "Select across directories" option will allow the shell to choose files even if they are contained in different directories.

```
Confirm on delete
Confirm on replace
Select across directories

Enter      Esc=Cancel    F1=Help
```

Figure 13.6   File Options submenu

Any or all of the three options can be marked. In graphics mode, they are marked with a box that will contain an X. An empty box shows that the option has not been selected. In text mode, a symbol is used.

The Show Information option This provides you with information about a particular file, the directory where it resides, and the disk on which it is located.

THE ARRANGE SUBMENU

This menu will allow you to choose how the File System displays files. The options are Single File List, Multiple File List, and System File List.

Single File List This is the default. It shows one set of panels, with the directory tree at the left and the file list at the right.

Multiple File List This optional display splits up the screen so you may display the files and directory trees of two directories at once. Each has its own scroll bars.

System File List This option allows displaying all the files on the drive, plus a panel that lists the file status. Information displayed includes the file's attribute, directory, and disk.

THE EXIT SUBMENU

This submenu has two choices. You may Exit the File System, or resume using the File System. You must go back to the Start Programs menu to leave the shell entirely.

SUMMARY

This chapter has been a comprehensive look at the DOS shell's Main Group features, with special emphasis on the File System. In the next chapter, we'll return to the DOS command line to show you some of the things that can be done with redirection of input and output, and DOS's built-in programs called *filters*.

CHAPTER

14

I/O Redirection and DOS Filters

INTRODUCTION

Although the computer works only with numbers, much of the information it processes is translated from numeric codes like ASCII into the familiar alphanumeric characters that are displayed on our CRTs and output by our printers. DOS has some special facilities for manipulating these streams of ASCII characters. This chapter will show you how you can *redirect* this input and output. You'll also learn how to *sort* it by parameters of your choosing, *find* a target string within a particular stream of characters, and *display* a set of characters in easy-to-read pages. Each of these capabilities has broad application.

REDIRECTION

ASCII text serves as a convenient format for the interchange of information between programs and between the user and programs. For example, you may wish to load and run a certain program. One way to accomplish this would be to type in the program's name and its loading parameters on a command line at DOS's *standard input device*, the keyboard. When the program is run, it might pass the information it needs to communicate to the user back as ASCII information. These characters would be displayed by the system's *standard output device*, the CRT screen.

This routing of standard input–program–standard output is the normal scheme of things when your PC is operating. However, DOS allows you to make some changes. The reason why you have this option is that DOS treats everything as if it were a *file*. Devices and files are treated more or less alike, so you may substitute just about any other file (or device) for the one that is normally in place.

You can prove to yourself that this is true by thinking about how batch files operate. You type the commands you want carried out into a file, rather than typing them sequentially at the keyboard console. In fact, you can enter batch files by using the COPY CON **filename** command. This tells DOS to COPY the output of the console (CON) to a second file, **filename**. In such cases, DOS treats the keyboard console as if it were just another file, which it copies to the target file name as you enter the keystrokes. In fact, you end the input by typing an ASCII end-of-file marker, Control-Z.

Not only will DOS treat a device as if it were a file, it will treat a file as if it were a device. When you execute the batch file later on, DOS will interpret each of the commands it contains in turn, *exactly* as if they had been entered at the keyboard.

We listed the various DOS device names earlier in this book when you were advised not to use them as root file names. Now you see that the reason for this is that DOS already thinks of each of these devices as a file, so you cannot name another file with the same name. The reserved device names are shown in Table 14.1.

You may experiment with these to confirm that DOS treats them as files by attempting to COPY a file to one of them:

```
COPY C:TEST.DOC CON
COPY C:TEST.DOC PRN
COPY C:TEST.DOC COM1
COPY C:TEST.DOC NUL
```

CON	Keyboard/screen combination
AUX	The first serial port (also called COM1)
PRN	The first parallel port (also called LPT1)
NUL	A dummy device
COM1	The first serial port
COM2	The second serial port
COM3	The third serial port
COM4	The fourth serial port
LPT1	The first parallel port
LPT2	The second parallel port
LPT3	The third parallel port

Table 14.1 DOS Device Names

In the first case, the document will be copied to your screen, and displayed if it is in ASCII form. An ASCII file can be directed to the printer using the second format, or to the serial port with the third. The final example will produce no effect; the NUL device is a computer black hole that is useful for tests and suppressing screen output.

DOS provides some special additional facilities for the console device, standard input and standard output. Instead of directing the output of a file (or device) to the standard output, you may redirect it somewhere else. And, instead of supplying the input to a file (or device) from the standard input you can specify that it comes from somewhere else. Let's start off with some simple examples to make this more clear.

If you were to enter the command TYPE TEST.DOC at the DOS command line, the DOS internal command TYPE would try to locate a file called TEST.DOC. It would then direct its output to the standard output device, the CRT screen. However, you can instead redirect that output to another file (or device) using the DOS symbol >. Look at the following example:

```
TYPE TEST.DOC>PRN
```

Here, standard output has been redirected to the PRN file/device, so TEST.DOC would be printed. However, we could also have entered:

```
TYPE TEST.DOC>FILE2.DOC
TYPE TEST.DOC>CON
TYPE TEST.DOC>NUL
```

In each case, the output would be directed to a different destination. In the first example, TEST.DOC would be sent to a new file called FILE2.DOC. You would have, in effect, copied the file without using the COPY command! You also could have redirected it to the console (CON), which would have listed it to the screen (not much point in this), or sent it to the NUL device (say, because you just wanted to test the TYPE command).

This type of redirection can come in handy, as we'll see shortly. Redirecting to a file is particularly handy, because you can store the ASCII text in permanent form. For example, you may type:

```
DIR >DIRFILE.ASC
```

and the output of the DIR command will be redirected to a file called DIRFILE.ASC. You can load it into your word processor or otherwise manipulate the information. However, DOS doesn't require you to create a new file each time you use redirection. The **>>** sign can be used to tell DOS to add the output to the end of the file by that name. If you typed:

```
DIR A:>DIRFILE.ASC
DIR C:>DIRFILE.ASC
```

when you looked at DIRFILE.ASC, you'd see that it contained only the output of the second command. But if you typed:

```
DIR A:>DIRFILE.ASC
DIR C:>>DIRFILE.ASC
```

you'd find that DIRFILE.ASC would contain *both* directory listings. In all these cases, the file or device specified by the **>** and **>>** symbols takes the place of the standard output device, your CRT screen.

As you might guess, redirection works the other way as well. The **<** sign can be used to tell a program to receive its input from a device or file other than the standard input (keyboard).

When you type TIME at the keyboard, this internal DOS command will prompt you with the current time and ask you to enter a new time. You may enter a new time, or simply press Enter to keep the existing time. Yet, the TIME command can receive its input from a file instead of the keyboard. To test this, first create a file that contains the response you want to provide to TIME. Since we don't want to really change our system time, let's just put a carriage return in the file. Type in these lines:

```
COPY CON CR.ASC<Enter>
<Enter>
<F6><Enter>
```

(Don't type the *characters* enclosed in angle brackets; press those keys instead.) What you'll have will be a file called CR.ASC that contains nothing but a carriage return. Now, type this line:

```
TIME<CR.ASC>TIME.ASC
```

The time command (which you typed at the keyboard) will be activated, but instead of expecting further input from the keyboard, it will get its input from the file CR.ASC. And instead of printing the current time to the screen, it will redirect its output to the file called TIME.ASC. If you type TIME.ASC you'll see something like this:

```
Current time is 10:27:19.94a
Enter new time:
```

Not very useful, you say? Well, if you changed the command to read:

```
TIME<CR.ASC>>TIMELOG.ASC
```

and then put it in a batch file, every time that batch file was run the current time would be added to the file TIMELOG.ASC. You could do something similar with the DATE command, so that your log could keep a running list of dates and times when the batch file was run. Later on, we'll show you some special tricks, such as how to filter out the "Enter new time:" line.

Redirection of input can be used to streamline tasks in which you want a given program to receive a set list of commands every time it is started. You'll discover other applications as you use this technique more.

DOS FILTERS

Filters are related to redirection and are often used with the redirection symbols. Filters in themselves don't send ASCII text anywhere different than the destination they were headed for in the first place. However, they *alter* the text in useful ways before passing it on. There are three DOS filters: FIND, SORT, and MORE. You can use them individually or in combination to provide some powerful new capabilities.

The Find Filter

FIND will search through a stream of ASCII text and attempt to locate a specific string that you request. It will list all the lines containing that string, or list all the lines that do *not* contain the target string, or provide a count of the number of lines in which the string appears. FIND will also tell you the line numbers of the lines in which the string does (or does not) appear. The syntax for FIND is as follows:

```
FIND   /switch(es) "string to look for"   file to search
```

You should substitute the string you want to find (placing it in quotation marks) and the name of the file you want to search. You may not include wild cards in the file name (and so search through a series of files) but you may enter several file names on the command line:

```
FIND "string" FILE1.ASC FILE2.ASC FILE3.ASC
```

This can be a bother, particularly since DOS's 128–character limitation on command lines can restrict the number of file names (or the length of the string) you enter.

You may use redirection so that FIND can work on the output of another program, file, or device. FIND will ordinarily display its output to the screen, but you may redirect that as well.

If you paid attention to the chapter on batch files, you've probably already figured out a way to bypass FIND's wild card limitation. Examine this line:

```
FOR %%a IN (*.*) DO FIND "string" %%a>>FND.ASC
```

In this example, the line will loop through each of the files meeting the specification *.* and for each attempt to find "string." Each line located will be redirected to a file called FND.ASC.

You could also use a similar trick to search for *two* or more different strings in a single file:

```
FOR %%a IN (str1,str2,str3) DO FIND "%%a" FILE.ASC>>FND.ASC
```

This time, each trip through the loop would provide a different string to search from the same file.

You gain even more flexibility from FIND's three switches. They may be used singly or in certain combinations. The possible applications are:

/C	count the number of lines containing the string
/N	display line numbers containing the string
/V	display the lines without the string
/V /N	display line numbers not containing the string

/V /C   count line numbers not containing the string

You may not use /N and /C together.

While you may use the **>**, **>>**, and **<** redirection symbols with FIND and the other filters, DOS provides a fourth symbol, the vertical bar **I**, which serves as a *pipe*. With the pipe, DOS simply passes the ASCII text along to the filter unchanged. For example:

```
TYPE FILE.ASC | FIND "string"
```

serves the same function as

```
FIND "string" FILE.ASC
```

You'll find the pipe symbol to be most useful in order to direct the output of a program or command to the filter, or to pass information from one filter to another. For example:

```
DIR | FIND "<DIR>"
```

will create a display *only* of the subdirectories in a listing. Some of the utilities later in this book make use of the FIND filter.

The MORE Filter

This filter works like FIND, and uses the same redirection syntax, except that the only effect it has on the ASCII text is to break it up into "pages" of text.

```
MORE<TEST.DOC
TYPE TEST.DOC | MORE
DIR | MORE
```

The first two will display the contents of the file TEST.DOC in pages and the third will simply give you your directory by pages. DOS will pause at the end of each screen full with the prompt "—More—". You can press a key to see the next page. MORE is smart enough to notice when you have changed the number of lines in the screen display (using MODE with DOS 4.0) and will show you more lines. MORE has no switches or optional parameters. You can halt the display by pressing Control-Break.

The SORT Filter

This filter will take your ASCII text and reorder it through an alphabetical or numeric sort. If the input for SORT is a file, the original file is unchanged. You must redirect SORT's output to another file in order to save the sorted list. The largest file you can sort is about 63K. Look at these examples:

```
SORT<TEST.DOC>SORTED.DOC
TYPE TEST.DOC | SORT | MORE
```

The first will direct SORT to take its input from a file called TEST.DOC, and direct it to a file called SORTED.DOC. The second example will TYPE the file called TEST.DOC, and pipe it to SORT, which will then send its output to MORE. You'll see a sorted file in separate pages on your screen.

SORT has several optional parameters. You may follow the SORT filter with /R, which tells DOS to sort the file in reverse order. Or, you may sort based on something other than the first column of a line by using the /+n, where n is the column to sort on. When SORT operates, it doesn't differentiate between uppercase and lowercase letters. Examine this example, which uses both switches:

```
DIR | SORT /R /+14
```

In this case, the DIR command will be directed to SORT, which will sort the directory in reverse order, starting with column 14. That column happens to be where the size of the file in bytes is listed, so the sorted list will show your files with the largest first.

If you left off the /R switch, the files would be presented smallest first. Suppose you needed to remove some files from a floppy disk to make additional room. This command would provide you with a way of looking at the largest files to find a likely candidate for deletion.

To sort directories by other parameters, you could use:

/+9	to sort by extension
/+23	to sort by date, newest first
/+23 /R	to sort by date, oldest first
/+32	to sort by time, newest first
/+32 /R	to sort by time, oldest first

You can combine the FIND and MORE filters with SORT to produce lists of directories meeting specific file name types and combinations. You may also apply SORT to any other ASCII files you may have.

SUMMARY

This chapter has introduced you to the DOS concept of redirection. We've seen ways of redirecting standard input and output, and how to put this capability to work with the DOS filters SORT, MORE, and FIND.

CHAPTER

15

Copying Files and Backing Up Hard Disks

INTRODUCTION

You scarcely could have come this far without learning how to use the COPY command. However, we'll review COPY and all its variations in this chapter before moving on to another topic of key interest to hard disk users: how to back up your files.

THE COPY COMMAND

As we saw in the last chapter, COPY can be used to copy files between disk drives, directories, or even other devices. You may apply a new file name to the copy (and you must when you are copying a file to the same directory in which the source file resides) or you may keep the same name. COPY can also be used to append one file to another. There are quite a few options to COPY, so the syntax can become quite complex. Here is a summary of the correct syntax for this command:

```
COPY /switch1 filename1 /switch2 filename2 /switch3
```

Let's look at each of these elements one at a time. **Filename1** is the source file to be copied. You may include a path and drive specification if the source file is not in the current directory. **Filename2** is the name of the new file. You may also include a path and drive specification here. Or, you may include only the drive (or drive and path) and DOS will copy the old file to the specified drive and path using the same name. So, a simple COPY might look like one of these examples:

```
COPY C:\WP\FILE1.DOC A:\FILE2.DOC
COPY C:\WP\FILE1.DOC A:
COPY FILE1 C:\FILE2.DOC
```

You may use wild cards to copy more than one file at a time:

```
COPY C:\WP\*.DOC A:
COPY C:\WP\*.DOC A:*.BAK
```

In the second example, the files from C: would be copied to A:, but given a new extension, BAK.

You may also copy all the files in a subdirectory, without using the *.* file specifier:

```
COPY C:\WP A:
```

would copy all the files in C:\WP to drive A:, for example.

Optional Switches

The optional switches tell DOS to perform a special function during the copy process.

/V This verifies that the copy matches the source file. You should place the /V switch at the end, in **switch3's** position.

/A This tells DOS to treat the file as an ASCII file. If applied to the source file, the contents will be copied up to but not including the first Control-Z DOS encounters. DOS will automatically add a Control-Z to the end of the copy (unless you tell it not to).

When applied to the destination file, the /A switch will tell DOS to add the Control-Z at the end (for example, when it is copying a binary file and would not ordinarily add one).

/B Use this to tell DOS to treat the file as a binary (non-text) file. Applied to the source file, it will cause DOS to copy the entire file, including any Control-Z's that are encountered. If used with the destination file, DOS will *not* add a Control-Z to the end.

DOS applies the /A and /B switches to files depending on their position on the command line. When it finds one of these, the switch is applied to the file immediately preceding and all the files listed after that, until another /A or /B is found. You can see that **switch1** won't ordinarily be needed, since there are no file names preceding it. It functions much the same as if the switch had been placed after the file name.

If you use wild cards for **filename1**, all the files meeting that specification will be concatenated or joined together to form the destination file. You may also add files together by separating them with plus signs:

```
COPY FILE1+FILE2+FILE3 CLUMP.ASC
```

This command would combine the contents of FILE1, FILE2, and FILE3 into CLUMP.ASC. In this case, we could also have used:

```
COPY FILE? CLUMP.ASC
```

but that command wouldn't work if file names had no shared characters.

THE XCOPY COMMAND

Introduced with DOS 3.2 to provide support for 3.5–inch disk drives, **XCOPY** also has some features of particular interest to hard disk users. XCOPY is an enhanced version of COPY. It will allow you to copy files, subdirectories, and all the files in subdirectories, as you desire. You may also initiate a prompted copying sequence, and specify that only unbacked-up files, or files created after a date you indicate, be copied. The syntax for XCOPY is as follows:

```
XCOPY sourcefile destinationfile /switches
```

As always, the source file name and destination file name can include the full path name. Note that the default source file name is *.* and that XCOPY will not change the date of the copied files. The creation date and time are the same as for the original file.

Optional Switches

The switches used can be entered in any order.

/A This switch selects only those files that have changed since the last backup. However, the attribute byte of the source file is not changed to indicate that you have copied the file with XCOPY. This in effect leaves the file marked as "unbacked-up" so that you can later use the BACKUP command to copy it.

/M This switch can be used to copy files that have changed since the last backup, but with the archive attribute now reset. You may back up files onto several diskettes by repeatedly issuing the XCOPY command followed by the /M switch. Each time the command is issued only the unbacked-up files will be copied to the new diskette. If any one file is larger than the capacity of your diskette, XCOPY will be unable to copy it. In such cases, use BACKUP, which can break up very long files into several parts and then join them together through RESTORE.

/D This switch, when followed by the date (in **/D:mm-dd-yy** format) copies only those files that have changed since the date supplied.

/D This switch copies all subdirectories below the source directory. XCOPY will create new directories on the destination disk as needed, except if those directories will be empty. If you want all directories duplicated, use the /E switch.

/E This causes XCOPY to create subdirectories on the destination disk to match those of the source disk, even if they will end up being empty.

/P This switch initiates prompted copying. XCOPY will ask you to confirm that you want each file copied. The /W switch forces XCOPY to wait for you to insert diskettes before beginning a search for the source files.

/V As with COPY, the /V switch verifies that the information written to the destination disk is the same as that on the source disk. This switch is not needed if VERIFY has been set to ON.

THE ATTRIB COMMAND

ATTRIB was introduced with DOS 3.x. Its syntax is as follows:

```
ATTRIB [+R] [-R]  [d:] [path]  [filename]
```

Use +R to set a file to read-only status, or –R to set a file to read/write, which allows it to be changed, erased, or overwritten. The drive where the file resides is entered in the place of d:. The path where the file resides and the path name are entered immediately following. Below is an example of the use of ATTRIB:

```
ATTRIB +R C:\WP\LETTERS\DB*.*
```

This would protect all the files in subdirectory C:\WP\LETTERS that begin with DB from accidental erasure or overwriting.

THE REPLACE COMMAND

Another command introduced with DOS 3.2, REPLACE will copy files from the source disk to replace those with the same name on the destination disk. You might think of it as a sort of "updating" command.

For example, if your hard disk has files called INVOICE.86, INVOICE.87, and INVOICE.88, invoking REPLACE to copy them to a floppy disk (if the /A switch is not used) will cause the files to be copied only if files by those names already reside on the destination floppy. The syntax for the command is:

```
REPLACE sourcefilename destinationdrive /switches
```

The source file name, which can include wild cards, names the file or files that you wish to copy to the destination drive.

Optional Switches

The switches provide you with some flexibility.

/A This switch reverses the action of the command, causing REPLACE to copy only those files that do *not* exist on the target disk. Instead of replacing files, it will *add* files to the existing files on the disk.

/S This switch causes REPLACE to search all directories on the target disk for files that match the source file name. It cannot be used with the /A switch; they are mutually exclusive.

/P   Because it forces DOS to ask you Y/N before replacing a file, this prompting allows you to be selective in which files are replaced.

/R   You can use this to replace files that are marked as read-only. If used with care, this lets you update files without bothering to change their status with ATTRIB.

/W   This switch causes DOS to wait for you to insert a diskette before beginning to search for files. It is useful in batch files where you want to prompt the user to insert a certain disk before updating begins.

/U   A new parameter added with DOS 4.0, /U tells DOS only to update files on the target diskette if they have a date that is older than the same file on the source disk. This switch cannot be used with /A; they are mutually exclusive.

BACKING UP YOUR HARD DISK

How often should you back up your hard disk? Well, how much data can you afford to lose? What method should you use to back up your hard disk? How much time can you spend, and how quickly do you have to get your data back when (or if) your hard disk crashes?

If most of your disk storage is consumed by applications programs, you won't need to back up the disk very often. Presumably, backup copies of the software have been made, and won't change. Users such as executives who write memos, letters, and proposals that are immediately transferred to another computer over a network or by disk exchange for printout, filing, permanent storage, etc., are generally protected in the event of a hard disk crash, since the files are effectively backed up elsewhere.

Hard disks that are the sole repository of data must be backed up more frequently. The frequency rises in direct proportion to the importance of the data and the number of people served. A

hard disk used as a file server on a network may have to
be backed up daily or, in rare cases, several times a day.

There are a few applications where the data is sensitive.
Government agencies and defense contractors may have such environments. In these cases, it may be forbidden to permanently
(or even temporarily) store data on hard disks at all. All data may
be relegated to removable media that can be locked up when
authorized people are not using them.

All the different situations calling for hard disk backup also
may require different solutions. Here are a few of them to consider.

File-by-File Copying

It is possible to back up a hard disk onto floppy disks simply by
making copies of each file you create. You can format a blank disk
for each subdirectory on your hard disk, and copy files over to the
diskette either en masse or a few files at a time as they are created.
This method requires no software expertise, and is particularly
effective if a given user creates only a few files a day and can
remember to back them up to floppy disks at the end of the day.

You can also create a batch file that automates the chore somewhat. The batch file can use COPY or (preferably) XCOPY to copy
all the files from specified subdirectories to the backup disk. In
this way, you can avoid copying meaningless files. XCOPY's /M
switch can be used to ensure that you are copying *only* those files
that have not been previously copied with XCOPY or BACKUP.

Your custom batch file can include IF EXIST lines that will
cause files to be backed only if they already exist on a given floppy, to update with the latest version, or only if they do *not*, to avoid
overwriting files with the same name. REPLACE may also be
used. However, REPLACE does not reset the archive bit, so you
won't be able to copy only unbacked-up files. You *can* tell
REPLACE to copy files with more recent dates than those on the
backup diskette, however.

THE BACKUP COMMAND

These methods above all copy your files to the backup media in the form of ordinary DOS files. You may individually access them from the floppy disk and copy them back to your hard disk or to any other storage device.

DOS also provides a special command, BACKUP, and its complementary RESTORE command. These store hard disk information onto floppy diskettes in a special format that gets the most use from the space available on the diskettes. The syntax for the BACKUP command is as follows:

```
BACKUP [d1:][path][filename] [d2:][/S][/M][/A][/D:mm-dd-yy]
```

d1: With DOS 2.x, this source drive specification must be C:, except in those cases where the user has more than one hard disk (D:, etc.). With DOS 3.x and later versions the source diskette can be any drive, allowing the BACKUP command to be used to back up from one diskette to another.

path The path name of the directory to be backed up can be specified; otherwise the currently logged directory is used by BACKUP.

filename You may use wild cards to represent more than one file. If *.* is used, or if this parameter is omitted, all the files in the directory indicated will be backed up.

d2: With DOS 2.x and systems with one floppy drive, this destination drive specification must be A:. With DOS 3.x and higher, any drive can be used.

Optional Switches

/S As with XCOPY, the /S tells DOS to copy all the files in the subdirectories beneath the one indicated. So:

```
BACKUP C:\ A: /S
```

would copy all the files on a hard disk to A:, with the user prompted to put in new diskettes as they fill.

/M As with XCOPY, the /M switch tells DOS only to copy those files that have not been backed up, that is, which have an attribute bit set to 1. If you wish, you can reset this bit using AT-TRIB as described earlier in this chapter.

/A This switch tells DOS *not* to erase the files that may currently be on a diskette. New files will be added to those already on the diskette.

/D:mm-dd-yy Like XCOPY, BACKUP can be used to copy only the files that have been created or changed after the date included with the /D switch.

Using Backup

To use BACKUP, make sure you have sufficient diskettes on hand. With 360K floppies, you will need 28 to 30 for a 10-megabyte hard disk and 56 to 60 for a 20-megabyte disk. When high-capacity diskettes are used, eight or nine will be needed for a 10-megabyte drive, and 17 or 18 for a 20-megabyte drive. BACKUP will supply numbers for the diskettes as they are used, which you can apply to them using labels. Most users keep double sets of backup disks. That is, each new backup is made to the oldest set, so if a problem occurs the more recent backup floppies are still available. Then, the newer set becomes the oldest to be used for the next backup.

Changes in BACKUP for DOS 3.3 and DOS 4.0

Other switches used with the BACKUP command introduced with DOS 3.3 and later versions include /T, /F, and /L.

/T:hh:mm:ss This switch is accompanied by a time in the format hh:mm:ss, and directs DOS to back up only files created on or after that time. It must be used with the /D command in order to indicate the date after which the time specified is relevant.

/F This switch tells DOS to format the backup disk, much like DISKCOPY does, except that with BACKUP the user must request this function, while with DISKCOPY formatting is automatic.

A change was made to BACKUP with DOS 4.0 so that the /F switch is no longer needed. BACKUP will automatically FORMAT a diskette if it is unformatted.

/L This switch requests the creation of a log file that lists all the files on the backup disk. This will be useful if you need to reconstruct a crashed hard disk and wish to know which files are stored on which disk.

With DOS 3.3 and later, DOS creates only two backup files on each diskette, CONTROL.xxx and BACKUP.xxx (the xxx being the number of the diskette: 001, 002, etc.). CONTROL.xxx contains the names of the files on the diskette, along with other useful information, such as file size, date and time of creation, etc. BACKUP.xxx is the file containing the backed-up files themselves. Compared with earlier versions of DOS, this new system is much more efficient, improving backup times by a third or more.

BACKUP now labels each diskette with a volume name of 11 characters. The label is in the format BACKUPbbxxx. The two **b**'s are blanks, while xxx will correspond to the number of the diskette (001, etc.).

Note that with versions 3.x of DOS, BACKUP cannot be used when SHARE is active. Since SHARE must be used with DOS

4.0 when you have disk volumes larger than 32 megabytes, BACKUP *can* be used with SHARE. Also note that the log file won't record error messages. So, if the backup of a file was thwarted because SHARE was active, or the function was aborted because Control-Break was pressed, there will be no indication in the log file.

THE RESTORE COMMAND

RESTORE is the complement to the BACKUP command, and must be used to put the files back on your hard disk. The syntax for RESTORE is as follows:

```
RESTORE [d1:] [d2:][path][filename] [/S][/P]
```

d1: The source drive paameter is not optional.

d2: If the destination drive is not specified, C: will be used.

path You can specify the directory where the files restored are to be routed. Otherwise, the currently logged directory on the destination drive is used.

filename You may use wild cards to specify restoring only certain file names. If this parameter is omitted, all the files in the specified directory are restored.

Optional Switches

/S This causes all the subdirectories below the one specified to be restored as well.

/M This switch tells DOS to restore files that were changed or removed from the hard disk since the last time they were backed up.

/P This handy feature will prompt the user before overwriting files that have been changed since the last backup, or files that have been marked by ATTRIB as read-only. This prevents the accidental restoration of a file that has been changed and hence is more up to date than the one that was backed up. You can also mark files with ATTRIB to protect them from being overwritten by RESTORE.

/B:mm-dd-yy This switch allows restoring files only if changed on or *before* the date specified.

/A:mm-dd-yy This allows restoring files only if changed on or *after* the date indicated.

Both the /A and the /B switches can be used with the /E and /L switches to indicate the time of day before which or after which the files to be restored must last have been modified. The syntax for these is:

```
/E:hh:mm:ss
```

```
/L:hh:mm:ss
```

/N This option restores files that have been deleted from the target disk since the backup.

Even though the file formats have changed with DOS 3.3's version of RESTORE, the command will still handle files backed up with earlier versions of DOS. However, in all cases, RESTORE will no longer restore the two invisible system files (IBMBIO.COM and IBMDOS.COM with PC-DOS; IO.SYS and MSDOS.SYS with earlier versions of MS-DOS) or COMMAND.COM. One reason for this is that the user may have upgraded to a new version of DOS (or switched to OS/2) since the backup. Restoring the system files would cause problems for the hard disk user, up to and including making the disk unbootable.

BACKUP ALTERNATIVES

Those who don't want to use the DOS commands for backup will find a wealth of third-party backup programs available to do the job for them. One popular alternative is the shareware program ARC.COM, which will compress your files as it prepares a back-up version of them.

ARC is available in a number of versions from bulletin boards and user groups. You can also obtain it from its creator, System Enhancement Associates, 21 New Street, Wayne, NJ 07470. The license fee for commercial organizations is modest. Syntax for ARC is:

```
ARC command option g password archivename file to arc...
```

For "command" you may substitute one of the following:

A :   add files to archive
M :   move files to archive
U :   update files in archive
F :   freshen files in archive
D :   delete files from archive
X :   extract files from archive
E :   extract files from archive
R :   run files from archive
P :   copy files from archive to standard output
L :   list files in archive
V :   verbose listing of files in archive
T :   test archive integrity
C :   convert entry to new packing method

For "option" you may use:

B :   retain backup copy of archive

S :   suppress compression (store only)
W :   suppress warning messages
N :   suppress notes and comments
O :   overwrite existing files when extracting
G :   encrypt/decrypt archive entry; add *password*

For **archivename** use the name of the file the compressed files will be stored in. **File to arc** may be a list of one or more files to archive.

There are also many commercial backup programs besides ARC to choose from. We haven't tried any of these with DOS 4.0 and disks larger than 32 megabytes. However, if any of them don't work with DOS 4.0, their vendors will surely have an updated version on the market by the time this book is published.

SUMMARY

This chapter has been an introduction to one of the most important aspects of hard disk management with DOS; copying files and making backups. These are also the least well understood and most neglected aspects of the operating system. We learned about several new commands, including XCOPY, REPLACE, BACKUP, RESTORE, and ATTRIB. Now it's time to turn to a command that can take up a whole chapter by itself, MODE.

PART

3

Advanced
DOS
Commands

16

MODE and Some Related Commands

INTRODUCTION

The rest of this book will cover the remaining commands of DOS, including some of the more complex ones. MODE is not a particularly difficult command to use. However, it does have almost two dozen completely different applications, and can be used to control everything from your CRT screen to your printer.

Consequently, we'll devote this entire chapter to sorting out different uses for MODE, and explaining their syntax.

THE MODE COMMAND AND PERIPHERAL EQUIPMENT

MODE is an external DOS command that has been designed specifically for use in configuring peripheral equipment, from printers to EGA adapter card. *Peripheral equipment* is a general name given to any external equipment that can be attached to the PC. Generally, it interfaces through one of the card slots inside the PC.

Any device attached to the PC through a slot can be thought of as a peripheral. This, of course, includes memory cards, video interface cards, disk controllers, hard disk cards, and the like, even though these are so integral to the system that they are seldom referred to as peripherals. The term has come to mean external equipment attached to the PC. The most common of all peripherals is the printer; other examples include modems, graphics digitizers, scanners, analogue controllers, speech synthesizers, pen plotters, and joysticks.

One of the key uses of the MODE command is to control printers and other devices attached to the parallel and serial ports of the PC. However, it can also be used to change the mode of your display adapter and other hardware. Let's look at each use of MODE separately.

USING MODE TO SET THE DISPLAY ADAPTER

The syntax for this version of the MODE command is:

```
MODE n
```

The options for the **n** parameter are as follows:

40 specifies a 40-column display with the color/graphics adapter (CGA)

80 specifies an 80-column display with the CGA

BW40 changes the active display to the CGA adapter and selects a 40-column black-and-white display

BW80 changes the active display to the CGA adapter and selects an 80-column black-and-white display

CO40 changes the active display to the CGA adapter and selects a 40-column color display

CO80 changes the active display to the CGA adapter and selects an 80-column color display

MONO changes the active display to the monochrome display adapter (MDA) (note that you can have more than one display adapter installed in your PC)

You may also add an R or L parameter, which will move your screen display over right or left, and a T parameter, which requests a screen test pattern to help you align your screen. Most monitors today are properly aligned; this option was of most use back in the days when PCs were likely to be connected to composite video monitors or (gasp) television sets.

You would use the screen alignment options like this:

```
MODE CO80,L,T
```

MODE would display a pattern, such as a series of numbers, which you could use to check proper display of the image.

With DOS 4.0, the added ability to specify the number of screen lines was included, along with a new syntax for specifying the number of screen columns. The commands are as follows:

```
MODE CON LINES=n
MODE CON COLS=n
```

The number of lines specified by **n** can be either 25, 43, or 50 (you must have a display adapter that supports 43 or 50 lines). The number of columns can be either 40 or 80. MODE will ignore other values. You may also add the number of lines you want onto one of the other MODE screen specifications:

```
MODE CO80,50
```

```
MODE CO40,50
```

The latter display, 40 characters wide by 50 lines, looks *really* squashed, by the way. Any programs that you run that take control of the display have probably not been set up to sense the changes MODE has made and so may return you to default display mode. However, DOS 4.0 has added a switch for ANSI.SYS in your CONFIG.SYS file (more on CONFIG.SYS later) that you can use to keep the application program from overriding your setting.

Your application program may still be unable to use the extra lines. Most of the software we tried simply confined their display to half the screen, still using only 25 lines.

USING MODE TO CONTROL THE PRINTER

Five other versions of MODE can be applied to your line printer. These are listed separately:

```
MODE LPT#
MODE LPT#=COMn
MODE LPT# COLS=col
MODE LPT# LINES=lines
MODE LPT# RETRY=E, B, R, or NONE
```

In all five cases, you would substitute for # the LPT port you wish to configure, 1 to 3. The first example cancels rerouting of the output to LPT port #. In other words, all the output intended to go to that port actually goes to that port.

The second example does the rerouting, sending output directed to that LPT port to a COM port, either 1, 2, 3, or 4. You'd substitute a value for **n** to indicate which COM port is to be used.

The third example is used to define the line length for the printer, either 80 or 132 characters per line.

The fourth example is used to set the line spacing per inch, either 6 or 8 lines per inch.

The final example tells MODE how to respond to a status check from the computer to a given printer port. With earlier versions of DOS, you would include a ,P with the MODE command to tell DOS to keep trying until the printer is ready. In current versions, you may enter:

E   to return an error from a check of a busy port.
B   to instead return a busy signal from a busy port.
R   to return a ready message from a busy port
NONE   no retry action if the port is busy

The last three may be used together on a single command line to set columns and lines and retry action at once. Later versions of DOS will no longer accept the ,P parameter.

USING MODE TO SET THE KEYBOARD

DOS 4.0 added the capability to set your enhanced keyboard's rate with the MODE command. The syntax is:

```
MODE CON RATE=r DELAY=d
```

For **r** you would substitute a value indicating the approximate number of repetitions per second when a key (such as the underscore key) is held down. A higher number will provide a faster *typematic* rate. For **d**, you would indicate the delay time before the automatic repeat feature starts. Experiment with these values to see which ones suit your particular typing speed. A long delay helps clumsy typists, but also slows down the response of your keyboard.

USING MODE TO CONTROL THE COM PORTS

MODE can also be used to control the COM ports. With DOS 4.0, additional options were added to allow setting COM parameters. The basic syntax is as follows:

```
MODE COMx:baud,parity,databits,stopbits,P
```

For **x** you would substitute the number of the COM port you wish to define, 1 through 4. Then, you would enter a baud rate for **baud**; you may use baud rates from 110 to 19,200. The other settings are optional. N, O, E (None, Odd, or Even) may be used for parity, 7 or 8 for databits, 1 or 2 for stopbits, and P for continuous retries on timeout.

With DOS 4.0, instead of P you would use the same retry syntax as for the LPT version of mode:

```
MODE COM1:1200,RETRY=E
```

The options would include:

E   to return an error from a check of a busy port
B   to instead return a busy signal from a busy port
R   to return a ready message from a busy port
NONE   no retry action if the port is busy

As with MODE and LPT, the default is no retry action if the port is busy.

DOS 4.0 also allows additional syntax specifications for MODE. The optional way of setting asynchronous parameters looks like this:

```
MODE COMx BAUD=b DATA=d STOP=s RETRY=r
```

While BAUD must be specified, you may enter only one of the others, or more than one, in any combination. Substitute appropriate values shown above for b, d, s, or r. For parity, you may use ODD, EVEN, MARK, SPACE, or NONE, as well as O, E, M, S, or N.

USING MODE FOR CODE PAGE SWITCHING

DOS 3.3 was enhanced with four new versions of the MODE command intended for use in supporting additional foreign language character sets. The first move in this direction was taken with

DOS 3.0 in 1984, with 15 new sets of time, date, numeric, and currency formats, along with six different keyboard layouts.

The user wishing to add support for foreign language formats first specifies the time/date/numeric/currency format and keyboard layout by including the relevant COUNTRY command in the CONFIG.SYS file. (CONFIG.SYS will be covered in detail in Chapter 19.) However, the foreign language characters that DOS had available to draw from were limited to those of the standard IBM PC character set. This "page" of characters, referred to as Code Page 437, or CP437 for short, is lacking in many of the symbols needed for comprehensive foreign language display and printing.

In 1987, IBM adopted a new multilingual code page for its mainframe computers, conforming to a new International Standards Organization character set. The new set includes letters from the alphabets of all the Latin-based languages. A version of the code page, called CP850, was set up for PCs. While the first 128 characters of the set are the same as those currently used on PCs, some graphics symbols, Greek characters, and math symbols have been replaced by foreign language symbols.

In addition, IBM introduced three other code pages: CP860 (Portuguese), CP863 (Canadian French), and CP865 (Norwegian and Danish). Overall, DOS can now support eleven different languages used in a total of 19 countries.

Obviously, files created under the original code page that use any of the second 128 characters will not be displayed or printed properly when one of the new code pages is active. DOS 3.3 provides the capability of switching from one code page to another. Thus, the user can embed the appropriate MODE command in a batch file when starting up a program that needs a character set different from the one currently active.

Note that code page switching requires compatible hardware. You must have an EGA graphics subsystem, or a compatible system with an EGA mode. Your printer must also support code-page switching to print out the symbols properly. Most frequently, this will be accomplished through special font files you can load and designate.

In this chapter, we'll look in detail at the use of MODE to switch code pages. However, you should know that you must also select a default code page with the COUNTRY command in CON-FIG.SYS, and allow buffer memory for your display and printer through the DEVICE=DISPLAY.SYS and DEVICE=PRINT-ER.SYS device drivers. These, too, will be discussed in more detail in Chapter 19.

Finally, code-page support for your keyboard must be accomplished through the KEYBxx command, which reads keyboard definitions for the desired country from the KEYBOARD.SYS file.

The four new forms of MODE for code page switching are as follows:

```
MODE device CODEPAGE PREPARE=cplist d:path/
   filename.ext
MODE device CODEPAGE SELECT=cp
MODE device CODEPAGE /status
MODE device CODEPAGE REFRESH
```

In all four cases, **device** can be CON, PRN, LPT1, LPT2, or LPT3, depending on whether you want to configure your display screen or your printer with the command. The first format sets up DOS to handle a series of code pages. You may enter as many code page numbers as you plan on using from a list, as a substitute for **cplist**, from 437, 850, 860, 863, or 865. The **d:path/file-name.ext** should include the name of the file containing the code page information.

The next format selects the active code page. Substitute for **cp** the actual code page number you wish to use. The third format displays the active code page, while the fourth refreshes the specified device with the current code page information.

THE CHCP AND NLSFUNC COMMANDS

You also should know that the code page can be changed from the command line with the new command CHCP. For this command to operate, you must first activate support for the command with the NLSFUNC command. Syntax for that command is as follows:

```
NLSFUNC filename
```

Substitute for **filename** the name of the file containing country information. Then, the code page can be changed by typing:

```
CHCP nnnn
```

Substitute the number of the code page you wish to activate for **nnnn**.

Chances are you will never need to fiddle with the code pages of your PC or PS/2 system. Should you need to do so, your application program will likely provide additional information.

THE KEYBxx COMMAND

You can load a keyboard information file from a batch file or from the command line with the KEYBxx command. You would replace **xx** with two characters representing the country you wish to activate for your keyboard characters. This command uses about 2K of memory. Formats include:

KEYBUK	United Kingdom
KEYBGR	Germany
KEYBFR	France
KEYBIT	Italy
KEYBSP	Spain

There are other keyboard definitions that support various code pages and keyboard IDs. You should check with someone in the country where you will be using the PC to determine the best setup for that language and country.

You may switch back to the U.S. keyboard at any time by pressing Control-Alt-F1. To return to the keyboard specified by KEYBxx, press Control-Alt-F2.

If you enter KEYB on a line by itself, DOS will return the current setting for the keyboard and display terminal, as well as the ID, but only if these have already been specified.

KEYBxx has a number of syntaxes to allow several different functions. Exploring all of them in detail is beyond the scope of this book. However, here is a brief summary:

KEYBxx	selects special keyboard layout
KEYBxx,yyy	identifies the code page to be used
KEYB xx,,file	defines the file name of the keyboard definition file (if not KEYBOARD.SYS, the default file name)
KEYBxx /ID:nnn	defines a keyboard identification code
KEYB xx,yyy,file /ID:nnn	defines keyboard layout, code page, file name of the definition file, and keyboard ID code

THE SELECT COMMAND

With versions of DOS earlier than 4.0, SELECT is a command used only to create a system diskette set up for a particular keyboard layout and time/date format. The syntax is as follows:

```
SELECT d: d2: xxx yy
```

The **d:** parameter should be the source drive, which must contain a DOS diskette. Only A: and B: can be used for **d:**, and A: is the default. The **d2:** parameter, added as an option with DOS 3.2, is the target drive, and must be different from the source drive. The **xxx** specification is the country code for the date and time format. Your options are shown in Table 16.1.

The **yy** parameter is the keyboard code that instructs DOS which keyboard layout to use. Your options are shown in Table 16.2.

Country	Code
DOS 3.0, 3.1, and later	
France	033
Germany	049
Italy	039
Spain	034
United Kingdom	044
United States	001
DOS 3.2 and later	
Australia	061
Belgium	032
Canadian-French	002
Denmark	045
Finland	358
Israel	972
Middle East	785
Netherlands	031
Norway	047
Portugal	351
Sweden	046
Switzerland	041

Table 16–1

SELECT functions differently with various versions of DOS 3.x. With DOS 3.0 and 3.1, it will use DISKCOPY to make a copy of a diskette, and then use DISKCOMP to compare the new copy. Because of this, it works only with diskettes (not hard disks) and both external DOS command must be available on the disk in drive A:. The key difference between the two diskettes is that SELECT adds a CONFIG.SYS file with the COUNTRY com-

Country	Code
United States	US
France	FR
Spain	SP
Italy	IT
United Kingdom	UK
Germany	GR

Table 16–2

mand, and an AUTOEXEC.BAT file with the KEYBxx invoked for the selected country.

With DOS 3.2 and DOS 3.3, SELECT uses FORMAT and XCOPY instead of DISKCOPY, so the command will work with all disk types and formats.

As you can probably guess, the functions of SELECT can just as easily be carried out manually. For that reason, this earlier version was dropped when DOS 4.0 was introduced.

SUMMARY

This chapter was devoted to the many uses for the MODE command. You learned how to use MODE to control your printer, serial port, keyboard, and CRT screen. Use of MODE to set code page information and related foreign language setup commands were explored. In the next chapter, we'll look at some advanced commands for DOS, including one very useful command introduced with DOS 4.0.

CHAPTER

Advanced DOS Commands for Hard Disks

INTRODUCTION

By now you should have a good understanding of how DOS works, and will be ready for some more advanced commands. Each of the versions of DOS from 3.0 on have included some significant enhancements. Some of the commands detailed in this chapter have been added to DOS in one of the later releases. Others are old standbys that qualify as advanced commands because they are more complex, or less often used than the "standard" DOS commands. You'll find that all these features provide useful enhancements that let you get more from the operating system.

THE VOL COMMAND

Strictly speaking, VOL is hardly an advanced command, since its function is not difficult to understand or use. It *is* a rarely used command, simply because most of us will have little use for it. All

VOL does is display the name or label of the drive specified. Its syntax is as follows:

```
VOL d:
```

Substitute for **d:** the drive for which you wish to see the volume label. If no drive is specified, the currently logged drive is used. If you typed:

```
VOL C:
```

you might see a message like this:

```
Volume in drive C is HARD DISK
Volume Serial Number is 2611-1DF8
```

The serial number is only displayed with versions of DOS from 4.0 on. The DIR command also shows you the volume name, if any, whenever you ask for a directory of a disk. So, VOL appears on the surface to have no useful function. However, you could conceivably use VOL in your batch file programming, by redirecting the output of the command to a file. For example, the following is a batch file that would allow you to insert floppy disks one after another into A:, and store in a file, DISK.LOG, a listing of the volume names of each:

```
echo off
:LOG
echo Place next disk in A:
echo Press Control-C if finished.
pause
VOL a:>>disk.log
goto log
```

THE LABEL COMMAND

This command is used to apply, change, or remove volume labels from disks. It was added to DOS with version 3.0. Its syntax is as follows:

```
label d:volumelabel
```

You would substitute for **d:** the drive containing the disk you wish to label. **Volumelabel** can be an 11-character name. The allowable characters are the same as in a file name. If you do not supply the label when typing the command line, DOS will ask you for the label. Note that you can't change the volume label of a drive that has been named through the SUBST command (explained later in this chapter). Also, LABEL will not work with networks or on *ASSIGN*ed drives (ASSIGN will also be explained later in this chapter).

THE FASTOPEN COMMAND

This command was added with DOS 3.3. It is actually a memory-resident utility that stores in memory the locations of frequently accessed subdirectories and files to speed disk access. The syntax for this command under DOS 3.3 is as follows:

```
FASTOPEN c:=nnn
```

The **c:** is the drive specification for your hard disk. For **nnn** you should substitute the number of entries to be "remembered" by DOS.

When you open a file that is buried several levels deep in subdirectories, DOS must first search the root directory to locate the top subdirectory in the path. Remember that a subdirectory is stored on the disk as just another file. DOS must then search the file containing the first subdirectory's entries to find the next subdirectory. This is repeated for each level until DOS locates the file you want to open.

When FASTOPEN is used, DOS will store in the special memory, or cache, the location of the **nnn** specified entries. The minimum you can require is 10. The default is 34, and you can request as many as 999. When 34 entries are specified, FASTOPEN consumes about 3,000 bytes of memory.

As files are accessed, DOS will first search the cache to see if the file being requested is listed. If so, it can retrieve the information needed without accessing the disk, then go directly to the disk to open the file. If the entry has not been cached, DOS must access the disk's directory as usual. DOS will store the locations of these files until the maximum number that can fit in the cache are memorized. Then, it will discard old entries on a least-recently used basis.

The data cached in memory includes the file name, its attribute, the date and time of creation, the beginning cluster number of the file, the sector number of the directory, and where in the directory its entry resides.

For DOS 4.0, the /X parameter was added to FASTOPEN, allowing DOS to use expanded memory for its functions. It can also be installed through the use of the INSTALL command (discussed in the next chapter). With the DOS 4.0 version of FASTOPEN, you may specify both directory or file entries and the number of extents to be used:

```
FASTOPEN c: (dir/files,extents) /X
```

You'd substitute for **dir/files** the number of directory or file entries to retain (10 to 999), and for **extents**, a number from 1 to 999. The /X parameter will help save your valuable conventional memory for running applications and storing data that cannot be directed to expanded memory.

THE VERIFY COMMAND

This command is used to turn on an extra checking step to verify that the computer information just written to the disk has been written correctly. It slows down operations somewhat, but may be especially useful when copying or backing up important information to floppy disks. Hard disks ordinarily have their own built-in verify-after-write routines, so using VERIFY all the time can increase write times by up to 100 percent with little benefit. Information written to floppy disks by hard disk users may be especially important, since floppies are mostly used for backup by these users.

VERIFY on a line by itself will report the current status of VERIFY. To set the status, you use the following syntax:

```
VERIFY ON
VERIFY OFF
```

THE RECOVER COMMAND

Magnetic data stored on hard disks or floppies is only as permanent as the flux changes that indicate a binary digit. It's possible for a minor electrical or physical change on the disk surface to ruin enough bits to generate an error the next time a particular sector is read.

RECOVER is a utility that makes a new copy of a file containing a bad sector, trying to read the sector if possible (in case the error was a "soft" one). If not, the sector is skipped during the copy process, and the sector marked as bad in the FAT so DOS won't try to use it again.

RECOVER is probably of most use in resurrecting ASCII files. Even though a minimum of 512 bytes will be missing from the new copy, the rest of the information can be retrieved. If the bad sector is located in a program file, you probably can't use that program anymore. Software just doesn't function well with half a kilobyte of instructions missing. It's remotely possible that the bad sector will be located in the middle of some instructional material or error messages stored in ASCII form in the program file. If you know what you're doing, you *might* be able to fix up a program like this using DEBUG or some other tool. However, if you've made backup copies of your software, the best answer is simply to copy a new version to your hard disk.

More serious are situations involving data files for programs. These files generally have special formats and may compress or encode the information. If you make a new copy of the file with RECOVER, the program may simply refuse to read any more of the file after the point where the bad sector was removed. If the bad sector was located deep within the file, you might save most of your data. Something is better than nothing.

Most serious of all are cases where the bad sector is located in a disk's directory or (horrors) the FAT itself. You may have to RECOVER the entire disk in an attempt to salvage what you can of its data files.

Obviously, you should never work with RECOVER unless you absolutely must, and particularly when attempting to retrieve an entire disk. As a last resort, the syntax for RECOVER is as follows:

```
RECOVER filename
RECOVER drive
```

The first example would be used to attempt to RECOVER a specific file. You would substitute for **filename** the name of the file you want to resurrect. Wild cards may be used. The fixed file is given the same name as the original file.

The second example is a little trickier. If you specify a drive name instead of a file name, or just type RECOVER by itself, the utility will attempt to retrieve the entire disk! Later versions of DOS won't let you RECOVER the current disk drive without explicitly typing in the drive name. You'll also see a message asking you to press Enter to start recovering the files on that drive.

However, be aware that the process *includes* creating a new root directory as well as all the files and subdirectories. Good files as well as bad are placed into new files with the name FILEnnnn.REC, with **nnnn** being replaced by a different four-digit number for each file. If you unintentionally RECOVER a disk you don't mean to, a lot of work is ahead of you at the very least.

RECOVERING FROM RECOVER

To sort out a hard disk that has been accidentally RECOVERed, you'll need to determine which files are ASCII text (such as batch files, etc.) and which are program files. You can try to TYPE all the files; the batch files and other ASCII files will show up plainly. You can RENAME them as you sort through them all.

You can try examining the remaining files with a disk editing program like the Norton Utilities or even DEBUG to see what information they contain. You might be able to tell program files from data files in this way. You could even rename some of the files with .EXE or .COM extensions and try to run them. If you recognize a program that comes up, you can RENAME it as well. DOS won't let you run a program that isn't a .COM, .EXE, or .BAT file even if you give it one of those extensions.

As with most serious errors, the best recourse may be to start over with a clean hard disk and your backup files. It's also a good idea to be *very* careful in using RECOVER. You might even want to rename RECOVER as something else, and write a batch file with the name RECOVER.BAT to check the command line for the correct parameters before running the program under its new name. The file might look like this:

```
:   ][ RECOVER.BAT ][
:   Adds Checking to RECOVER
:---------------------------:
"=="" GOTO WARNING
FOR %%a IN (C: D:) DO IF "%%A"=="%1" GOTO WARNING
REC %1
GOTO END
:WARNING
ECHO You have asked to RECOVER a hard disk or
ECHO the current drive!  All data on the disk may
ECHO be stored in new files.  To proceed type:
ECHO      REC %1
:END
```

Keep in mind that RECOVER won't work on a drive that has been changed through the ASSIGN, JOIN, or SUBST commands, described below.

THE ASSIGN COMMAND

This is the first of three commands that let you change how DOS interprets drive letters in commands. ASSIGN is used to tell DOS to use a *different* disk drive than the one specified. For example, you might wish to use drive C: instead of drive B: with an older software program that insists on storing its data files on drive B:. The syntax for this command is as follows:

```
ASSIGN d1=d2
```

You would substitute for **d1** the name of the drive that is normally used; for **d2**, substitute the name of the drive you want to use instead. Note that a colon is *not* used after the drive letter. You can put more than one assignment on a single command line. To return to normal operation, type ASSIGN on a line by itself. Examples:

```
ASSIGN B=C A=C to cause DOS to see A: and B: as C:
ASSIGN          to return to normal specifications
```

You should know that some programs manage to ignore or not work with ASSIGN, including the DOS DISKCOMP, DISKCOPY, CHKDSK, and FORMAT commands. Copy protection schemes that want the key disk to be placed in drive A: or B: may be deliberately set up to ignore any "attempt" to bypass this check. Finally, make sure you don't try to ASSIGN a disk drive letter higher than marked as available with your LASTDRIVE command in CONFIG.SYS.

THE JOIN COMMAND

This command allows connecting one drive to the directory on another drive, resulting in what DOS sees as a single directory. The syntax is as follows:

```
JOIN d: d2:directory
```

Replace **d:** with the name of the drive you wish to JOIN to **d2:directory**, which is the drive and directory path name you wish to append **d:** to. For example:

```
JOIN A: C:\COMM
```

would JOIN drive A: to the directory C:\COMM. When you issue a command like DIR C:\COMM, DOS would display the files in C:\COMM as well as those on A:. You may not JOIN a drive to the root directory. When JOIN is invoked, all of the disk **d:** is attached to the second directory, including all the files in the subdirectories below the root directory in **d:**.

To remove a connection, type

```
JOIN d: /D
```

where **d:** is the drive you want disconnected. When JOIN is in effect, don't use the ASSIGN, SUBST, BACKUP, DISKCOMP, DISKCOPY, FORMAT, or RESTORE commands, as the new connection will confuse them. Also, don't try to JOIN a network drive; DOS won't let you.

THE SUBST COMMAND

Yet another command for rerouting and joining disk drives and directories, SUBST allows you to substitute a drive name for a subdirectory that you specify. The syntax is simple enough:

```
SUBST d: d:path
```

For **d:**, you should substitute the drive name you wish to use in place of **d:path**. For example, entering the command

```
SUBST E: C:\COMM
```

would have the effect that every time you used the drive E: specification, DOS would substitute C:\COMM automatically. The command DIR E: would deliver, instead, the directory of C:\COMM.

SUBST provides a simple way of allowing the use of applications that don't accommodate path names. If you have an old program that won't allow you to enter the correct path to the subdirectory you want to use, SUBST would let you substitute a drive name instead. Or, you may have a directory that you use a lot and wish to type a drive specification only, instead of the whole directory path name.

To delete the substitution, use SUBST d: /D:

```
SUBST E: /D
```

If you enter SUBST at the DOS prompt without any parameters, DOS will display the list of current substitutions in effect. As with JOIN, you cannot use SUBST with commands like ASSIGN, BACKUP, DISKCOMP, DISKCOPY, FDISK, FORMAT, JOIN, LABEL, and RESTORE. To use a drive specification higher than E:, you must activate that specification as a valid one with the LASTDRIVE command in your configuration file, CONFIG.SYS.

THE SHARE COMMAND

Prior to DOS 4.0 this command was used only to load support for file-sharing under networks such as the IBM PC Network. This prevents two or more files from attempting to update the same file at the same time. With DOS 4.0, SHARE is also used to provide support for hard disks larger than 32 megabytes. When SHARE is activated, files currently in use are locked out from other users. The syntax is as follows:

```
SHARE /F:space /L:locks
```

You may substitute for **space** the amount of memory you want to reserve for recording file-sharing information. The default value is 2,048 bytes. Each open file requires the length of the full file name, plus 11 bytes, so you can calculate just how much **space** should be allowed.

The /L parameter allows specifying the number of locks you want, with 20 the default value.

THE CHKDSK COMMAND

CHKDSK is a multi-function command that has been available from the earliest versions of DOS, and that has gained new capabilities from time to time. It will check the directory and FAT of a disk, and report the status of the disk and memory. It can also be used to repair a limited number of errors, such as "lost" clusters that have not been allocated to any file. The syntax of CHKDSK is as follows:

```
CHKDSK filename /F /V
```

All the parameters following the CHKDSK command are optional. If you type CHKDSK on a line by itself, it will report on the status of the current disk with a display like this one:

```
Volume HARD DISK    created Jul 16, 1988 12:04a

21204992 bytes total disk space
45056 bytes in 3 hidden files
135168 bytes in 62 directories
16414720 bytes in 827 user files
4597760 bytes available on disk

655360 bytes total memory
187168 bytes free
```

If lost clusters are located, but the /F (fix) switch is not included on the command line, CHKDSK will report that they exist, but not convert them to files. In such cases, the display will look like this:

```
Volume HARD DISK   created Jul 16, 1988 12:04a

Errors found, F parameter not specified.
Corrections will not be written to disk.

6 lost clusters found in 2 chains.
Convert lost chains to files  (Y/N)? n
12288 bytes disk space
        would be freed.

21204992 bytes total disk space
   45056 bytes in 3 hidden files
  135168 bytes in 62 directories
16414720 bytes in 827 user files
 4597760 bytes available on disk

  655360 bytes total memory
  187168 bytes free
```

If you substitute a file name (including one with wild cards), CHKDSK will report if any of the files are stored in non-contiguous sectors. You may be able to speed up access to these files by recopying them until DOS is able to find a continuous set of sectors for them. If you typed this command:

```
CHKDSK C:\WP\DOS\*.*
```

CHKDSK would add the following information to the CHKDSK display:

```
C:\WP\DOS\DOSBAK.DOC
    Contains 17 non-contiguous blocks.
C:\WP\DOS\CH2.DOC
    Contains 6 non-contiguous blocks.
C:\WP\DOS\CH1.DOC
    Contains 6 non-contiguous blocks.
C:\WP\DOS\INTRO.DOC
    Contains 2 non-contiguous blocks.
C:\WP\DOS\CH3.DOC
    Contains 4 non-contiguous blocks.
```

The /V switch can also be used to provide you with a list of all the files on the disk. Your listing will look something like this:

```
Volume HARD DISK    created Jul 16, 1988 12:04a
Directory C:\
        C:\IO.SYS
        C:\MSDOS.SYS
Directory C:\BATCHES
        C:\BATCHES\A.BAT
        C:\BATCHES\B.BAT
        C:\BATCHES\BASIC.BAT
        C:\BATCHES\BATCHES.BAT
        C:\BATCHES\BBS.BAT
        C:\BATCHES\BW.BAT
        C:\BATCHES\C.BAT
        C:\BATCHES\CD.ASC

 . . .
 . . .
 . . .
```

Only a partial listing is shown.

CHKDSK was changed slightly for DOS 4.0. It will now display the volume serial number as well as the number of allocation units available. The display of non-contiguous blocks in files is also slightly different, with each listing on a single line where possible. Its report looks something like this:

```
Volume DOS4          created 08-19-1988 3:11p
Volume Serial Number is 2611-1DF8

44363776 bytes total disk space
   71680 bytes in 3 hidden files
  212992 bytes in 99 directories
36278272 bytes in 1812 user files
    6144 bytes in bad sectors
 7794688 bytes available on disk

    2048 bytes in each allocation unit
   21662 total allocation units on disk
    3806 available allocation units on disk

  655360 total bytes memory
  238816 bytes free

C:\WP\MS-DOS\CH01.DOC Contains 3 non-contiguous blocks
C:\WP\MS-DOS\CH09.DOC Contains 5 non-contiguous blocks
C:\WP\MS-DOS\CH10.DOC Contains 7 non-contiguous blocks
C:\WP\MS-DOS\CH16.DOC Contains 6 non-contiguous blocks
```

THE MEM COMMAND

This command was added with DOS 4.0 to provide additional reports on DOS memory usage beyond those available with CHKDSK. Those who have expanded memory or who use many memory-resident utilities will find it particularly helpful in sorting out what went where in memory. There have been a number of public domain and shareware utilities available for some time that provide some of the functions of MEM, but a lot of the information has not been readily available. MEM is a welcome utility. The syntax is:

```
MEM
MEM /PROGRAM
MEM /DEBUG
```

```
655360 bytes total memory
654336 bytes available
238816 largest executable program size

2097152 bytes total EMS memory
1949696 bytes free EMS memory

2490368 bytes total extended memory
 393216 bytes available extended memory
```

Figure 17.1 MEM command alone

To understand how the displays differ, it would be useful to look at each one separately.

In Figure 17.1 you can see the default display of MEM. It shows the total amount of memory installed in your system, as well as the number of bytes available for all uses. When you have loaded memory-resident utilities or other programs in memory, not all the memory will be available for any additional programs you want to run, of course. So MEM displays the latest executable program you can run in the remaining memory.

It will also display how much EMS (enhanced memory specification) memory you have, how much extended memory is installed, and how much of each is still available.

Address	Name	Size	Type
000000		000400	Interrupt Vector
000400		000100	ROM Communication Area
000500		000200	DOS Communication Area
000700	IBMBIO	002470	System Program
002B70	IBMDOS	008890	System Program

Figure 17.2 MEM with /PROGRAM Parameter

00B400	IBMBIO	00C440	System Data
	XMA2EMS	004B70	DEVICE=
		0001B0	
	DISPLAY	004700	DEVICE=
	ANSI	001190	DEVICE=
		000380	FILES=
		000100	FCBS=
		000A40	BUFFERS=
		000270	LASTDRIVE=
		000CD0	STACKS=
017850	COMMAND	000040	Data
0178A0	IBMDOS	000070	-- Free --
017920	SHARE	0018A0	Program
0191D0	FASTOPEN	000590	Program
019770	COMMAND	001A20	Program
01B1A0	COMMAND	0000A0	Environment
01B250	MSMOUSE	000090	Environment
01B2F0	MSMOUSE	002720	Program
01DA20	POPUP	000090	Environment
01DAC0	POPUP	006B40	Program
024610	KEYWORKS	000090	Environment
0246B0	KEYWORKS	010E90	Program
035550	SKC	000090	Environment
0355F0	SKC	00A4D0	Program
03FAD0	DW4PG	0000B0	Environment
03FB90	DW4PG	0242C0	Program
063E60	command	0000C0	Data
063F30	command	001640	Program
065580	command	0000B0	Environment
065640	MEM	0000C0	Environment
065710	MEM	012F60	Program
078680	IBMDOS	027570	-- Free --

```
  655360    bytes total memory
  654336    bytes available
  238816    largest executable program size
 2097152    bytes total EMS memory
 1949696    bytes free EMS memory

 2490368    bytes total extended memory
  393216    bytes available extended memory
```

Figure 17.3   MEM with /DEBUG Parameter

Address	Name	Size	Type
000000		000400	Interrupt Vector
000400		000100	ROM Communication Area
000500		000200	DOS Communication Area
000700	IBMBIO	002470	System Program
	CON		System Device Driver
	AUX		System Device Driver
	PRN		System Device Driver
	CLOCK$		System Device Driver
	A: - C:		System Device Driver
	COM1		System Device Driver
	LPT1		System Device Driver
	LPT2		System Device Driver
	LPT3		System Device Driver
	COM2		System Device Driver
	COM3		System Device Driver
	COM4		System Device Driver
002B70	IBMDOS	008890	System Program
00B400	IBMBIO	00C440	System Data
	XMA2EMS	004B70	DEVICE=
		0001B0	
	DISPLAY	004700	DEVICE=
	ANSI	001190	DEVICE=
		000380	FILES=
		000100	FCBS=
		000A40	BUFFERS=
		000270	LASTDRIVE=
		000CD0	STACKS=
017850	COMMAND	000040	Data
0178A0	IBMDOS	000070	-- Free --
017920	SHARE	0018A0	Program
0191D0	FASTOPEN	000590	Program
019770	COMMAND	001A20	Program
01B1A0	COMMAND	0000A0	Environment
01B250	MSMOUSE	000090	Environment
01B2F0	MSMOUSE	002720	Program
01DA20	POPUP	000090	Environment

01DAC0	POPUP	006B40	Program
024610	KEYWORKS	000090	Environment
0246B0	KEYWORKS	010E90	Program
035550	SKC	000090	Environment
0355F0	SKC	00A4D0	Program
03FAD0	DW4PG	0000B0	Environment
03FB90	DW4PG	0242C0	Program
063E60	command	0000C0	Data
063F30	command	001640	Program
065580	command	0000B0	Environment
065640	MEM	0000C0	Environment
065710	MEM	012F60	Program
078680	IBMDOS	027570	-- Free --

```
655360 bytes total memory
654336 bytes available
238816 largest executable program size
```

Handle	EMS Name	Size
0		000000
1	BUFFERS	010000
2	FASTOPEN	004000
3		010000

```
2097152 bytes total EMS memory
1949696 bytes free EMS memory

2490368 bytes total extended memory
393216  bytes available extended memory
```

MEM with the /PROGRAM parameter supplies additional information about programs that are loaded into memory (Figure 17.2).

When the /DEBUG parameter is used, MEM will add information about device drivers and other programs in use, the starting memory address where these have been installed, their size, and other data (Figure 17.3).

SUMMARY

This chapter has provided a description of key commands used by hard disk owners to manipulate their drives. We talked about ways to "alias" disk drives and directories so DOS and your programs would use a different drive or directory than the one supplied at the command line or by your application's requirements. We also explored the CHKDSK command and new DOS 4.0 MEM command.

CHAPTER

18

Some Miscellaneous DOS Commands

INTRODUCTION

By this point, we've covered most of the major DOS commands, and have certainly dealt with the ones of key interest to hard disk users. For the sake of completeness, this chapter will wind up with a discussion of the remaining DOS external and internal commands. You may find that you'll never use several of them at all, but at least after reading this chapter you'll know why not.

THE VER COMMAND

The VER command is a simple internal utility that tells you which version of the operating system is currently being used. You might want to use it when working with someone else's computer just to familiarize yourself with what DOS commands are and are not available. Should you discover you are using DOS 3.1, for example, you can forget about the XCOPY command. The output of

VER can also be redirected to a file and used by a batch file you write to determine which version of DOS is being used.

You'll need to prepare several batch files called VERSION.BAT, MS-DOS.BAT, and IBM.BAT. They would look like this:

```
: ] [ VERSION.BAT ] [
:   Captures DOS Version
:-----------------------:
@ECHO OFF
VER>RESULTS.BAT
RESULTS


: ] [ MS-DOS.BAT ] [
: Passes Parameters to IBM.BAT
:-----------------------------:
IBM %1 %2 %3


: ] [ IBM.BAT ] [
:   Inserts Version # in Environment
:-----------------------------------:
@ECHO OFF
ERASE FILE.BAT
:CHECK
IF "%1"=="Version" GOTO SET
SHIFT
GOTO CHECK
:SET
SET VERSION=%2
```

What happens when you type VERSION from the DOS command line? VERSION.BAT will redirect the output of VER to a file called RESULTS.BAT. That file will consist of a single line like one of these:

```
IBM DOS Version 4.00
IBM Personal Computer DOS Version 3.30
```

```
MS-DOS Version 3.21
```

The last line of VERSION.BAT tells DOS to *run* a program called RESULTS. Since DOS will be unable to find a program called RESULTS.COM or RESULTS.EXE, it will execute RESULTS.BAT. Since RESULTS.BAT contains the line indicating the DOS version, it will be interpreted as a command to run a program called IBM (or one called MS-DOS) with a series of command line parameters: "DOS", "Version", and "4.00" or some other combination of parameters depending on the version of DOS in use.

You've already prepared batch files called IBM.BAT and MD-DOS.BAT. If MS-DOS is in use, MS-DOS will be called with "Version" as %1 and the version number as %2. MS-DOS.BAT calls IBM.BAT and passes along %1 and %2 to it. If an IBM DOS is in use, IBM.BAT is called directly. That batch file SHIFTs as necessary until it finds the word "Version" as %1. When it does, %2 is assumed to be the version number. That's what you insert into the environment with the line SET VERSION=%2. From that point, any batch file you run can query the environment variable %VERSION% to see what version of DOS is being used, and make changes as required to accommodate it.

THE BREAK COMMAND

This command determines the actions DOS takes to see if a Control-Break has been entered by the user during the execution of a program. If BREAK is ON, DOS will look for Control-Break while performing *any* operation. If BREAK is OFF, DOS will only look for Control-Break when accessing the keyboard or screen, the serial ports or parallel ports.

The syntax for BREAK is:

```
BREAK ON
BREAK OFF
BREAK
```

The third version will ask DOS to report the current status of the BREAK command. It may be useful to turn BREAK ON when using programs that perform other DOS functions for long periods, but may not poll the keyboard, printer, or serial ports or update screen displays. If BREAK is OFF while such programs execute, you may be unable to interrupt the program with Control-Break easily. The BREAK ON and BREAK OFF commands can be embedded in the batch file that loads such programs. You can also Control-BREAK through an entry in the CONFIG.SYS file, explained in the next chapter.

THE CTTY COMMAND

This is a potentially useful and a potentially dangerous command that is rarely put to work. It allows you to redirect the standard input and standard output devices to an auxiliary console, and then change them back. However, you can only change back from the auxiliary device—so you must make sure one exists before using this command. The syntax for CTTY is as follows:

```
CTTY device
```

For **device**, you should substitute the name of a device that can handle both input and output (otherwise you'll be unable to communicate with your PC), and one that is character-oriented. So commands like:

```
CTTY PRN
CTTY TEST.DOC
CTTY NUL
```

have some obvious problems. DOS will let you know when you try to redirect to some inappropriate devices. However, setting up the NUL device as your console is entirely possible, and will leave you without a way to communicate with the computer. Your only choice in such cases is to reboot.

You *may* send control to one of your serial ports, using a command like:

```
CTTY COM1
```

If another computer is connected to the COM1 port (say, through a modem and a telephone line, or directly with a null modem adapter), the other computer can be used to control your system. To change back, type this command at the other computer:

```
CTTY CON
```

That changes standard input and output back to the console (the default devices). You should use care with this command—not only because of the risk of temporarily locking up your computer. Remember that the other keyboard can operate your computer just as if it were the other operator's own, so he can do anything, up to and including reformatting your hard disk!

THE GRAPHICS COMMAND

GRAPHICS has been a repeatedly enhanced utility that allows you to print a graphics display when using a suitable display adapter and printer.

The parameters vary according to DOS version. For example, originally GRAPHICS had no parameters at all. You typed the command at the DOS prompt to enable DOS to print out a graphics-screen when Shift-Prt-Sc was pressed.

The syntax of this command is as follows:

```
GRAPHICS printertype switches
```

By DOS 3.2, **printertype** was added, along with the /R and /B switches. The /LCD switch is new to DOS 3.3.

The /R switch causes GRAPHICS to print white (or light) images as white, and black (or dark) images as black. If the /R switch is not used, the tones are reversed.

The /B switch tells GRAPHICS to print the background color. This works *only* with printer types COLOR4 (such as an IBM 5182 color printer with red, green, blue, and black ribbon) or COLOR8 (such as the same printer with yellow, magenta, cyan, and black ribbon).

The /LCD switch allows printing of images as they appear on the IBM PC Convertible's liquid crystal display screen.

With DOS 4.0 **printertype** can currently be one of seven types:

COLOR1 = IBM Color printer with black ribbon

COLOR2 = IBM Color printer with red, green, blue, and black ribbon

COLOR8 = IBM Color printer with yellow, magenta, cyan, and black

COMPACT = IBM Compact printer

GRAPHICS = IBM Graphics printer or Proprinter

THERMAL = IBM Convertible printer

GRAPHICSWIDE = any of a series of IBM Graphics printers or Proprinters equipped with 11 inch-wide paper.

A complete list of the many different printers and display types supported (DOS 4.0 adds EGA and VGA support) are listed in your DOS manual.

Also new is the /PRINTBOX:*id* switch. This allows altering the size of the image, using the print box size indicated by **id**. That number should match the figure found in the Printbox statement in the printer profile. Consult your printer manual for the appropriate figure, if this feature is supported by your printer's manufacturer.

THE GRAFTABL COMMAND

This command lets you use the extended character set with a color/graphics adapter in the graphics mode. Its syntax is as follows:

```
GRAFTABL cp /status
```

The two parameters are permitted only with DOS 3.3 and later versions. Typed alone, GRAFTABL will load the default code page 437 graphics characters into memory, where they are available for use by your programs. With DOS 3.3 and later, you may specify the code page **(cp)** or add the /STATUS switch to show the current code page. Typing:

```
GRAFTABL ?
```

will provide a display of the current code page in use, along with a list of the code page options. A typical display might look like this:

```
Active Code Page: None

DOS command line parameters supported:

/STA - Request Status only
?    - Display this summary of parameters

Code Pages available:
437  - USA Graphic Character Set
850  - Multi-lingual Graphic Character Set
860  - Portuguese Graphic Character Set
863  - Canadian French Graphic Character Set
865  - Nordic Graphic Character Set
```

To display the graphics characters, you can hold down the *Alt* key and type in the code number of the character with the numeric key pad. (Do *not* use the numbers on the top row of your keyboard.) The numbers assigned to the upper 128 graphics characters for the standard code page (CP437) are shown in the manuals supplied with your computer.

THE COMP COMMAND

How far we've come in only a few years! In the early days of DOS, the COMP command was one of the first introduced in any book on the operating system. Users would learn how to get a directory with DIR, to FORMAT a disk, to COPY files, then to use COMP. That was because all early users had floppy disk-based systems, and had to copy files back and forth between disks as a matter of course every day. We were also a lot less sure of our software and hardware. Using COMP to compare a file that had just been copied with the original was a handy insurance policy and a way of providing peace of mind. Even VERIFY or COPY's /V option doesn't provide quite the assurance that a byte-by-byte comparison with COMP does.

Today, we use hard disks, don't bother with COMP much, and may not even know its syntax. The command is quite easy to use:

```
COMP file1 file2
```

You would substitute the name of the source file for **file1** and the name of the file you want it compared to for **file2**. As (almost) always with DOS commands, you can include the path and directory for each file. Wild cards may be used to compare sets of files. For example:

```
COMP C:\*.BAK A:\*.BAK
```

would compare the files on C:\ ending in the .BAK extension with the corresponding files on A:\ with the same extension.

If you do not enter the file names, DOS will prompt you for the primary and secondary file names. COMP cannot be used with files of different sizes, and will only report the first ten mismatches between them. After that, the utility aborts and asks if you'd like to compare more files.

THE DISKCOPY COMMAND

This command is used to make a mirror image copy of a diskette. It can only be used with floppy disk drives; you can't DISKCOPY to the hard disk. Nor can you make copies between drives of different capacities. You must make identical 360K (or 160K, 180K, or 320K) or 1.2M 5.25–inch copies, or 720K or 1.44M 3.5–inch copies. The syntax of the command is:

```
DISKCOPY drive1 drive2 /switch
```

For **drive1** you would substitute the name of the source drive. For **drive2** include the name of the destination drive. You may include the /1 switch if you wish to copy only one side of a 5.25–inch normal density disk.

If you do not include **drive2**, DISKCOPY will make the copy using the single disk drive, **drive1,** and prompt you to exchange disks at the correct time. You can also use drive A: and drive B: with systems having a single disk drive. DISKCOPY will prompt you to insert the correct disks in drive A:. Since all this disk shuffling can lead to errors, remember to write-protect your source diskette—just in case you insert it at the wrong time.

THE DISKCOMP COMMAND

This is the DISKCOPY equivalent of COMP. It will allow you to make a track-by-track comparison of two diskettes. Either COMP or DISKCOMP should have been made with the DISKCOPY command. The syntax for the command is as follows:

```
DISKCOMP drive1 drive2 /switch
```

As with DISKCOPY, you would substitute for **drive1** the name of the source drive, and for **drive2** the name of the drive containing the disk to be compared. **Switch** may be either /1 (compare only one side of the disk) or /8 (compare only eight sectors per track). DOS will not allow you to compare two different types of diskettes. DISKCOMP may not work properly with 360K diskettes that have been produced with a 1.2M drive, if you try to compare them on a standard 360K drive.

THE EXE2BIN COMMAND

This is a command that is on its way out. The most recent versions of DOS don't include it at all. EXE2BIN is a utility that converts .EXE files into .COM or .BIN files. The .COM and .BIN files use less disk space and may load faster.

However, the need for this has diminished over the years. The smaller cluster size of recent versions of DOS mean that .EXE files that are small or that "spill over" into additional clusters are likely to waste less space. Faster hard disks and computers mean that the gains in quicker program loading may be minimal. Only certain .EXE files can be converted successfully. The syntax for this command is:

```
EXE2BIN filename1 filename2
```

There are no optional parameters, except that you may leave off the extension for the source file (DOS will assume .EXE) and the extension for the destination file (DOS will use .BIN as default). If you don't include a root file name for the destination file, DOS will use the root name of the source file.

THE PRINT COMMAND

PRINT, once an essential command, allows background printing of a group of files. Today, most of us have applications programs and special spoolers that perform this task for us automatically and more flexibly. Many users may put PRINT to work only to quickly print an ASCII file or other text on the spur of the moment. Since you can do the same thing with commands like

```
TYPE filename >PRN
```

it's now possible to get by without ever using PRINT at all.

Even so, let's review the command's complicated syntax and capabilities:

```
PRINT   /D:device   /B:buffersize  /M:maxtick
/Q:maxfiles  /S:timeslice  /U:busytick  filename
/P /T /C....
```

This is a lot to digest. The switches /D, /B, /M, /Q, /S, and /U can only be specified the first time PRINT is used during a session with the computer (a session is any usage without rebooting the system). Further, the /D parameter must be placed first if it is used. If it is left off, DOS will ask you to enter the name of the list device, and offer PRN as the default.

/D:device   Substitute for *device* any valid DOS device. You can use this switch to redirect printer output to some other device or file, including the serial port or a file you wish to store the output in.

/B:buffersize   For *buffersize*, insert amount of memory you'd like to set aside to use as a printer buffer to store your files as they print. Up to 32K may be used for the buffer.

/M:maxtick   Here, you enter the number of clock ticks (about 1/18th second on IBM PCs and PS/2 systems) the printer is allowed to send characters to the printer when PRINT is given its turn from the background. This number can range from 1 to 255.

/S:timeslice   This indicates the number of divisions to slice each second into, from 1 (a whole second) to 255 (each 1/255th second long).

/U:busystick   This indicates the clock that ticks the program should wait for a printer that returns a busy or unavailable signal. You may use a number from 1 to 255.

/Q:maxfiles   The number of files PRINT can handle at one time, from 1 to 32.

The default values for these are as follows:

```
buffersize      512 bytes
maxtick         2 ticks (about 1/9th second)
maxfiles        10 files
timeslice       8 slices per second
busytick        1 tick (about 1/18th second)
```

You may include as many file names on the command line as you can fit within DOS's 128–character limitation. Each can be followed by one of three switches, /P, /T, or /C.

/P This optional switch puts the file in the queue for printing.

/T When encountered, DOS stops printing all files, including the current one.

/C This cancels background printing of files.

THE PROMPT COMMAND

We've talked about the PROMPT command from time to time in this book. PROMPT can be used to perform some special tasks with the ANSI.SYS device driver (to be explained in the next chapter). Every DOS book published in the past five years has discussed using PROMPT to redefine keys, change screen colors, and redefine the system prompt in useful ways. You'd feel cheated if we didn't cover the material in this volume, so here goes!

One of the ways we use ANSI.SYS is to interpret special sequences of characters. ANSI.SYS commands always include the *Escape* character to alert ANSI.SYS that a command follows. However, the Escape character can't simply be typed in from the keyboard. When you press Escape, DOS aborts the current line and drops down to the next.

Earlier we showed you how to use PROMPT to change the system prompt. DOS has another capability when ANSI.SYS has been activated. You can send to ANSI.SYS certain special characters that control the cursor movement on the screen.

The PROMPT command allows representing the Escape code in the form of a *metastring*. That is, PROMPT followed by the metastring **$e** will cause an Escape character to be sent to ANSI.SYS, so long as you have not turned ECHO off.

You probably know that you can clear the screen in DOS by typing CLS. If you do that, the cursor character (and the prompt) will appear on the blank screen starting at row 1, column 1. Each subsequent character typed will be located one space farther to the right, until you reach the right side of the screen, and the line wraps around, or you press Enter, and DOS interprets the line. Each new line begins one line farther down from the last.

However, the cursor can also be moved *directly* with ANSI.SYS commands. These sequences all begin with the Escape character and a left bracket: **Esc[**. Other characters follow the Escape and left bracket to tell ANSI.SYS specifically what to do. Here are some of the allowable sequences:

Esc[row;colH Substitute the row and column you want the cursor to move to for **row** and **col**. If you do not specify row and column, the cursor is moved to the home position. To move the cursor to row 2, column 5, type:

```
ESC[2;5H
```

Esc[linesA Substitute for **lines** the number of rows you want the cursor to move *up*.

Esc[linesB Substitute for **lines** the number of rows you want the cursor to move *down*. In both these cases, the column in which the cursor appears remains unchanged.

Esc[columnsC Substitute for **columns** the number of positions you want the cursor to move *forward* (right). Default value is 1, and this sequence is ignored if the cursor is already at the far right of the screen; in other words, there is no wraparound to the next line.

Esc[columnsD Substitute for **columns** the number of positions you want the cursor to move *backward* (left). The default and lack of wraparound is identical to the sequence above.

Esc[row;col1F This is the same as ESC[**row,col1**H above.

Esc[S This saves the current cursor position.

Esc[U This restores the cursor to the value it had when the above sequence was delivered.

PROMPT can also send other metastrings to ANSI.SYS that do more than move the cursor. Table 18.1 shows the allowable strings.

```
$t    current time
$d    current date
$v    DOS version number
$n    default drive name
$g    > symbol
$l    <  symbol
$p    current drive and path
$b    vertical bar symbol
$q    equals sign
$h    backspace
$e    escape character
$_    underscore
```

Table 18.1 Metastrings used with PROMPT

Some of these are supplied because DOS won't let you enter them from the keyboard. Others are included as variables so the current value (time or date, for example) can be substituted at the time the command is issued. You may use these along with the cursor control commands and PROMPT in flexible ways to redefine the default prompt for DOS.

For example, you might type in the following prompt statement:

```
PROMPT $n$g$e[s$e[1;4H$d$e[u
```

To translate, the first two metastrings, **$n** and **$g**, would start off the prompt with the standard system prompt that displays the default drive. Next, the **$e[s** sequence would store the current cursor position. After that, the **$e[1;4H** sequence would position the cursor at row 1, column 4. The **$d** metastring would cause the system date to be printed there, and, finally, **$e[u** would restore the cursor to its former position. With this prompt, each time you typed a new line, the standard prompt would seem to appear on its appropriate line, but the system date would be printed each time at the top of the screen (thereby writing over anything that had been written or scrolled up to that point).

Another set of ANSI commands can be used to change the attributes of the video images displayed on your CRT screen. With a color monitor, you may change the colors of the screen (or the prompt), while those using monochrome monitors can alter the screen images to include reverse video, blinking, and other attributes.

The screen attribute commands all begin with Esc[followed by a number or numbers and a lowercase **m**. Several of the numbers can be used together to include more than one attribute in a single command line. The allowable attribute numbers are shown in Tables 18.2 and 18.3.

Table 18.2 is for monochrome monitors. If used with color monitors, it will produce different results, as the IBM color/graphics adapter doesn't produce underlined characters with the standard character set.

Number	Result
0	normal characters
1	high intensity characters
4	underlined characters
5	blinking characters
7	reverse video characters
8	invisible characters

Table 18.2

Number	Result
30	black characters
31	red characters
32	green characters
33	yellow characters
34	blue characters
35	magenta characters
36	cyan characters
37	white characters
40	black background
41	red background
42	green background
43	yellow background
44	blue background
45	magenta background
46	cyan background
47	white background

Table 18.3

Table 18.3 is for all monitors; different colors may be displayed in different ways on your monochrome monitor, however.

You might change colors using examples like the following:

```
PROMPT $e[0;1;31
PROMPT $e[5;30;47
```

The first example would produce high-intensity red characters, using the default background color. The second would provide blinking black characters on a white background.

One final application for ANSI.SYS is in redefining the keys on your keyboard. When you press a key, the keyboard sends out a scan code representing the key that was pressed. This scan code is generally passed on to COMMAND.COM by ANSI.SYS. However, ANSI.SYS can be told to provide a different character, or even an entire string of characters, when that key is pressed.

You would not want to redefine keys that are commonly used. However, you can easily define function keys, Shift function keys, and Alt key combinations. The syntax is as follows:

```
PROMPT $e[0;(scan code);"new string"p
```

Obtain the scan codes for the keys you'd like to redefine from the listing provided in your computer's manuals. Scan codes can vary from machine to machine, although it is usually only such keys as the F11 and F12 keys that don't conform to the standard set by IBM. For example, the scan codes for the function keys F1 through F10 are 59 through 68.

If you'd like the new key definition to end with a carriage return, substitute 13p for p. We could change F1, F2, and F3 to produce "DIR A:<Enter>", "DIR B:<Enter>", and DIR C: /P<Enter>" by the following lines:

```
PROMPT $e[0;59;"DIR A:";13p
PROMPT $e[0;60;"DIR B:";13p
PROMPT $e[0;61;"DIR C: /P";13p
```

The initial zero in the above lines tells the driver that we are defining a function or Alt key. The second number is the scan code of the key to be redefined. Next, we have the actual string and, in this case, a carriage return signified by the final "13."

You may change a key back to its normal definition at any time by replacing the new string with the old scan code for the key involved.

```
PROMPT $e[0;59;0;59p
```

would return F1 to normal.

SUMMARY

This chapter has rounded up some of the remaining DOS commands. You learned such things as how to redefine the keyboard, change your system prompt, and alter the colors DOS uses to display information on the CRT screen. The only thing left to cover are the configuration commands and options for the CONFIG.SYS file. We'll address those in the next chapter.

19

Customizing Your System

INTRODUCTION: CONFIG.SYS

When DOS starts, a file called CONFIG.SYS is read and its commands carried out before the AUTOEXEC.BAT file is begun. CONFIG.SYS is a simple ASCII file, like AUTOEXEC.BAT, but can contain only those commands already allowed for it by DOS. On the positive side, the end user cannot accidentally or intentionally "bypass" CONFIG.SYS by pressing Control-Break.

Each release of DOS has brought us new CONFIG.SYS commands. DOS 4.0, in particular, has benefited from the latest software technology. Some enhancements that originally appeared in OS/2 have been provided in the latest DOS release of CONFIG.SYS. A total of three new CONFIG.SYS commands, two brand new device drivers, and improvements to six other CONFIG.SYS commands or drivers were made.

You can create a CONFIG.SYS file with any ASCII text editor, including EDLIN, which is explained in Chapter 20. Once you have altered or created a CONFIG.SYS file, you must reboot the computer to put the new commands into effect. DOS 4.0 will report any errors it finds in the CONFIG.SYS file when the computer is started up, including the line number of the mistakes.

With earlier versions, you are on your own in locating errors; DOS will tell you only that an unrecognized command was encountered, or that a device driver was bad or missing.

This chapter will examine each of the commands in turn, and explain how device drivers are used.

THE BREAK CONFIGURATION COMMAND

This command functions in the same manner as the DOS BREAK command discussed in Chapter 18. When BREAK is turned ON, DOS will check for Control-Break during many different functions. When BREAK is OFF, DOS will only check for Control-Break when sending output or reading input. To use BREAK in your CONFIG.SYS file, include lines like these:

```
BREAK=OFF
BREAK=ON
```

THE BUFFERS CONFIGURATION COMMAND

The BUFFERS command is used to tell DOS how many 512- to 532-byte memory buffers to set aside to store information read from or written to a disk. DOS can manipulate data in memory much faster than it can using the disk drive, so any time information can be read from the buffer instead of the disk drive, your application saves time. Similarly, data can be stored in the buffer much more quickly than it can be written to the disk. The danger, of course, is that power may be lost to the computer before the buffer has been written to disk permanently. Even so, the considerable amount of time you can save using the BUFFERS statement generally justifies the risk.

You may include a BUFFERS statement in your CONFIG.SYS file to set aside from 1 to 99 buffers. For versions of DOS prior to DOS 4.0, the syntax is:

```
BUFFERS=nn
```

DOS 4.0 considerably enhances the BUFFERS statement. First, you may add a /X switch to tell DOS to use expanded memory if it is available. This allows you to save conventional memory for your applications, and you may specify as many as 10,000 buffers if sufficient expanded memory is available.

We also gain from DOS 4.0 the capability to assign from 0 to 8 *look-ahead* buffers. These are buffers used to store disk sectors *ahead* of the current sector. When processing sequential files, this can save considerable time. Look-ahead buffers each consume 512 bytes of conventional memory. The syntax for this command is:

```
BUFFERS=rr,la /X
```

where **rr** is the number of regular buffers (0 to 99, or 0 to 10,000 if expanded memory is available), and **la** is the number of look-ahead buffers (0 to 8).

If you specify eight look-ahead buffers, when DOS reads a sector it will also read the seven sectors that follow that sector. If it turns out those sectors are needed, no additional disk read is necessary.

You may need to experiment to determine the optimum number of buffers for your system. Hard disk users can usually use a minimum of three and up to about 30 buffers. The number can also be affected by whether or not you use a disk *cache* program. Cache programs function somewhat like buffers in that disk information is stored in memory for faster access. However, a cache uses built-in intelligence to make some decisions on which disk sectors to keep in memory to optimize usage.

THE COUNTRY CONFIGURATION COMMAND

The use of this configuration command was mentioned obliquely in Chapter 16 when we talked about code page support. The COUNTRY command allows you to specify country data, including time and date format, when the computer is booted. The syntax is:

```
COUNTRY=xxx,yyy,filename
```

You would replace **xxx** with the country code for the time and date format you wish to have as the default. Ordinarily a value of 001 for the United States is the default. However, you can specify any of the countries listed in Table 19.1.

DOS 3.0, 3.1 and later

Country	Code
France	033
Germany	049
Italy	039
Spain	034
United Kingdom	044
United States	001

DOS 3.2 and later

Country	Code
Australia	061
Belgium	032
Canadian-French	002
Denmark	045
Finland	358
Israel	972
Middle East	785
Netherlands	031
Norway	047
Portugal	351
Sweden	046
Switzerland	041

DOS 4.0 and later

Country	Code
Japan	081
Korea	082
People's R.O.C.	088
Taiwan	086

Table 19.1

With DOS 3.3 and later versions only, you may also specify **yyy**, the code page of the character set you want to use, and **filename**, the data file containing country data.

COUNTRY is an advanced CONFIG.SYS command. If you need it, you'll know it.

THE FCBS CONFIGURATION COMMAND

This command allows you to specify the number of file control blocks (FCBs) that DOS can use at one time. Most software doesn't use this method any more, but the FCBS command has been included for compatibility. The syntax is as follows:

```
FCBS=f,n
```

You would substitute for **f** the number of files opened by FCBs at one time. You may indicate any value from 1 to 255; the default value is 4. The **n** should be replaced by a number equal to or smaller than **f**. It indicates the number of FCBs that DOS must not close automatically to allow for opening new files in excess of those allowed by **f**. For example, if you had specified four FCBs and three were already open when your software tried to open two more, DOS would not allow five open files at once, since only four FCBs had been indicated; DOS would automatically close enough files to allow the additional open files. The **n** parameter would block DOS from closing **n** files, thus protecting them. You'll rarely, if ever, need this command. You might find that a program that operated under earlier versions of DOS does not work with DOS 3.0 or later versions. In such cases, it is probably older software that uses FCBS. Allow for some in your CONFIG.SYS file until the program operates properly.

THE FILES CONFIGURATION COMMAND

This command sets the maximum number of files that DOS may have open at one time. The minimum number is 8; the maximum you can set is 255. The syntax is as follows:

```
FILES=n
```

Each of the files that you allow through this command above the default of 8 will require an additional 64 bytes of conventional memory. Expanded memory cannot be used.

THE INSTALL CONFIGURATION COMMAND

This command was added with DOS 4.0 to allow installing memory-resident utilities from CONFIG.SYS rather than through the AUTOEXEC.BAT file. IBM recommends using INSTALL with FASTOPEN, KEYB, NLSFUNC, and SHARE. It may also be used to install some third-party utilities such as SIDEKICK.

If you install SHARE from the CONFIG.SYS file rather than through AUTOEXEC.BAT, you can avoid seeing the DOS warning message that requires use of SHARE with DOS 4.0 and disk volumes larger than 32 megabytes. The syntax for INSTALL is:

```
INSTALL=utility
```

THE LASTDRIVE CONFIGURATION COMMAND

LASTDRIVE tells DOS the highest drive letter in use by your system. The syntax is:

```
LASTDRIVE=x
```

You would replace **x** with the letter representing the highest drive letter you want available. The default value is E, allowing five drives, or A: through E:. If you have several hard disks, or wish to create a number of RAM disks, or want to create "false" disk drives using SUBST, you might want to redefine the last drive in your system.

You cannot set this value to fewer than the actual number of drives you have, or to a drive beyond Z.

THE REM CONFIGURATION COMMAND

The ability to put REMarks in the CONFIG.SYS file was introduced with OS/2 1.0 and was included with DOS 4.0. It lets you put notations in the CONFIG.SYS file explaining what a command does, or why it was included. You may also insert REM at the beginning of a line to "deactivate" a command you want to temporarily disable. DOS will not display REMarks when executing the CONFIG.SYS commands.

THE SHELL CONFIGURATION COMMAND

This command will start the DOS command processor, COMMAND.COM, or another one of your choice. You may also elect to put COMMAND.COM somewhere other than in the root directory of the boot disk, by listing its directory path here. In addition, SHELL lets you specify the size of the DOS environment.

The syntax for SHELL is different for DOS 3.0, DOS 3.1, and DOS 3.2 and later versions.

DOS 3.0 uses the following syntax:

```
SHELL file1 file2 /P
```

The /P switch makes the command processor permanent, which you'll probably find to be a good idea. For **file1** you'll want to substitute the path, drive, and name of the command processor to be used (almost always COMMAND.COM). For **file2** substitute the command processor used for the COMSPEC environmental variable. This will generally be the same as **file1**.

HDOS 3.1 syntax is:

```
SHELL file1 file2 /P /E:size
```

This version is identical to the last, except that you may add the switch /E to indicate the size of the DOS environment. With DOS 3.1 you replace **size** with the number of 16–byte chunks or *paragraphs* you'd like to use. Both DOS 3.0 and 3.1 use 128 bytes as a default value. You can't change the environment size with

DOS 3.0 and earlier versions. With DOS 3.1 you may indicate 11 to 62 chunks (176 to 992 bytes).

DOS 3.2 and later versions use:

```
SHELL file1 file2 /P /E:size
```

These versions of DOS use the same SHELL command, except that for **size** you may enter the size of the environment in bytes, from 160 to 32,768 bytes. DOS rounds up the actual value to the next 16–byte paragraph, and will default to 160 bytes if an invalid entry is given.

DOS 4.0 did add the /MSG parameter to SHELL. This must be used with the /P parameter. If specified, DOS will load DOS messages, such as error messages, into memory. Those using floppy disk-based systems may want to use this option, but hard disk users won't generally need it; DOS can access its messages at any time from the hard disk.

THE STACKS CONFIGURATION COMMAND

This command, new to DOS 3.2, sets the stack resources of your system. Again, if you don't know why you would want to use this command, you probably don't need it.

A *stack* is a portion of memory used to hold information temporarily. Although there are many types of stacks used by your computer system, one type is used to store information used by DOS to handle requests from hardware called *interrupts*.

Earlier versions of DOS used a single stack for these, which could sometimes overflow. DOS 3.2 introduced nine different stacks, and the STACKS command lets you set aside even more, from 8 to 64, as well as define how large each stack should be in bytes, from 32 to 512. The default value for these will vary depending on what computer you have. The syntax is as follows:

```
STACKS=n,s
```

Substitute for **n** the number of stack "frames" you want to use, either 0 or in the range 8 to 64. For **s**, you may enter the frame size, either 0 or 32 to 512. As in the case of buffers, the ideal values are determined by your equipment configuration, including memory size, disk capacity, and machine type. No stack support is installed for the IBM PC, XT, and Portable PCs.

THE SWITCHES CONFIGURATION COMMAND

This command tells DOS to use only the non-extended keyboard functions even if you have an enhanced keyboard, thus restoring compatibility with earlier versions of software that cannot support features like the F11 and F12 function keys. The syntax is:

```
SWITCHES=/K
```

to disable extended keyboard functions.

THE DEVICE CONFIGURATION COMMAND

We've saved the DEVICE command for last because it has the greatest number of options of any of the configuration commands. It allows you to install specific files called *drivers* that provide support and control for a variety of advanced DOS functions. Let's go through the drivers one at a time to see what they can do.

VDISK.SYS

One of the most commonly used device drivers is VDISK.SYS, which is the virtual disk program supplied with DOS 3.0 and later versions. It will create RAM disks in unused portions of your PC's memory. These can be treated as fast disk drives, faster even than a hard disk. However, the information they contain will disappear when the computer is turned off. If you don't have DOS 3.x or 4.0, you may still have a similar device driver, supplied by the maker of your memory expansion board. To use VDISK.SYS, you insert lines in your CONFIG.SYS file using the following syntax:

```
DEVICE=VDISK.SYS comment ddd sss eee /e:m
```

The **comment**, new to DOS 3.3 and later versions, is any string of ASCII characters from ASCII code 32 to 126, except for the slash character, which you can use to label your RAM disk.

Replace **ddd** with the size of the RAM disk you wish to create, in kilobytes. The default value is 64, which would produce a RAM disk 64K (65,534 bytes) in size.

The **sss** parameter specifies the sector size. You may specify 256 or 512 bytes;128 bytes is the default. Sector size specification is a tradeoff for the user. The larger the sector size, the more data read by DOS at one gulp and, therefore, the faster the access. However, larger sectors tend to be more wasteful. Even a few extra bytes spilling over from one sector will consume all of the next sector, since DOS cannot use partial sectors for anything else. So, with a 512–byte sector size you may have many partially filled sectors and much waste. With a 128–byte sector size, odds are good that each sector will contain less wasted space.

You can choose the appropriate sector size by looking at your application for the RAM disk. Will you store many short files on the disk, thus increasing the chance of having many partially filled sectors at the tail end of files? Or, will you store long files, which will make it beneficial to allow DOS to read big chunks through a larger sector size? RAM disks are so fast that speed may not be an issue. For most users, memory space is limited, making efficient consumption of a RAM disk important, so it is usually best to err on the side of the smaller sector. Thus 128 bytes is the default.

The **eee** parameter controls the number of directory entries that can fit on your RAM disk. The default is 64, but you may specify 2 to 512. Since each directory entry takes up valuable space on your RAM disk, you can reclaim some space by indicating fewer than 64 entries when the RAM disk is created. Or, if you know many small files will be stored, you can create more directory space.

The **/e:m** switch lets you indicate that extended memory (if available) be used for the RAM disk. The **m** parameter is the maximum number of sectors of information read from the disk at one time. The default is eight, but you can indicate any figure from 1 to 8. If your files are consistently very short, a number smaller than 8 can speed up operations. Instead of always reading 8 sectors, whether it needs them or not, DOS will read only a smaller number. If the number required is greater than that number, it must read the RAM disk again, slowing down operations. So, you must be certain that your application will benefit from a smaller figure before changing the default value.

The /X switch, introduced with DOS 4.0, allows using expanded memory for RAM disks.

You may create more than one RAM disk by repeating the DEVICE command. For example, if you had these lines in your CONFIG.SYS file:

```
DEVICE=VDISK.SYS 100
DEVICE=VDISK.SYS 50
```

DOS would create one RAM disk with 100K available for storage, and a second one with 50K set aside, assuming you have sufficient memory to spare. DOS uses the next available drive name to indicate the RAM disks. If you have two floppy disk drives in your system, the two RAM disks will be defined as drive C: and drive D: respectively.

DRIVER.SYS

This device driver originated with DOS 3.2. It allows you to connect an external diskette drive, or to assign a second drive letter to a disk. The syntax is as follows:

```
DEVICE=driver.sys /D:ddd /T:ttt /S:ss /H:hh /C /N
/F:f
```

That's quite a lot to chew off. Let's look at the switches and parameters one at a time.

The **/D:ddd** parameter allows you to enter the drive number of the drive being affected by DRIVER.SYS. Although it may seem confusing, diskette drives are numbered 0–127, and hard disks are numbered 128–255, by the system. Of course, no one would have so many drives. Your A: would be drive 0, your B:, drive 1. Any external floppy disk drives would be numbered drive 2, drive 3, etc. The first hard disk, usually C:, is numbered 128, and so forth.

The default values for the remaining switches are those for the 3.5–inch 720K microdisk drive. The **/T:ttt** switch indicates the number of tracks per side for the disk. Replace the **ttt** with the number of tracks. The default value is 80. The **/S:sss** switch indicates the number of sectors per track, from 1 to 99. Default is 9 sectors per track, as found in a 360K 5.25–inch floppy.

The **/H:hh** switch allows you to enter the number of read/write heads in the disk drive. The default value is 2, as found in a double-sided floppy disk drive.

The /C switch specifies support for the diskette changeline, as found in drives like those in the PC/AT. The /N switch specifies a nonremovable disk as a hard disk.

The final switch is the **/F:f** parameter. The **f** following the colon should be a number that indicates the *form factor* or type of drive. You can choose from 0 for single or double-sided 160/180/320/360K 5.25–inch drives; 1 for 1.2-megabyte 5.25–inch drives; 2 for 3.5–inch drives.

One use for DRIVER.SYS is to allow applying another drive letter to a disk drive. For example, if you wanted to designate an external 3.5–inch disk drive as both D: and E: (so you could copy files from one to the other simply by entering the drive names), you would use lines like these:

```
DEVICE=DRIVER.SYS /d:2
DEVICE=DRIVER.SYS /d:2
```

This assumes that you have a fixed disk drive installed as C:. On bootup, DOS will see the external 3.5–inch drive as both D: and E:.

Or, you might have a PC/AT with a single 1.2 megabyte drive, and you want to assign a drive letter to the 360K mode of that drive. You would do that by entering:

```
DEVICE=DRIVER.SYS /d:0 /t:40 /s:9 /h:2 /f:0
```

If your system has one or two internal disk drives and one fixed disk, the 1.2-megabyte drive will still be assigned as A:, but a new drive, D:, will exist as an imaginary or "virtual" 360K version of that same A:.

DISPLAY.SYS

Discussed in Chapter 16, DISPLAY.SYS is the driver you use to set up for code page switching of your display. The syntax is as follows:

```
DEVICE=DISPLAY.SYS type,hwcp,n,m
```

The **type** parameter is replaced with the type of monitor you are using, either MONO, CGA, LCD, or EGA. Those with PS/2 systems and the VGA adapter should use the EGA specification.

The **hwcp** stands for hardware code page, and should include the code page number (437, 850, 860, 863, 865, etc.) that you want to use. Replace **n** with the number of prepared code pages (from 0 to 12), and **m** with the number of subfonts used per page. Again, this is a complex command that you probably will not need to use unless you are setting up a system for use in a foreign country. It is most often a one-time operation.

For DOS 4.0, DISPLAY.SYS was changed so that it checks your hardware to determine the type of active display if you don't include the display adapter type.

PRINTER.SYS

This driver is the equivalent of DISPLAY.SYS, but for printers. The syntax is as follows:

```
DEVICE=PRINTER.SYS LPT#:=type,hwcp...,n
```

Here, you would substitute for **#** the parallel port you want to use (1, 2, or 3). The printer type would be a number representing your particular printer. At this writing, only the IBM Proprinter (4201) and the IBM Quietwriter III (5202) have been defined.

As before, for **hwcp** substitute the relevant code page. You may enter a list of code pages, separating them by commas. For **n** substitute the number of prepared code pages.

IBM introduced extended support for several of its printers with the DOS 4.0 version of PRINTER.SYS.

ANSI.SYS

ANSI.SYS is the most common device driver used with, or, at least, tied with VDISK.SYS. This driver was written to replace the default screen and keyboard driver built into the operating system and your computer's BIOS.

What ANSI.SYS does is intercept characters received from the keyboard. It either passes them on to DOS unchanged, or supplies new, redefined characters or strings of characters.

ANSI.SYS also allows control of the display, including the colors shown on the screen, the position of the cursor, and the characters used to supply the system prompt itself. To activate ANSI.SYS, simply include this line in your CONFIG.SYS file:

```
DEVICE=ANSI.SYS
```

As with any of the device drivers described thus far, the driver itself does not have to reside in your root directory. CONFIG.SYS must be there, but the drivers can be placed anywhere on the disk, as long as you include the proper path name in the configuration command. For example:

```
DEVICE=C:\DOS\ANSI.SYS
```

would allow you to put your ANSI.SYS driver out of sight in the C:\DOS subdirectory, cleaning up your root directory.

ANSI.SYS was enhanced for DOS 4.0 by the addition of three new parameters: /X, /L, and /K.

/X Allows the extended keyboard keys such as F11 and F12 to be redefined using the method discussed in Chapter 18.

/L Lets you override your software when you have redefined the number of rows displayed by your CRT using the MODE command. Many applications simply change the number of rows back to 25. When the /L parameter is included, they will not be able to do so. However, you may end up with only a partial-screen display if you are using particularly stubborn software. You'll still have 43 or 50 lines, but only the first 25 will be used.

/K This is yet another way of preventing use of the extended keyboard functions with software that doesn't support those features.

XMA2EMS.SYS

This new DOS 4.0 driver is the first of two device drivers that represent IBM's recognition that the rest of the world has already found the Lotus-Intel-Microsoft expanded memory specification (EMS) to be useful.

Expanded memory differs from *extended memory*. The latter is an extension of regular memory (which is 0 to 1M), from 1M to as much as 16M. Only 80286- and 80386-based systems can use extended memory, and even then only for applications written especially for them. VDISK.SYS, for example, is a driver written to take advantage of extended memory.

Expanded memory, on the other hand, is more flexible. It can be used by any PC equipped with a special EMS memory board and a driver like XMA2EMS.SYS. Most memory boards provide their own drivers. This is the first supplied with DOS. Expanded memory is not viewed by DOS as continuous memory, but rather as "pages" that are mapped in and out of DOS's view by the driver. You might visualize EMS memory as a book of many pages, each of which is held up in front of a window for you to read as you request it.

XMA2EMS.SYS can be used if you have one of the following:

★An expanded memory adapter—IBM mentions several in the DOS 4.0 manual; it worked just fine with the ORCHID Ramquest 50/60 in a PS/2 Model 60.

★An 80386–based computer with the XMAEMS.SYS driver installed before this one.

The syntax for this driver is:

```
DEVICE=XMA2EMS.SYS    FRAME=xxxx    P254=yyyy
P255=zzzz /X:aa
```

You would substitute for **xxxx** any page from C000 to E000. Each will be 64K in size. P254 and P255 represent 16K pages of memory used by FASTOPEN and BUFFERS, respectively, to perform their functions in expanded memory. The /X parameter is used to prevent the driver from using less than the maximum total available memory. If you substitute a value of **aa** in multiples of 16K pages, XMA2EMS.SYS will use only that amount for EMS. For example, if /X:8 were used, 128K of EMS memory would be defined from the total memory on your expanded/extended memory board.

Your applications programs that can use EMS memory will include recommendations on allocating your expanded memory.

XMAEM.SYS

This driver is used with 80386–based systems, and allows using the extended memory that can be addressed by such systems as if it were EMS memory. You can use this driver to define the number of 16K pages of extended memory to be devoted to expanded memory. The syntax is as follows:

```
DEVICE=XMAEM.SYS aa
```

For **aa** you would substitute the number of pages to allocate (divide the amount of memory by 16 to calculate this figure). This driver must be loaded *before* XMA2EMS.SYS in your CONFIG.SYS.

SUMMARY

In this chapter, you learned about the DOS CONFIG.SYS file, and how to set up and use the various configuration commands provided with DOS through version 4.0. We addressed the many different device drivers provided with DOS, and covered how they can be used to create RAM disks, control printers or displays, and allocate extra memory.

CHAPTER

Using EDLIN and DEBUG

INTRODUCTION

Although we're done with our discussion of DOS's commands and features, we still haven't covered two valuable utilities provided with the operating system. This chapter will present a pair of short tutorials on using DOS's two editing programs, EDLIN and DEBUG. They've been placed at the back of the book for a simple reason: Only a few readers will actually ever use either of them. However, no discussion of DOS would be complete without an explanation of these two useful programs.

Should the need for them ever arise, you'll find that EDLIN and DEBUG have three advantages: They are free, they are easy to use, and simple instructions for them are right in this book. This becomes particularly important for those with DOS 3.3 and later versions: The documentation for DEBUG has been moved from the DOS manual to the DOS technical manual, although the program itself remains on the DOS Supplementary disk. EDLIN is also included with DOS 4.0.

EDLIN: A LINE-ORIENTED TEXT EDITOR

Unless your use of personal computers dates back to before 1981, you probably have not had much exposure to line-oriented text editors. It's more likely that you have always used a screen-oriented editor, such as WordPerfect, Microsoft Word, or Word-Star.

With a screen-oriented editor, you are shown a screen full of text at a time. The cursor can be moved anywhere on the screen, with either the cursor keys or special Control key combinations. Editing document text would be inconvenient without this screen orientation.

However, the first text editors for personal computers weren't designed for word-processing documents. Instead, they were developed for use by programmers, particularly those working with compilers. Since program code can't be run as-is (it must be compiled first), a separate text entry and editing program that allows listing individual program lines, deleting them, etc., is a handy tool. Line-oriented text editors were developed for this application.

With such editors, each line of text is treated as a separate entity. That is, you may move the cursor around in that line, but not between *lines*. As an aid to the programmer, line numbers are applied to the lines being edited. Thus, you may ask the program to *list* lines 1 to 10, to *delete* lines 20 to 25, or to *move* lines 30 to 40 and place them after line 105.

EDLIN is such a line-oriented editor. It works on pure ASCII files, and does not taint them with the special control codes that word processors need to indicate formatting and such. EDLIN is handy for creating and editing DOS ASCII files, such as AUTOEXEC.BAT, CONFIG.SYS, or any batch file. Its commands are few and easy to learn, and as a free program, it makes a good choice for those without any other means of entering and editing ASCII files.

Before you learn EDLIN, you might want to investigate your alternatives. Most word processing programs have a "nondocument" or plain ASCII mode. You may be able to import ASCII into your documents. With some programs, such as DisplayWrite 4, you must then perform a search-and-replace to substitute DW4's "hard" carriage returns for the "soft" carriage returns that are applied to the end of each line of ASCII text. Once the text has been imported, you may edit it using your WP program's screen-oriented editor. Then, you can save it in ASCII form using your program's ASCII text option.

Many utility programs also provide an ASCII text option. Sidekick's Notepad, for example, edits and saves text in pure ASCII format. Keyworks has a Text Edit feature that you may pop up at any time to create and edit ASCII text. If none of these options are available to you, read on to learn more about EDLIN.

EDLIN can create lines with lengths of up to 253 characters. As you enter text, line numbers are shown on the screen for your reference. As new lines are inserted, the line numbers following are automatically renumbered to reflect the new order. These numbers are used only during the creation and editing process; they do not become part of the finished file.

To use EDLIN, you must first make sure that the EDLIN program is available on the disk you'll be using, or, if you have a hard disk, that DOS has been told where to find it through a PATH command. If you know which directory stores EDLIN and you are using DOS 3.0 or later versions, you may type the full path name from anywhere to bring up the editor. To start EDLIN, use this syntax:

```
[path1]EDLIN [d:][path2] filename to edit[.extension] [/B]
```

Everything on the above line except EDLIN and the file name to edit are optional. **Path1** is the path name of the directory where EDLIN can be found, and can be used if you are operating with DOS 3.x, which allows running system files by typing the full path name. **D:** is the drive where the file to be created or edited resides. If the file is present on the currently logged drive, D: is optional. **Path2** is the path name to the file to be created or edited, and is optional if the current directory will be used. The file name to edit and its extension, if any, should be entered next on the line. Note that the extension is optional *only* when creating the file. To edit that file, the extension *must* be included.

The /B switch tells EDLIN to continue loading the file even after a Control-Z, the ASCII end-of-file marker, is encountered. When editing most ASCII files, such as batch files, you won't need to use the /B switch. However, if you should need to load a file that is likely to contain a Control-Z somewhere in the middle, such as a binary file, this switch will tell EDLIN to load the entire file regardless of any Control-Z's that might be encountered.

Try out EDLIN for yourself by typing in this simple batch file:

```
Type A:EDLIN TEST.BAT
```

If EDLIN is not stored on A:, log over to the disk or directory where EDLIN is stored, and omit the drive specification A:.

EDLIN will display **New File** and an asterisk cursor.

Type **I** to begin entering text.

EDLIN will display **1**.

Type the following lines as each line number is displayed. Press Enter at the end of each line:

```
1. echo off
2. echo This is Line 2
3. echo This is Line 3
4. echo This is Line 4
5. <Control C>
```

At the EDLIN prompt, enter E to exit. The new file will be written to disk. You can summon this new batch file by typing TEST at the DOS prompt when you are logged onto the disk containing TEST.BAT.

EDLIN will handle just about any file you care to create or edit. EDLIN does have some limitations. Because it works in memory, EDLIN is limited to files that will fit in the amount of memory that EDLIN can address at once. If a file is too long, EDLIN will load only up to 75 percent of it, to allow room for additions. You can then save that section of the file and load the next portion, processing the long file in sections.

EDLIN'S COMMANDS

The EDLIN prompt is an asterisk. When you have typed the **I** (for Insert) command, you may type each line of text, ending the line by pressing Return. You may backspace within a line to make changes. However, once you have advanced to the next line, special commands are needed to return to any previous text for further changes. EDLIN line specification commands *follow* the listing of relevant line numbers.

To *list* lines, you may use the **L** command. Type the beginning line number you want to list, a comma, and then the last line you wish to have displayed. Follow the line numbers with an **L**. The default first number is the beginning of the file, so you may omit that number if you want to see all lines up to a given line.

```
30,60L
```

This will display all lines between Line 30 and Line 60.

```
,25L
1,25L
```

Both these commands will display all lines that exist between 1 and 25.

To insert lines between two existing lines, use the **I** command. Type the line number where the insertion is to begin, and follow that with the **I** command. If you don't enter a line number, or use a period as the line number, the insertion will begin just before the current line. Line numbers higher than the last line in the file will cause the insertion to begin at the end of the file. Press Control-Break to get out of Insert mode. Here are some examples:

```
30I
.I
999I
```

The first example would cause the insert to begin after line 30. All later lines in the file would be renumbered to accommodate the insert. The second example would start insertion after the current line (last line referenced), while the third example would jump to the end of the file and begin the insert there (as long as the file had fewer than 999 lines, of course).

To delete lines of text, use the **D** command. Syntax is similar to the **L** command. Type the beginning and last line numbers you want deleted, separated by commas. For example:

```
20,30D
```

will cause EDLIN to delete all the lines between 20 and 30 inclusive, and renumber the remaining lines to account for the deletion. Omitting the first number will result in the delete lines starting with the current line up to the line specified. Omitting the second parameter will cause EDLIN to delete only the line shown. Typing D on a line by itself will delete only the current line.

To edit a line of text, simply type in the line number to be edited, or a period to indicate the current line, or just Enter to edit the line *after* the current line. To abort a line edit, press Esc or Control Break instead of Enter, or move the cursor to the beginning of the line and press Enter. To delete the remainder of a line, move the cursor to that point and press Enter.

When you are finished editing a file, you may save it to disk with the **E** command. The file will be written to disk under the name you used when you started up EDLIN. You will also exit the program and return to DOS.

Several other commands are available. For example, the **W** command allows you to write lines in memory to disk, beginning with the first line in memory. The syntax:

```
[n]W
```

will write **n** lines of text to the disk. If you omit **n**, EDLIN will write lines that take up the equivalent of 25 percent of available memory. This command is used to save files to disk, and to edit very large files by allowing you to write part of the file to disk to make room for additional lines brought in through the **A** (append) command.

The **A** command will add lines from a disk file to the file currently being edited in memory. These new lines are placed at the end of the current lines. Syntax is:

```
[n]A
```

where **n** is the number of lines to be loaded. If you do not specify a number, EDLIN will load lines equivalent to 75 percent of the available memory to be loaded.

The **T** command transfers or merges a disk file into the file being edited. You could use this to import one batch file's contents into a new batch file you are editing in order to reuse (after editing) some of the lines. Syntax is:

```
[line]T[d:]filename
```

If specified, **line** will indicate the number of the line before which the file is to be inserted. If not indicated, the current line will be used.

To search text for a string of characters, use the **S** command. It will search the text for your string within the indicated range of lines. Syntax is as follows:

```
[line],[line][?]S[string]
```

Both the beginning and ending line numbers to be searched can be indicated. However, these are optional following the usual line specification rules already described. If you want a prompt that will cause EDLIN to pause after each line is displayed, enter the question mark immediately preceding the **S** command. The string to be searched follows; if you do not indicate a string, the last string previously searched (by Search or the Replace command) will be used.

As with any good text editor, EDLIN also has a replace option. The **R** command is used similarly to **S**, except that **string1** (to search for) is followed by a Control-Z (or F6) and **string2**, to be used as a replacement for **string1**. You may insert the question mark to be queried before each placement. If **string2** is not specified, the **string1** will be deleted where it appears. Syntax is as follows:

```
[line],[line][?]R[string][<F6>string2]
```

It is also useful to move lines from one place to another in a file. The **M** command will let you move a range of lines to the location specified by a third line. Syntax is as follows:

```
[line1],[line2],line3M
```

The first two **line** entries indicate the range, while the third indicates the new location. You can also specify a quantity of lines to be moved:

```
10,+20,200M
```

This would move 20 lines beginning at line 10 to a location starting at line 200. All the lines in the file would be renumbered to reflect the change.

You may *copy* lines from one place to another with the **C** command. Use this syntax:

```
[line1],[line2],line3[count]C
```

The first two entries show the range of lines to be copied, the third shows the location they are to be copied to, and *count* represents the number of times the operation is to take place. If you had a set of basic lines you wanted to reuse in the file, you could make two, three, four, or more copies of those lines at one step with this command.

The **P** command is akin to the **L** command and uses the same syntax. The chief difference is that the new current line becomes the last line of those displayed by this command.

To quit EDLIN, type the **Q** command. The program will ask you if you wish to leave without saving any changes that have been entered. If not, first write the lines to disk with the **W** command, then quit.

USING DEBUG

DEBUG is also an editing program, albeit one that treats files at an even lower level. Instead of working with lines, DEBUG handles individual bytes. You can use DEBUG to display and change any byte of information on your disk or in memory.

As a result, DEBUG can be dangerous if misused. You might accidentally change a byte in a key file on your disk—including one within your FAT or DOS itself. However, the chances of doing this are fairly remote. Given the instruction on using DEBUG provided in this chapter, you should be able to edit and create files with aplomb.

As you might think, DEBUG is used to enter or modify program and data files. You can also *assemble* machine language programs and carry out some specialized functions, such as a low-level format of your hard disk, with DEBUG. Most of these are beyond the scope of this book. Here, we'll provide you with some basic instruction on using DEBUG. You'll find the information handy if you need to enter a patch to a program (a "fix" of a bug, or enhanced feature), or wish to enter a machine language utility you find printed in a magazine.

To use DEBUG, first make a copy of a file that you would like to practice on:

```
COPY TEST.BAT TEST.BAK
```

Then, making sure that DEBUG is available on the disk or directory you are using, type:

```
DEBUG TEST.BAK
```

You may also enter DEBUG without accessing a particular file in order to create a brand-new file rather than editing an existing file.

After DEBUG has loaded, all you'll see is a hyphen cursor that is even less obvious than EDLIN's asterisk. DEBUG is ready for a command. If you have loaded a file into DEBUG, you can display or *dump* a portion of the file now in memory using the **D** command.

D

will display the first 128 bytes of the file on eight lines which will look something like this:

DEBUG Dump

```
xxxx:0100 65 63 68 6F 20 6F 66 66 0D 0A 65 63 68 6F 20 54  echo off..echo T
xxxx:0110 68 69 73 20 69 73 20 4C 69 6E 65 20 31 0D 0A 65  his is Line 1..e
xxxx:0120 63 68 6F 20 54 68 69 73 20 69 73 20 4C 69 6E 65  cho This is Line
xxxx:0130 20 32 0D 0A 65 63 68 6F 20 54 68 69 73 20 69 73   2..echo This is
xxxx:0140 20 4C 69 6E 65 20 33 0D 0A 00 00 00 00 00 00 00   Line 3.........
xxxx:0150 00 00 00 00 00 00 00 00 00 00 00 00 00 00 00 00  ................
xxxx:0160 00 00 00 00 00 00 00 00 00 00 00 00 00 00 00 00  ................
xxxx:0170 00 00 00 00 00 00 00 00 00 00 00 00 00 00 00 00  ................
```

(Your display won't look exactly like this. The zeros that finish out the block will probably contain a mish-mash of bytes left behind by the previous file written to that disk sector. We've just placed zeros in those positions here for clarity.)

The column of xxxx's to the left of the colon will contain different values depending on the memory address where DEBUG loaded your program. Those four numbers represent the address of the first of the sixteen bytes displayed on that line. Ignore that part of the address entirely. The second four digits provides the *relative* position of the bytes within the file. This is the important figure to you. In this, for example, 0100 is the starting address of the first byte, while 0101 is the address of the second byte, and so forth.

As you might have surmised, DEBUG uses *hexadecimal* notation. This is the base-16 numbering system, where each digit represents a number from 0 to 15. The characters 0,1,2,3,4,5, 6,7,8,9,A,B,C,D,E,F are used to represent these 16 numbers. So, the number FF in hex would stand for 255—15 units plus 15 x 16.

With this numbering system, the last byte in the first line would be 010F and the first byte in the second line, 0110. Hexadecimal numbering is mentioned here only for your information; you don't need it to use DEBUG.

The pairs of 16 numbers on each line represent consecutive bytes in memory, and can have a value of 00 to FF (0 to 255). Next to that listing are 16 characters that represent the ASCII value, if any, of the bytes. You'll note that since this is an ASCII file, each of the hexadecimal numbers can be represented by appropriate characters. The exceptions are the last two of the file, hex 0D (13 decimal) which is the carriage return at the end of the line, and hex 0A (10 decimal), which is the line feed character. Characters that cannot be translated into alphanumerics are shown as periods.

Most files you examine with DEBUG will be longer than the 128 initial bytes shown. You can see the next 128 bytes after whatever "page" was just shown by typing **D** again. You may also dump specific areas of memory by typing in the addresses. For example,

```
D 300-310
```

will show you the bytes in the range 300 to 310 (hexadecimal).

You may enter bytes directly into DEBUG. You might want to do this when you have a listing of unassembled machine language code and want simply to type in the hex values shown. You may enter bytes with the following syntax:

```
E <address to change><byte to enter>
```

For example, if you wanted to enter the file shown in our example, you would type:

```
-E 100 65 63 68 6F 20 6F 66 66 0D 0A 65 63 68 6F
```

```
20 54 68 69 73 20 69 73 20 4C 69 6E 65 20 31 0D 0A
65 63 68 6F 20 54 68 69 73 20 69 73 20 4C 69 6E 65
20 32 0D 0A 65 63 68 6F 20 54 68 69 73 20 69 73 20
4C 69 6E 65 20 33 0D 0A
```

However, since the information is an ASCII string, you could type the string and enclose it in quotation marks to tell DEBUG to translate the string into the ASCII equivalent:

```
e "echo off"
```

The Enter command can be used to *change* the values found in memory. You can use this command to edit an ASCII file (or a program file, too—use caution). The changes will exist only in memory until you write them back to disk.

You may also enter machine language utilities using the **A** assemble command. This is a more convenient way of entering bytes that make up a machine language program instead of simple ASCII text. Machine language programmers find it convenient not to constantly look up the hexadecimal values of the instructions they write for the computer. Instead, they use DEBUG's Assemble command (or, if a program is more than just a few lines long, an assembler). It isn't necessary to type in the bytes corresponding to the machine language instructions. You may type *mnemonic* abbreviations, which DEBUG will translate into the correct values when the bytes are assembled. Consider the following example, which consists of nonsense commands presented only to illustrate the concept.

```
A 100
xxxx:0100 MOV AH,0
xxxx:0102 INT 21
xxxx:0104 CMP AH,0
xxxx:0106 <Enter>
```

The first line tells DEBUG to begin assembling code at relative memory location 100. When you press Enter, DEBUG will respond with:

```
xxxx:0100
```

You then respond with the mnemonics **MOV AH,0** and press Enter again. DEBUG will supply the next memory location, and you continue with **INT 21**. Respond with nothing but Enter when finished. The "program" you have typed in will be assembled in memory, ready to be written to disk. To check on it, you can either *dump* the memory locations (you would type **d** 100 104) or *unassemble* the locations with:

```
U100 106
```

In the latter case, DEBUG will respond with a display something like this:

```
xxxx:0100 B400 MOV AH,0
xxxx:0102 CD21 INT 21
xxxx:0104 3D00 CMP AH,0
```

You must be sure to *write* your file to disk before exiting DEBUG. The **W** or Write command can be typed alone, or followed by the number of bytes to be written from memory to disk.

```
W
W108
```

With the first example, DEBUG will default to a start address of 100. In the second case, DEBUG will start writing to disk the data starting at memory location 108. The information will be written to a file with the same name as the one you typed when you entered DEBUG (if you are *editing* an existing file) or one that you enter by using the N command:

```
N filename
```

Once that command has been entered, DEBUG will respond to any W commands using that file name as the new default.

DEBUG determines how many bytes of memory to include in the file by looking at a special memory location, called a **register**. This register, CX, is loaded with the length of the file when you access a particular file through DEBUG. If you add to the file's length, or if you are creating a new file, you must change the value in CX before attempting to save the file. That can be done using the DEBUG **R** or Register command:

```
R cx
CX 00
:1A
```

We could type the first line to see the contents of the CX register. DEBUG would respond with the current value, supply a colon, and pause while we entered a new value.

To summarize, creating a file with DEBUG consists of the following steps:

1. Type DEBUG at the DOS prompt.
2. Begin to Enter or Assemble the program starting at relative memory location 100 by typing either E 100 or A 100 at the prompt.
3. If using Enter, type in the hexadecimal numbers. With Assemble, enter the mnemonics. Press Enter on a line by itself to quit.
4. Provide a name for the file with the N command.
5. Tell the CX register how many bytes long the file will be.
6. Write the file to disk using the W command.
7. Quit DEBUG with the Q command.

Such a session would look like this:

```
C>DEBUG<Enter>
A 100
```

```
xxxx:0100 MOV AH,0
xxxx:0102 INT 21
xxxx:0104 CMP AH,0
<Enter>
N TEST.COM
R cx
CX 00
:6
W
Q
```

Many of the magazine articles presenting short machine language programs that can be entered using DEBUG suggest a shortcut called a DEBUG *script*. In this mode, you type all the commands you will be entering into an ASCII file, using EDLIN or some other ASCII text editor. For the TEST.COM file shown above, the script might look something like this:

```
A 100
MOV AH,0
INT 21
AH,0
<Enter>
N TEST.COM
R cx
6
W
Q
```

This looks much like the session shown above, without DEBUG's responses. The <Enter> shown should consist of a blank line in your script file that includes only the carriage return.

To use the script, you would store it on your disk under a name like TEST.SCR, then type:

```
DEBUG<TEST.SCR
```

DEBUG would then use the ASCII file TEST.SCR for its input, taking advantage of DOS's redirection feature.

While there is more to using DEBUG than has been covered here, we've discussed all the basic information that the beginner needs. You may have had your interest piqued enough to explore some simple books on assembly language. DEBUG is a good beginner's tool for learning assembly language, but if you become deeply immersed in the topic you'll want to purchase a macro assembler that has many more tools and features.

In the next chapter, we'll provide you with some machine language utilities. You'll need to use the instructions in this chapter, either to type the utilities in directly, or to create a DEBUG script that can create the file for you.

SUMMARY

This chapter has been an introduction to EDLIN and DEBUG. All the functions of neither were provided. However, you learned enough about EDLIN to use it to create and edit the batch files in the next chapter. You also learned enough about DEBUG to type in the machine language utilities in the next and final chapter.

CHAPTER

21

Some DOS Utilities

INTRODUCTION

This chapter is intended to get you started in creating some utilities of your own for DOS. Many of the most powerful can be put together using batch file programming, particularly if used with some of the machine language utilities presented in this chapter. In addition, a selection of sample batch file utilities is included to give you some ideas.

The machine language routines can all be entered using the DEBUG methods discussed in Chapter 20. If you need to, review them before trying to type any of these in. The batch files can be entered using your favorite ASCII text editor.

ADDING INTERACTIVITY TO BATCH FILES

One failing of batch file language is that it does not allow the user to input information while the batch file is running. However, DOS does include the ability to compare ERRORLEVELS from within a batch file. Utilities that allow you to press a key and have your batch file know which key was pressed abound. Here's one you can use called INPUT.COM.

Only the commands required to enter this program are provided below. If you need help, review the last chapter.

INPUT.COM

Type in the following lines, or put them in a DEBUG script:

```
DEBUG
A 100
MOV AH,08
INT 21
CMP AL,41
JLE 010A
AND AL,DF
CMP AL,00
JNZ 0110
INT 21
MOV AH,4C
INT 21
<ENTER>
R CX
14
N INPUT.COM
W
```

INPUT.COM will load into the register storing **ERRORLEVEL** a value corresponding to the scan code of the key that was pressed. The scan codes for IBM PCs and compatibles are as shown in Table 21.1.

To use INPUT.COM, put tests in your batch files to examine the scan codes and then direct control to the labels you want, depending on which key was pressed. For example:

```
:ENTER CHOICE
ECHO Enter your choice (1-5):
INPUT
IF ERRORLEVEL 49 IF NOT ERRORLEVEL 50 GOTO 1
```

Table 21.1 Scan Codes for IBM PC

Key	Code	Shift	Control	Alt
A	97	65	1	0;30
B	98	66	2	0;48
C	99	67	3	0;46
D	100	68	4	0;32
E	101	69	5	0;18
F	102	70	6	0;33
G	103	71	7	0;34
H	104	72	8	0;35
I	105	73	9	0;23
J	106	74	10	0;36
K	107	75	11	0;37
L	108	76	12	0;38
M	109	77	13	0;50
N	110	78	14	0;49
O	111	79	15	0;24
P	112	80	16	0;25
Q	113	81	17	0;16
R	114	82	18	0;19
S	115	83	19	0;31
T	116	84	20	0;20
U	117	85	21	0;22
V	118	86	22	0;47
W	119	87	23	0;17
X	120	88	24	0;45
Y	121	89	25	0;21
Z	122	90	26	0;44
1	49	33		0;120
2	50	64		0;121
3	51	35		0;122
4	52	36		0;123
5	53	37		0;124
6	54	94		0;125
7	55	38		0;126
8	56	42		0;127
9	57	40		0;128

Table 21.1 (Continued)

Key	Code	Shift	Control Alt
0	48	41	0;129
-	45	95	0;130
=	61	43	0;131
TAB	9		0;15

Extended Scan Codes For Numeric Keypad and Function keys

Key	Code	Shift	Control	Alt
F1	0;59	0;84	0;94	0;104
F2	0;60	0;85	0;95	0;105
F3	0;61	0;86	0;96	0;106
F4	0;62	0;87	0;97	0;107
F5	0;63	0;88	0;98	0;108
F6	0;64	0;89	0;99	0;109
F7	0;65	0;90	0;100	0;110
F8	0;66	0;91	0;101	0;111
F9	0;67	0;92	0;102	0;112
F10	0;68	0;93	0;103	0;113
F11	0;133			
F12	0;134			
Home	0;71	55	0;119	
Crs-Up	0;72	56		
Pg Up	0;73	57	0;132	
Crs-Lf	0;75	52	0;115	
Crs-Rt	0;77	54	0;116	
End	0;79	49	0;117	
Crs-Dn	0;80	50		
Pg Dn	0;81	51	0;118	
Ins	0;82	48		
Del	0;83	46		
PrtSc			0;114	

```
IF ERRORLEVEL 50 IF NOT ERRORLEVEL 51 GOTO 2
IF ERRORLEVEL 51 IF NOT ERRORLEVEL 52 GOTO 3
IF ERRORLEVEL 52 IF NOT ERRORLEVEL 53 GOTO 4
IF ERRORLEVEL 53 IF NOT ERRORLEVEL 54 GOTO 5
GOTO ENTER
```

Since ERRORLEVEL only reveals if the ERRORLEVEL is equal to or greater than the value indicated, you must test twice to see if a value is exactly what you expect. That is, if ERROR-LEVEL equals 49, and it also does not equal 50, then it must be exactly 49. The double tests on each line take care of this automatically. You would need to write routines in your batch files labeled :1, :2, etc. to handle the individual choices selected by the user.

AN IMPROVED PAUSE

The problem with PAUSE is that it doesn't display the prompt you want (see p.xxx). You may not want the user to press any key, particularly since *any* key won't work. The improved version of PAUSE, called PAUZE, will let you type a prompt of your own— or leave the prompt off entirely if you wish. The syntax is:

```
PAUZE prompt
```

The routine will wait until the user presses a key, and then allow the batch file to continue. As before, use DEBUG to enter the following commands that create PAUZE:

```
PAUZE.COM
DEBUG
A 100
MOV SI,0080
MOV BL,[SI]
CMP BL,00
JZ 011D
XOR BH,BH
```

```
MOV BYTE PTR [BX+0081],20
MOV BYTE PTR [BX+0082],24
MOV DX,0081
MOV AH,09
INT 21
MOV AH,08
INT 21
MOV AH,4C
INT 21
<ENTER>
R CX
26
N PAUZE.COM
W
```

UTILITIES TO CAPTURE THE YEAR, MONTH, AND DAY OF WEEK

The following machine language utilities will capture the current year, day of the month, month, and day of the week and store a value in ERRORLEVEL that your batch files can interpret. Some sample batch files follow that use these utilities.

Type in each of the following using DEBUG.

YEAR.COM (Captures the Year)

```
DEBUG
A 100
MOV AH,2A
INT 21
MOV AL,CL
MOV AH,4C
INT 21
<ENTER>
R CX
```

```
10
N YEAR.COM
W
```

DOM.COM (Captures the Day of the Month)

```
DEBUG
A 100
MOV AH,2A
INT 21
MOV AL,DL
MOV AH,4C
INT 21
<ENTER>
R CX
10
N DOM.COM
W
```

MONTH.COM (Captures the Month)

```
DEBUG
A 100
MOV AH,2A
INT 21
MOV AL,DH
MOV AH,4C
INT 21
<ENTER>
R CX
10
N YEAR.COM
W
```

DATER.COM (Captures the Day of the Week)

```
DEBUG
A 100
MOV AH,2A
INT 21
MOV AH,4C
INT 21
<ENTER>
R CX
08
N DATER.COM
W
```

Using the Routines

These batch files put the previous machine language routines to work, storing the day of the week, day of the month, month, and year in environment variables that your batch files can check. For example, you may run these all at the beginning of each day from your AUTOEXEC.BAT file. Then, you might check to see if it is the first day of the month, first day of the week, etc., and perform some necessary periodic task when the relevant environment variable is found. Note that you may have to enlarge your environment to accommodate all these variables. Review the SHELL command in Chapter 19 to see how to do this.

If you don't want to use these routines, here is a brief summary of what ERRORLEVELS to look for with each routine:

DATER.BAT sets the day of the week in the environment, in a variable called WEEK. When DATER.COM is called, it stores a value in ERRORLEVEL corresponding to the day of the week, from 0 (for Sunday) to 6 (For Saturday).

MONTH.BAT sets the month in the environment, in a variable called MONTH. When MONTH.COM is called, an ERROR-LEVEL is returned ranging from 1 (January) to 12 (December).

DOM.BAT sets the day of the month in the environment, using a variable called DAY. When DOM.COM is called, an ER-RORLEVEL is returned that ranges from 1 to 31, corresponding to the current day of the month.

YEAR.BAT sets the current year in an environment variable called YEAR. When YEAR.COM is called, an ERRORLEVEL is returned that ranges from 0 to 255. The figure 190 corresponds to 1982; 200 represents 1991. The numbers in between equal the intervening years.

ALL.BAT calls up all of these date parameters and displays them. This is another sample batch file showing you how to use the utilities.

```
:  ] [ DATER.BAT ] [
:  Sets Day of Week in Environment
:  --------------------------------:
DATER
IF ERRORLEVEL 6 IF NOT ERRORLEVEL 7 SET
  WEEK=Saturday
IF ERRORLEVEL 5 IF NOT ERRORLEVEL 6 SET
  WEEK=Friday
IF ERRORLEVEL 4 IF NOT ERRORLEVEL 5 SET
  WEEK=Thursday
IF ERRORLEVEL 3 IF NOT ERRORLEVEL 4 SET
  WEEK=Wednesday
IF ERRORLEVEL 2 IF NOT ERRORLEVEL 3 SET
  WEEK=Tuesday
IF ERRORLEVEL 1 IF NOT ERRORLEVEL 2 SET
  WEEK=Monday
IF ERRORLEVEL 0 IF NOT ERRORLEVEL 1 SET
  WEEK=Sunday
:END
```

```
ECHO %WEEK%

: ][ MONTH.BAT ][
:  Sets Month in Environment
: -------------------------:
@ECHO OFF
MONTH
IF ERRORLEVEL 12 GOTO 12
IF ERRORLEVEL 11 GOTO 11
IF ERRORLEVEL 10 GOTO 10
IF ERRORLEVEL 9 GOTO 9
IF ERRORLEVEL 8 GOTO 8
IF ERRORLEVEL 7 GOTO 7
IF ERRORLEVEL 6 GOTO 6
IF ERRORLEVEL 5 GOTO 5
IF ERRORLEVEL 4 GOTO 4
IF ERRORLEVEL 3 GOTO 3
IF ERRORLEVEL 2 GOTO 2
IF ERRORLEVEL 1 GOTO 1
GOTO END
:12
SET MONTH=December
GOTO END
:11
SET MONTH=November
GOTO END
:10
SET MONTH=October
GOTO END
:9
SET MONTH=September
GOTO END
:8
SET MONTH=August
GOTO END
:7
SET MONTH=July
```

```
GOTO END
:6
SET MONTH=June
GOTO END
:5
SET MONTH=May
GOTO END
:4
SET MONTH=April
GOTO END
:3
SET MONTH=March
GOTO END
:2
SET MONTH=February
GOTO END
:1
SET MONTH=January
:END
ECHO %MONTH%

: ][ DOM.BAT ][
:  Sets Day of Month in Environment
: --------------------------------:
@ECHO OFF
Sets Day of Month
DOM
FOR %%a IN (1 2 3 4 5 6 7 8 9 10 11 12 13 14
   15 16 17 18 19  20 21 22 23 24 25 26 27 28 29
   30 31) DO IF ERRORLEVEL %%a  SET DAY=%%a
ECHO %DAY%

: ][ YEAR.BAT ][
:  Sets Year in Environment
: --------------------------------:
@ECHO OFF
YEAR
```

```
IF ERRORLEVEL 200 IF NOT ERRORLEVEL 201 SET
   YEAR=1991
IF ERRORLEVEL 199 IF NOT ERRORLEVEL 200 SET
   YEAR=1992
IF ERRORLEVEL 198 IF NOT ERRORLEVEL 199 SET
   YEAR=1990
IF ERRORLEVEL 197 IF NOT ERRORLEVEL 198 SET
   YEAR=1989
IF ERRORLEVEL 196 IF NOT ERRORLEVEL 197 SET
   YEAR=1988
IF ERRORLEVEL 195 IF NOT ERRORLEVEL 196 SET
   YEAR=1987
IF ERRORLEVEL 194 IF NOT ERRORLEVEL 195 SET
   YEAR=1986
IF ERRORLEVEL 193 IF NOT ERRORLEVEL 194 SET
   YEAR=1985
IF ERRORLEVEL 192 IF NOT ERRORLEVEL 193 SET
   YEAR=1984
IF ERRORLEVEL 191 IF NOT ERRORLEVEL 192 SET
   YEAR=1983
IF ERRORLEVEL 190 IF NOT ERRORLEVEL 191 SET
   YEAR=1982
ECHO %YEAR%

: ][ ALL.BAT ][
:  Displays Month, Day, Year, Day of Week
: ----------------------------------------:
@ECHO OFF
CALL MONTH
CALL DOM
CALL YEAR
ECHO The day is
CALL DATER
```

LOGGING COMPUTER USAGE

The next three utilities let you log your computer usage in a file.

They make use of the batch files MONTH.BAT, DOM.BAT and YEAR.BAT.

The first file, USELOG.BAT, calls all three of them in succession. If your system already has the equivalent batch file commands in its AUTOEXEC.BAT file, you can skip USELOG.BAT and call TIMER.BAT instead. Otherwise, USELOG.BAT will call TIMER.BAT when it is finished.

```
:  ] [ USELOG.BAT ] [
:   Logs Use of Computer
:  ----------------------:
@ECHO OFF
CALL MONTH
CALL DATER
CALL YEAR
TIMER
```

Next, TIMER.BAT will post the current time in the environment, using a trick introduced earlier in this book as applied to the VER command. In this case, the output of the TIME command is redirected to a file called FILE.BAT, which is then called. FILE.BAT will contain a line like this:

```
Current Time is: 00:02:04
```

DOS will interpret that as a command to run an executable program called CURRENT with three parameters, the third of which is the current time.

Of course, you have prepared CURRENT.BAT, which stores that time along with the date in a file called LOG.ASC. You can examine LOG.ASC at any time to see when the computer was booted.

```
:  ] [ TIMER.BAT ] [
:   Enters Time in Environment
:  ---------------------------:
ECHO | MORE | TIME>FILE.BAT
FILE
```

```
:  ] [ CURRENT.BAT ] [
:  Makes Log Entry
:  ------------------:
SET TIMENOW=%3
ERASE FILE.BAT
ECHO Booted: %MONTH% %DAY% %YEAR%
   %TIMENOW%>>C:\LOG.ASC
```

SOME UTILITIES USING FIND

The next set of utilities are included to demonstrate the use of the FIND filter to build your own helpful DOS commands. They use DOS 4.0's MEM command or the earlier CHKDSK to locate specific bits of information about your system. You can use these as simple commands from the command line, or put the values in the DOS environment for ready access by other batch files.

These utilities report the amount of EMS memory available, the bytes of storage available on your hard disk, the total size of the disk, the amount of conventional memory you have installed, and the amount of that memory available for your applications. There are numerous public domain utilities that also provide this information. You may also obtain the same data by typing CHKDSK or MEM. However, we think you'll like learning how to build your own commands from these examples.

```
:  ] [ EMS.BAT ] [
:  Shows Amount EMS Memory
:  -------------------------:
@ECHO OFF
MEM>FILE.$$$
TYPE FILE.$$$ | FIND "EMS"
ERASE FILE.$$$

:  ] [ AVAIL.BAT ] [
:  Shows Bytes Available on Disk
:  -----------------------------:
```

```
@ECHO OFF
CHKDSK ----->FILE.$$$
TYPE FILE.$$$ | FIND "bytes available"
ERASE FILE.$$$


: ][ SIZE.BAT ][
:  Shows Total Size of Disk
: ------------------------:
@ECHO OFF
CHKDSK ----- FILE.$$$
TYPE FILE.$$$ | FIND "space"
ERASE FILE.$$$


: ][ MEMORY.BAT ][
:  Shows Total Memory Installed
: ---------------------------:
@ECHO OFF
CHKDSK ----- FILE.$$$
TYPE FILE.$$$ | FIND "Memory"
ERASE FILE.$$$


: ][ FREE.BAT ][
:  Shows Amount of Free Memory
: ---------------------------:
FREE.BAT
@ECHO OFF
CHKDSK ----- FILE.$$$
TYPE FILE.$$$ | FIND "free"
ERASE FILE.$$$
```

SUMMARY

This chapter has provided a number of interesting utility
programs you can use as a foundation to build your own. Both

machine language routines and batch file programming were used. Hard disk users—even those who use the DOS 4.0 shell—will find that the ability to put together a handy program like these on an *ad hoc* basis will let them get the most from their systems.

PART

4

Appendixes

DOS Command Summary

This command summary will provide you with a quick reminder of the syntax and options for each DOS command. For a more complete explanation of each command, consult the main text. Note that the operation of some commands changes from one DOS version to another. The syntax shown is for DOS 3.3, since most readers will have this version. We've noted where changes were made for DOS 4.0.

Conventions used in this summary include:

d:, d1:, d2:, etc:	drive specifications
\path	any full path name
filespec	file specification
[ ]	optional
...	parameter may be repeated

Lowercase parameters should be substituted with some other value. Uppercase parameters should be included as they are. Parameters separated by a slash are mutually exclusive: choose one.

Command: APPEND
Type: External Command
Version: DOS 3.3

Syntax	*Result*
APPEND d:path[;d:]path...]	Add data file path
APPEND /E	Store path in environment
APPEND /X	Add function calls SEARCH FIRST, FIND FIRST, and EXEC
APPEND ;	Remove APPEND path
APPEND /X:OFF	Turn off search for DOS executable files (DOS 4.0)
APPEND /X:ON	Turn on search for DOS executable files; same as /X (DOS 4.0)
APPEND /PATH:ON	Turn on search for files that have drive or path specified; default condition (DOS 4.0)
APPEND /PATH:OFF	Turn off search for files that have path or drive specified (DOS 4.0)

Command: ASSIGN
Type: External Command
Version: DOS 2.0

Syntax	*Result*
ASSIGN d1:=d1:	Assign name d2: to d1:
ASSIGN	Clear assignments

Command: ATTRIB
Type: External Command
Version: DOS 3.0

Syntax	*Result*
ATTRIB +Rd:\path\filespec	Make files read-only
ATTRIB -Rd:\path\filespec	Make files read/write
ATTRIB +Ad:\path\filespec	Set archive bit

ATTRIB -Ad:\path\filespec   Reset archive bit

Options
/S   Include subdirectories

Command: BACKUP
Type: External Command
Version: DOS 2.0

Syntax   *Result*
BACKUP d1:\path\
  filespec d2:   Backup files from d1: to d2:

Options:
/S   Include subdirectories
/M   Only modified files
/A   Add files to backup disk
/D:mm-dd-yy   Only files after mm:dd:yy
/T:hh:mm:ss   Only files after hh:mm:ss
/L d3:\path\filespec   Use log file specified
/F   Format backup diskette (not
                              required by DOS 4.0, which
                              FORMATs automatically)

Command: BREAK
Type: Internal Command
Version: DOS 2.0

Syntax   *Result*
BREAK ON   Check during DOS functions
BREAK OFF   Check only during I/O
BREAK   Display BREAK status

Command: CHCP
Type: Internal Command
Version: DOS 3.3

Syntax	*Result*
CHCP nnnn	Select code page nnnn

Command: CHDIR
Type: Internal Command
Version: DOS 2.0

Syntax	*Result*
CHDIR d:\path	Change to specified directory
CD d:\path	Change to specified directory
CHDIR	Display current directory
CD	Display current directory

Command: CHKDSK
Type: External Command
Version: DOS 1.0

Syntax	*Result*
CHKDSK	Analyze disk and provide disk and memory status report
CHKDSK filename	Examine file name(s) to see if their sectors are contiguous
CHKDSK /F	Fixes sectors
CHKDSK /V	List of files, directories; with DOS 4.0, display serial number of the disk

Command: CLS
Type: Internal Command
Version: DOS 2.0

Syntax	*Result*
CLS	Screen clears

Command: CommAND
Type:Internal Command
Version: DOS 3.0:

Syntax	*Result*
CommAND [d:\path]	Start command processor

Options
/P	Make permanent
/C string	Pass command string
/E:xxxx	Set environment size

Command: COMP
Type: Internal Command
Version: DOS 1.0

Syntax	*Result*
COMP d1:\path\filespec d2: \path\filespec	Compare files

Command: COPY
Type: Internal Command
Version: DOS 1.0

Syntax	*Result*
COPY d1:\path\filespec d2:\path\filespec	Copy from d1: to d2:
COPY d1:\path\filespec+ d2:\path\filespec d3:\path\filespec	Combine files

Options
/A	Stop copying when ASCII end-of-file marker encountered; add EOF marker (Control-Z)
/B	For binary files: ignore Control-Z EOF marker
/V	Verify after copying

Command: CTTY
Type: Internal Command
Version: DOS 2.0

Syntax   *Result*
CTTY device   Change standard I/O device;
                                 device may be AUX, COM1,
                                 COM2, COM3, COM4

Command: DATE
Type: Internal Command
Version: DOS 1.0

Syntax   *Result*
DATE mm-dd-yy   Date set
DATE mm.dd.yy   Date set
DATE   Display date

Command: DELETE
Type: Internal Command
Version: DOS 1.0

Syntax   *Result*
DELETE d:\path\filespec   File(s) erased
DEL d:\path\filespec   File(s) erased
DEL d:\path\filespec /P   With DOS 4.0, ask to verify each
                                 file deleted

Command: DIR
Type: Internal Command
Version: DOS 1.0

Syntax   *Result*
DIR d:\path\filespec[switch]   List files

Options
/W   Display wide
/P   Page display

Command: DISKCOMP
Type: External Command
Version: DOS 1.0

Syntax
DISKCOMP d1: d2:

Result
Compare disks

Options:
/1
/8

Check only first side
Check only 8 sectors per track

Command: DISKCOPY
Type: External Command
Version: DOS 1.0

Syntax
DISKCOPY d1: d2:[switch]

Result
Diskette copied

Options:
/1

Copy only first side

Command: ERASE
Type: Internal Command
Version: DOS 1.0

Syntax
ERASE d:\path\filespec
ERA d:\path\filespec

Result
File(s) erased
File(s) erased

Command: FASTOPEN
Type: External Command
Version: DOS 3.3

Syntax
FASTOPEN d: nnn

Result
Remember nnn files and
directories on drive d: for faster
file operations

FASTOPEN d: nnn /X

With DOS 4.0, allow using expanding memory

Command: FDISK
Type: External Command
Version: DOS 3.3

Syntax
FDISK

Result
Manipulate DOS partitions

Command: FIND
Type: External Command
Version: DOS 2.0

Syntax
FIND [switch] "string"
  d:\path\filespec

Result

Locate string in file

Options
/V

Find lines without
string specified

/C

Display count of lines

/N

Display line numbers of
matching entries

Command: FORMAT
Type: External Command
Version: DOS 1.0

Syntax
FORMAT d1:[switches]

Result
Format drive d1:

Options:
/S

Copy system files also

/1

Make single-sided disk

/8

Copy 8 sectors per track

/V

Ask for volume label

/B

Format 8 sectors, allow system

/4	Format 360K disk in 1.2M drive
/N:nn	Format nn sectors per track
/T:nn	Format nn tracks per disk
/V:label	DOS 4.0 enhancement
/F:size	DOS 4.0 enhancement; also displays serial number and allocation units

Command: GRAFTABL
Type: External Command
Version: DOS 3.0

Syntax	*Result*
GRAFTABL [code page /STATUS]	Load graphics table

Options:

437	U.S.A. code page
860	Portugal code page
863	French-Canadian code page
865	Norway/Denmark code page
/STATUS	Show code page status
850	Multilingual (DOS 4.0)

Command: GRAPHICS
Type: External Command
Version: DOS 2.0

Syntax	*Result*
GRAPHICS [printer type] [switch]	Graphics screen print

Options:

COLOR 1	IBM Color Printer: black
COLOR 4	IBM Color Printer: RGB/black
COLOR 8	IBM Color Printer: black, cyan, magenta, yellow
COMPACT	IBM Compact Printer

GRAPHICS   IBM Proprinter or Graphics
                                  Printer
THERMAL   IBM Convertible Printer

/R   Reverse black and white
/B   Use background color
/LCD   Print from IBM Convertible LCD

Command: JOIN
Type: External Command
Version: DOS 3.1

Syntax   *Result*
JOIN d1: d2:\path   Join d1: to d2:\path
JOIN d1: /D   Disconnect JOIN
JOIN   Display JOIN status

Command: KEYBxx
Type: External Command
Version: DOS 3.0

Syntax   *Result*
KEYBxx,yyy,d:\path   Load keyboard xx, using code
  \KEYBOARD.SYS   page yyy, with KEYBOARD.SYS
                                in location d:\path\KEYBOARD.
                                SYS
KEYB /ID:zzz   Keyboard code (DOS 4.0)

Command: LABEL
Type: External Command
Version: DOS 3.0

Syntax   *Result*
LABEL d:label   Add label to drive d:

Command: MEM
Type: External Command
Version: DOS 4.0

Syntax	*Result*
MEM	Show used and free memory, allocated and free memory areas, and programs loaded
MEM /PROGRAM	Show programs loaded into memory and locations
MEM /DEBUG	Show drivers, display programs, and other data

Command: MKDIR (MD)
Type: Internal Command
Version: DOS 2.0

Syntax	*Result*
MKDIR d:\path	Make directory
MD d:\path	Make directory

Command: MODE
Type: External Command
Version: DOS 1.1

Syntax	*Result*
MODE LPT#[:] [n] [m],[P]	Set mode of printer

Substitute 1, 2, or 3 for # to indicate LPT1, LPT2, LPT3, and line 80 or 132 for n to indicate characters per line

m	6 or 8 lines per inch
P	Continuous retry on timeout

MODE LPT# [n] [m] RETRY=xx switches

Options	
E	Return error from check of busy port
B	Return busy signal from check of busy port
R	Return ready signal from check of

	busy port
(none)	No retry
MODE LPT#[:]=COMx	Send LPT output to COM port; substitute

1, 2, or 3 for # to indicate LPT1, LPT2, LPT3, and 1 or 2 for x to indicate COM1 or COM2

| MODE n | Set video mode |
| MODE [n],m [T] | Align video |

Options

40	40-column mode
80	80-column mode
BW40	Black-white 40 columns
CO40	Color 40 columns
BW80	Black-white 80 columns
CO80	Color 80 columns
MONO	Monochrome display
m	R or L, shift display left/right
T	Set up test pattern
,25	25-line display (DOS 4.0)
,43	43-line display (DOS 4.0)
,50	50-line display (DOS 4.0)

MODE COM#[:]	
baud ,[parity],[databits],	
[stopbits],P	Set COM port

Substitute 1 or 2 for # to indicate COM1 or COM2; for baud rate; 110 to 19200
N (None), O (odd), E (even) for parity;
7 or 8 for databits;
1 or 2 for stopbits

| P | Continuous retry on timeout |

if COM port is attached to printer

Command: MODE
Type: External Command
Version: DOS 3.3

Syntax	*Result*
MODE device CODEPAGE PREPARE= list d:\path \filespec	Prepare code page

Options:
device	CON, PRN, LPT1, LPT2, LPT3
list	One or more of 437, 850, 860, 863, 865

Syntax	*Result*
MODE device CODEPAGE [/STATUS]	Display active code page

Options:
device	CON, PRN, LPT1, LPT2, LPT3
/STATUS	Show status

Syntax	*Result*
MODE device CODEPAGE REFRESH	Refresh code page

Options:
device	CON, PRN, LPT1, LPT2, LPT3

Command: MODE
Type: External Command
Version: DOS 4.0

Syntax	*Result*
Options	
MODE CON COLS=col	Set number of columns in display
40	40-column display
80	80-column display
Options	
MOD CON LINES=lines	Set number of lines in display
25	25-line display
43	43-line display
50	50-line-display
MODE CON RATE=rate	Keyboard rates
Delay=delay	set

Command: MORE
Type: External Command
Version: DOS 2.0

Syntax	*Result*
MORE	Page output to screen

Command: NLSFUNC
Type: External Command
Version: DOS 3.3

Syntax	*Result*
NLSFUNC [d:\path	Support extended country
\filespec]	information
Options:	
d:\path\filespec	Country information file

Command: PATH
Type: Internal Command
Version: DOS 2.0

Syntax   *Result*
PATH d:\path [;...]   Set system file search path
PATH ;   Nulls search path

Command: PRINT
Type: External Command
Version: DOS 2.0

Syntax   *Result*
PRINT [options] d:\path
\filespec   Background print file(s)

Options:
/D:device   Print device (PRN is default)
/B:nnnn   Size of print buffer (512)
/U:nn   Ticks to wait for printer
/M:nnn   Ticks to use for printing
/S:nnn   Time slice
/Q:nn   Max files in queue
/C   Cancel preceding file and all
                                      files until /P encountered
/P   Print preceding file and all files
                                      until /C encountered
/T   Cancel print queue

Command: PROMPT
Type: Internal Command
Version: DOS 2.0

Syntax   *Result*
PROMPT string   Set system prompt
PROMPT   Reset prompt to default

Command: RECOVER
Type: External Command
Version: DOS 2.0

Syntax   *Result*
RECOVER d:\path\filespec   Recover file(s)
RECOVER d: Recover all files on d:

Command: RENAME
Type: Internal Command
Version: DOS 1.0

Syntax   *Result*
RENAME d1:\path\filespec
  d2:\path\filespec   Rename d1: as d2:
REN d1:\path\filespec
  d2:\path\filespec   Rename d1: as d2:

Command: REPLACE
Type: External Command
Version: DOS 3.2

Syntax   *Result*
REPLACE d1:\path   Replace files on d1: with files on
  \filespec d2:\path\filespec   d2:

Options
/A   Copy files that don't
                                        exist on target disk
/P   Prompt when found on
                                        target before replacing
/R   Replace even read-only files
/S   Include all directories
/W   Pause for source disk
/U   Update older files (DOS 4.0)

Command: RESTORE
Type: External Command
Version: DOS 2.0

Syntax	*Result*
RESTORE d1: d2:\path \filespec [switch]	Restore backed up files

Options:

/S	Restore files in subdirectories
/P	Ask before restoring files changed since last backup
/B:mm-dd-yy	Restore if changed on or before mm-dd-yy
/A:mm-dd-yy	Restore if changed after mm-dd-yy
/M	Restore if changed since last backup
/N	Restore if not on target
/L:hh:mm:ss	Restore if modified since hh:mm:ss
/E:hh:mm:ss	Restore if modified on or before hh:mm:ss

Command: RMDIR (RD)
Type: Internal Command
Version: DOS 2.0

Syntax	*Result*
RMDIR d:\path	Remove directory
RD d:\path	Remove directory

Command: SELECT
Type: External Command
Version: DOS 3.0–3.3

Syntax	*Result*
SELECT A:/B: d:\path xxx yy	Set DOS

Options
d:\path	Target disk drive/path
xxx	Country code
yy	Keyboard code

DOS 4.0 version is a full utility program with complete installation functions for hard disks as well as floppy disks

Command: SET
Type: Internal Command
Version: DOS 2.0

Syntax	Result
SET variable=value	Set environment variable to value
SET variable	Erase this variable
SET	Display environment variables

Command: SHARE
Type: External Command
Version: DOS 3.0

Syntax	Result
SHARE [options]	Set file sharing

Options:
/F:xxxx	Set allocation for sharing
/L:xx	Set locks

For DOS 4.0, also is used as support for disks larger than 32 megabytes

Command: SORT
Type: External Command
Version: DOS 2.0

Syntax	Result
SORT [/R] [/+n]	Sort ASCII text

Options:

/R	Reverse sort
/+n	Start sort on column n

Command: SUBST
Type: External Command
Version: DOS 3.0

Syntax — *Result*

SUBST d1: d2:\path	Substitute path for d:1
SUBST d1: /D	Remove substitution
SUBST	Display substitutions

Command: SYS
Type: External Command
Version: DOS 1.0

Syntax — *Result*

SYS d:	Transfer system to d:

DOS 4.0 allows specifying optional source drive

Command: TIME
Type: Internal Command
Version: DOS 1.0

Syntax — *Result*

TIME hh:mm[:ss[:yy]]	Set time; DOS 4.0 allows entering time on a12-hour or 24-hour clock, depending on country code
TIME	Display time

Command: TREE
Type: External Command
Version: DOS 2.0

Syntax	*Result*
TREE [d:] [/F]	Display directory tree
Options:	
/F	Include file names; with DOS 4.0, uses block graphics and indents for each subdirectory

Command: TYPE
Type: Internal Command
Version: DOS 1.0

Syntax	*Result*
TYPE d:\path\filename	Display file

Command: VER
Type: Internal Command
Version: DOS 2.0

Syntax	*Result*
VER	Show DOS version

Command: VERIFY
Type: Internal Command
Version: DOS 2.0

Syntax	*Result*
VERIFY [ON/OFF]	Verification turned on/off

Command: VOL
Type: Internal Command
Version: DOS 2.0

Syntax	*Result*
VOL d:	Display label of d:

Command: XCOPY
Type: External Command
Version: DOS 3.2

Syntax	*Result*
XCOPY d1:\path\filespec d2:\path\filespec [option]	Copy files
/A	Copy only if modified since last backup or XCOPY
/D:mm-dd-yy	Copy if same or later date as mm-dd-yy
/E	Create subdirectories on target, even if empty
/M	Copy files that have been modified since last backup or XCOPY, and mark them as backed up
/P	Ask if each file should be copied
/V	Verify
/W	Pause until source disk inserted

DOS CommAND HISTORY

Command	Type	Introduced
CHKDSK	External Command	DOS 1.0
COMP	Internal Command	DOS 1.0
COPY	Internal Command	DOS 1.0
DATE	Internal Command	DOS 1.0
DELETE	Internal Command	DOS 1.0
DIR	Internal Command	DOS 1.0
DISKCOMP	External Command	DOS 1.0

DISKCOPY	External Command	DOS 1.0
ERASE	Internal Command	DOS 1.0
FORMAT	External Command	DOS 1.0
RENAME	Internal Command	DOS 1.0
SYS	External Command	DOS 1.0
TIME	Internal Command	DOS 1.0
TYPE	Internal Command	DOS 1.0
MODE	External Command	DOS 1.1
ASSIGN	External Command	DOS 2.0
BACKUP	External Command	DOS 2.0
BREAK	Internal Command	DOS 2.0
CHDIR	Internal Command	DOS 2.0
CLS	Internal Command	DOS 2.0
CTTY	Internal Command	DOS 2.0
FIND	External Command	DOS 2.0
GRAPHICS	External Command	DOS 2.0
MKDIR (MD)	Internal Command	DOS 2.0
MORE	External Command	DOS 2.0
PATH	Internal Command	DOS 2.0
PRINT	External Command	DOS 2.0
PROMPT	Internal Command	DOS 2.0
RECOVER	External Command	DOS 2.0
RESTORE	External Command	DOS 2.0
RMDIR (RD)	Internal Command	DOS 2.0
SET	Internal Command	DOS 2.0
SORT	External Command	DOS 2.0
TREE	External Command	DOS 2.0
VER	Internal Command	DOS 2.0
VERIFY	Internal Command	DOS 2.0
VOL	Internal Command	DOS 2.0
ATTRIB	External Command	DOS 3.0
CommAND	Internal Command	DOS 3.0
GRAFTABL	External Command	DOS 3.0
KEYBxx	External Command	DOS 3.0
LABEL	External Command	DOS 3.0

SELECT	External Command	DOS 3.0
SHARE	External Command	DOS 3.0
SUBST	External Command	DOS 3.0
JOIN	External Command	DOS 3.1
REPLACE	External Command	DOS 3.2
XCOPY	External Command	DOS 3.2
APPEND	External Command	DOS 3.3
CHCP	Internal Command	DOS 3.3
FASTOPEN	External Command	DOS 3.3
FDISK	External Command	DOS 3.3
NLSFUNC	External Command	DOS 3.3
MEM	External Command	DOS 4.0

Appendix

B

Glossary

ANSI.SYS An installable device driver that provides extended keyboard and screen control to the PC.

applications program Software such as a word processing program, spreadsheet, database manager, etc., that performs useful work not directly related to the maintenance or operation of the computer.

applications program interface A common interface allowing software engineers to write programs that will operate with a broad range of computer configurations.

archive To store files that are no longer active. Programs like ARC.EXE combine and compress files into an archive file for more compact, easier storage.

archive bit A bit within a file's attribute byte in the file allocation table that is set to a value of 1 or 0 to indicate whether or not the file has been backed up by XCOPY, BACKUP, or some other utility program designed to reset that bit.

assembler A program that allows the user to write software

357

using a higher level language than machine language, called *assembly language*. Once the program has been written, the assembler translates it into machine language.

assembly language The language used by an assembler that allows using mnemonic commands such as MOV and INT instead of machine language. The programmer can apply labels to certain sections of code and call these instead of keeping track of where specific modules are located. When the program has been finished, the source code produced can be assembled into machine language object code.

asynchronous Characteristic of communications method under which exact timing of the signals is not critical: The next set of information is sent whenever a confirmation signal is received. This is the opposite of *synchronous* communications, which send out data within an exact block of time. IBM PCs most commonly use asynchronous communications to exchange data over distances of more than a few feet, as with modems.

attribute byte A byte in the file allocation table that stores certain information about a file, such as whether it is read-only, invisible, or a system file, or has been backed up since it was last modified.

AUTOEXEC.BAT An ASCII file placed in the root directory of the disk. It contains a list of commands to be carried out by DOS automatically during the boot-up operation. This file allows the user to load memory-resident programs, specify a path to be used by DOS to search for system files, and perform other tasks that configure the system.

average latency The average time needed for the hard disk to finish rotating to the first sector of a track so the read/write head can begin writing information or reading the track. The average latency time is usually included in the access time of a given hard disk.

average seek time The average time required for the read/write head of a disk drive to move from one track to another, usually measured in milliseconds.

backup To make a copy of computer data as a safeguard against accidental loss. The copy that is made is also called the *backup*.

BASIC Beginner's All-purpose Symbolic Instruction Code. The high-level language built into IBM PCs, and furnished with DOS in compatibles. BASIC.COM is the simplest version with disk I/O capabilities. BASICA.COM and GW-BASIC.EXE are the most widely used versions.

batch A set stored for later processing as a whole. Batch files, for example, contain sets of DOS commands that can be interpreted and carried out by DOS one after another when the batch file is called.

baud A data transmission rate of 1 bit per second, used to measure asynchronous communications speed.

Bernoulli drive A mass storage device using flexible magnetic media, and relying on the "Bernoulli effect" to keep the disk and read/write heads separated by a thin cushion of air. These drives offer the same storage capacity as smaller hard disk drives, with access times that are somewhat slower, but have the advantage of providing removable media and freedom from data-damaging head crashes.

binary Base-two arithmetic, which uses only 1's and 0's to represent numbers. 0001 represents 1 decimal, 0010 represents 2 decimal, 0011 represents 3 decimal, etc.

BIOS The Basic Input/Output System of a computer, which is a set of computer code, provided on read-only memory (ROM) chips, and used to govern basic system level functions.

bit A binary digit, either a 1 or a 0.

bits per inch Abbreviated *bpi*, used as a measure of data density along a track.

boot To start a computer, either when the power is turned on or when the system is reset (through Control-Alt-Delete).

bootstrap A very short set of computer instructions, usually designed to do nothing but load into the computer a longer program that carries out the actual loading of the operating system. On hard disks, the boot sector is found on the first sector of the first track of the first surface to be read by the system.

buffer An area of computer memory set aside to store information meant for some sort of I/O, such as printing, writing to disk, etc. This allows the device supplying the information to feed it into memory faster, if necessary, than the device meant to accept it can handle it. A printer buffer, for example, allows DOS or an applications program to quickly dump a document for printing and then go on to something else. The buffer can then feed the information to the printer at a more suitable slower rate.

bug An error in a program that results in some unintended action.

byte Eight bits, which can represent any number from 0000000 to 11111111 binary (0 to 255 decimal).

cache A memory buffer used to store information read from disk, to allow DOS to access it more quickly. Cache programs use various schemes to make sure that the most frequently accessed sectors as well as the most recently accessed sectors remain in the buffer as long as possible.

CD-ROM Compact Disk-Read-Only Memory. An optical disk mass storage device that, like all optical disks, uses pits written on the disk by laser to convey information. CD-ROMs are encoded with information during manufacture, and cannot be written by the user. They provide a means of distributing large databases on one compact medium.

character An alphanumeric character, punctuation mark, or other symbol available from the PC keyboard.

child directory A directory created below a parent directory. C: \ is the root directory of drive C: ; C: \WP would be a child directory of C: \; while C: \WP\LETTERS would be a child directory of C: \WP.

cluster The smallest unit of disk space that can be allocated by DOS. For hard disks, a cluster may be 4 sectors (512 bytes each) totalling 2,048 bytes, or 16 sectors for a total of 8,192 bytes. Cluster size has a bearing on how efficiently DOS operates. Smaller clusters waste less space on the disk, but larger clusters allow DOS to collect more information at one time.

.COM file A disk file, 64K or less in size, which is a DOS executable program.

command A word or phrase used to tell a computer what to do next.

COMMAND.COM The DOS command interpreter, which takes the commands supplied by the user or software and determines what DOS services are needed to carry them out.

command processor A program like COMMAND.COM that serves as an interface between the user and the DOS files that actually carry out various functions.

compiler A program that translates source code written in a higher level language into machine language object code.

concatenate To add together.

control character A nonprinting character used to send information to a device, such as the control characters used to communicate special commands to a printer.

current directory The *default* directory that DOS assumes you mean unless you explicitly type some other within a command.

cursor A symbol that indicates the current screen display position.

CONFIG.SYS An ASCII file that is interpreted by DOS on booting, if present in the root directory of the boot disk. CONFIG.SYS is acted on *before* AUTOEXEC.BAT, but may not contain anything other than commands that specify device drivers to be used, or that set other system configuration factors such as the number of buffers to be allocated, size of the environment, etc.

contiguous In reference to hard disks, contiguous sectors are those that are arranged consecutively on the disk. DOS tries to allocate sectors to a file contiguously so that the disk drive can read as many sectors of a file as possible with a minimum amount of read/write head movement. However, as a hard disk fills, the unallocated sectors gradually become spread out and fragmented, forcing DOS to choose more and more noncontiguous sectors. Fragmented files can be much slower to access.

coprocessor An additional microprocessor used in tandem with the main processor. IBM PCs and compatibles typically have sockets for an 8087, 80287, or 80387 math coprocessor designed to offload number-crunching tasks from the main microprocessor, producing much faster operation for applications involving much computation, such as spreadsheet recalculation.

cylinder The "stack" of tracks on all the platters of a hard disk drive that can be read simultaneously by the read/write heads.

data transfer rate The maximum speed that data can be moved from the disk to memory.

debug The process of removing errors from a program, as well as the name of a program, DEBUG.COM, that allows changing the value of bytes stored in memory and on disk.

device driver A software module that tells DOS how to control a given piece of hardware, such as a printer, monitor, disk drive, or keyboard. ANSI.SYS and VDISK.SYS are device drivers supplied with DOS. Others are supplied by manufacturers of peripherals.

diagnostic A utility that tests components of a computer to locate potential defects and problems. When the PC is turned on, built-in diagnostics programs in ROM perform the power-on self-test.

direct memory access Abbreviated DMA, this is the movement of data directly from memory to some other device, such as the disk drive, without first being loaded into the microprocessor.

directory The list of file names stored on a disk, along with the size of each file, the date and time it was created or last changed, and the type of file.

disk drive A mass storage device that can read and write information. Disk drives can be floppy drives, hard disks, optical disks, Bernoulli devices, or other types.

DOS Disk Operating System. The control program of the computer that oversees how the system interfaces with the user and peripherals, including disks.

drive specification The letter used by DOS to identify a disk drive, from A: to Z: .

dynamic RAM Type of memory that must be electrically refreshed many times each second, or else the contents will be lost. PCs and compatibles use dynamic RAM to store programs, data, and the operating system.

EBCDIC A code system like ASCII, used with IBM mainframes and some software, such as DisplayWrite.

EDSI Enhanced Device Systems Interface.

EMS Expanded memory specification. A special kind of memory using hardware and software drivers designed for it. DOS sees this memory in pages, using a window located in conventional memory.

end-of-file marker A character used to mark the end of a file. DOS uses the Control-Z character (ASCII code 26).

environment An area of memory set aside to keep track of information, such as the system prompt. The user can also define variables to be placed in the environment through the SET command.

escape A special key that produces the ASCII code 27, which represents the Escape character. Many programs use this code to back out of, or escape, from menus. The Escape character can also be used to send information to the ANSI.SYS device driver.

.EXE file A more complex type of DOS executable file that allows running programs requiring more than 64K of memory.

extended memory Continuous memory from 1 megabyte to 16 megabytes, which can be used by 80286- and 80386-based computers with applications written to use this form of memory.

extended partition The second DOS partition, which is not bootable like the primary partition. May contain up to 32 megabytes, divided into separate volumes. Extended partitions were introduced with DOS 3.3.

external command A command that is not built into IBMDOS.COM, but that must be accessed through a separate utility program. These are executable files like FORMAT.COM, DISKCOPY.EXE, etc.

FAT File allocation table. A special area on the disk that tracks how each cluster is assigned to various files.

file A collection of information, usually data or a program, that has been given a name and allocated sectors by the FAT.

file control block A file management tool that is used only by older software. The number of such blocks of memory that can be made available is specified by the FCBS command in the CONFIG.SYS file.

file name The name given a file, consisting of eight characters and a three-character extension.

file oriented backup Any backup system that stores information in files, just as they are stored on the disk. Such systems allow easier access or restoration of a particular file.

filter A DOS program that accepts data from the standard input device, modifies it, and then sends it to the standard output device. DOS filters SORT, FIND, and MORE will sort, locate specific strings, or display the output in pages, respectively.

fixed disk Another name for a hard disk drive, so called because such disks are not commonly removed from the computer while in use.

floppy disk drive A type of disk drive with removable media. Today, most floppy disks are 5.25 inches square, although an earlier type was 8 inches square. The 3.5 inch-square microdisks such as those found in PS/2 computers are also sometimes called floppy disks, even though their rigid shells are not flexible.

flux changes Reversals in the orientation of the magnetic material on a disk, used to indicate the presence of a binary 1.
FM Frequency modulation. A disk encoding scheme in which each data bit is followed by a clock bit.

FM Frequency Modulation. A disk encoding scheme in which each data bit is follwed by a clock bit.

formatting Preparing a disk for use by writing certain information in magnetic form. Formatting divides the disk into tracks and sectors and sets up a directory structure.

hard error An error in reading or writing data caused by hardware. Since such errors are usually the result of damage to the computer, they are more difficult to recover from than soft errors.

hardware The physical components of a computer system, including the CRT, keyboard, microprocessor, memory, and other peripherals.

head seek time The time needed for movement of the read/write head of a disk drive over the disk surface to a specified track.

hexadecimal The base-16 number system, used with PCs to make binary information easier to interpret by humans. The numbers 0 to 16 are represented by the numerals 0 to 9, plus A, B, C, D, E, and F. An eight-bit byte storing a number from 0 to 255 can readily be represented by the hexadecimal values 0 to FF.

hidden file A file whose attribute byte is marked so that it will not be displayed by the DOS DIR command.

hierarchical In hard disk terminology, characterized by a structure of directories such that each subdirectory has one parent, but may have several child directories, branching out in a tree-like structure.

high-density disks Floppy disks that store more than the standard 360K of information. For example, 5.25-inch high-density floppies can hold up to 1.2 megabytes of information; high-density 3.5-inch microdisks can store 1.44
  megabytes of data.

high-level format The formatting performed by FORMAT.COM, in which information needed by DOS to use the disk is written.

high-level language A language that allows representing machine-level operations by mnemonic keywords rather than 1's and 0's. BASIC, COBOL, PASCAL, C, and FORTRAN are all high level languages.

IBMBIO.COM The DOS system file that contains low level information for handling the hardware, and that directs the computer to load IBMDOS.COM during boot-up. Under MS-DOS, this file is called IO.SYS.

IBMDOS.COM The file that contains the program code needed to carry out various DOS services, and that directs the computer to load COMMAND.COM during boot-up. Under MS-DOS, this file is called MSDOS.SYS.

image-oriented backup Any backup system that creates a mirror image of the disk, without regard to the files themselves. With such systems, the entire disk has to be restored from the backup medium to allow access to the files.

induce To cause an electrical field to be generated. As the read head of a disk drive passes over the media, the flux changes that have been written to the disk induce an electrical signal that can be interpreted by the drive controller to reconstruct the original information written to the disk.

I/O Input/output. Used to describe the process whereby information flows to and from the microprocessor or computer through peripherals such as disk drives, modems, CRT screens, printers, etc.

input   Incoming information. Input may be supplied to the computer by the end user, or to a program by either the end user or a data file.

instructions   the basic set of capabilities of a microprocessor, allowing the chip to load information in registers, move it to other registers, increment the data, add or subtract data from registers, and so forth.

Intel 8086   The microprocessor used in the IBM PS/2 Models 25 and 30 and some other systems.

Intel 8088   The microprocessor used in the IBM PC, IBM PC-XT, PCjr, PC Convertible, Portable PC, and many clones.

Intel 80286   The microprocessor used in the IBM PC-AT, PS/2, Model 30 286, Models 50 and 60, and many compatible computers.

Intel 80386   The microprocessor used in the IBM PS/2 Model 80 and other systems.

intelligent   Having sufficient programming built in to carry out certain tasks independently. An intelligent disk drive can accept requests from DOS, locate the data, and deliver it without detailed instructions on how to do the physical I/O.

interactive   Allowing user input during run-time.

internal command   A command loaded into memory at boot-up time and available to DOS thereafter without the need to access the disk.

interpreter   A program that interprets and carries out each line of another program written in a high level language like BASIC or COBOL. These languages can also be *compiled* so that DOS can carry out a program's commands directly.

interrupt   A signal to the microprocessor to stop what it is doing and do something else. Simple processes like pressing a key can generate an interrupt.

interleave   The alternating of logical disk sectors to allow the hard disk time to process the information from one sector before the next is presented. Without interleave, a slow controller would allow reading only one sector per revolution.

K   Kilobytes.In computer teminology, 1,024 bytes, so that 16K represents 16,384, 64K equals 65,536, 512K corresponds to 524,288, etc.

label   On a hard disk, the volume name applied immediately after high level formatting, if the /V switch was specified, or by use of the LABEL command. In batch files, a label is a line prefixed with a colon, and is used to direct control from other parts of the batch file using the GOTO subcommand.

latency   The time needed for the hard disk to finish rotating to the first sector of a track so the read/write head can begin writing information or reading the track. The average latency time is usually included in the access time of a given hard disk.

logical   Characteristic of any feature not physically present, but defined functionally for convenience. The physical sectors on a hard disk are arranged contiguously. Logically, they may be arranged in alternating fashion through interleaving.

low-level formatting   The most basic formatting done on the hard disk to prepare it for partitioning and high-level formatting. Often done by the manufacturer, it locks out bad sectors before the disk is used.

macro   A series of commands that can be triggered at the press of a key or two. Many applications programs, as well as utilities like SuperKey and ProKey, allow the users to develop their own macros for frequently used command sequences.

mass storage Permanent storage of computer information, usually on magnetic disk but also including magnetic tape, optical disk, bubble memory, and other nonvolatile storage media.

memory-resident program Also called a *terminate and stay resident program* (TSR). A utility that is loaded into high conventional memory (or into high memory plus extended or expanded memory) and that remains active while DOS executes other programs. It may be called by pressing a hotkey (like SIDEKICK), or may simply work in the background (like FASTOPEN).

MFM Modified frequency modulation. A way of encoding information on a hard disk such that greater capacity is achieved. The code varies depending on the way the previous bits were set, resulting in a 50 percent increase in the amount of information that can be recorded.

microprocessor The computer-on-a-chip that is the brains of a personal computer.

millisecond One-thousandth of a second.

multitasking The handling by a computer system of several different chores simultaneously. Since microcomputers have only one main processor, this is usually done by "slicing" the processor's time into individual segments and allowing each program to share these in rotation. DOS is not generally a multitasking operating system, although third-party enhancements can give it these capabilities.

multiuser Characterized by the ability of a computer system to handle several different tasks by several different users simultaneously. UNIX is the best known multitasking system among microcomputer users (it is also available for larger systems.)

oersted A measure of the coercivity of a magnetic medium, or, its ability to capture and retain information. Usually abbreviated Oe.

overlays Portions of a program that are called into memory as needed, overlaying the previous redundant section of the program. Using overlays allows programs that are much bigger than those that could fit into memory all at once.

parallel Moving data several bits at a time, rather than one at a time. Usually, parallel operation involves sending all eight bits of a byte along eight separate data paths at one time. This is faster than serial movement.

parameter A qualifier that defines more precisely what a program such as DOS is to do.

parent directory The directory immediately above a child directory.

partition A part of a disk drive set aside for use by a particular operating system. One partition on a hard disk is bootable. The others, if any, may become the active partition through use of the FDISK program.

path A listing of parent-and-child directory names in order that defines the location of a particular file.

peripheral Any device of a computer system other than the microprocessor itself and its directly accessible memory. We usually think of peripherals as printers, modems, etc.

physical Characteristic of a feature that exists materially, as opposed to one existing by virtue of logical definition only.

pipe DOS's way of communicating between programs.

pixel A picture element of a screen image: one "dot" of the collection that makes up an image.

port A channel of the computer used for input or output with a peripheral. The serial port and parallel ports of the PC are the most widely used.

primary partition With DOS 3.3 or later, the bootable DOS partition, which may be up to 32 megabytes in size.

program Code that instructs the computer how to perform a function.

prompt A character or series of characters that lets the user know that the program is waiting for input. PROMPT is also a DOS command.

read-only memory Memory that can be read by the system, but not changed. Abbreviated ROM, read-only memory often contains system programs that help the computer carry out DOS services.

redirection Re-routing input or output to or from the device for which it was originally headed. For example, you may send screen output to the printer using a command like DIR>PRN, or send it to a file: DIRMYFILE.ASC.

registers The basic memory locations of a microprocessor, through which all information that is processed passes.

RISC Reduced Instruction Set Computer. A computer system that has a special microprocessor with fewer instructions, and that therefore operates faster. Such systems depend on the software for functions that formerly were handled by the microprocessor.

RLL Run Length Limited. An encoding system for hard disks that is 50 percent more efficient in the density of information that can be recorded. Therefore, hard disks using RLL have 50 percent more capacity, and a data transfer rate that is 50 percent faster.

SCSI Small Computer Systems Interface. An intelligent interface.

sector The smallest section of a track, containing 512 bytes of data.

segment A section of memory that is manipulated as a block by DOS, 64K in size. Up to four segments can be controlled by DOS at one time.

serial Passing information one *bit* at a time in sequential order.

shell A program layer designed to simplify things for the end user. Often provides menus to replace a harder-to-learn command-line interface.

source code The program code generated by the programmer, which may not be directly executable by the computer. If not, it is translated by an assembler or compiler into machine language object code.

ST506/412 The most popular hard disk interface.

static RAM Memory that does not need to be refreshed, and that therefore does not lose its contents when power to the computer is turned off.

string A series of characters.

subdirectory A directory, created within *another* directory, that stores its own separate files.

substrate A base material that is coated with another. For example, flexible polyester forms the substrate onto which a floppy disk's magnetic coating is placed. For hard disks, the substrate is most frequently a rigid aluminum platter.

system level interface An interface over which information is passed in logical form.

text file Usually, an ASCII file.

track One of the concentric circles on a disk platter, made up of sectors of information, and marked by the read/write head through a series of changes in the direction of the magnetic poles on the disk.

tracks per inch The number of tracks on a disk per inch of radius; a measure of the capacity of the disk.

track-to-track access time A measure of the time needed to move the read/write heads between adjacent tracks on the disk.

transfer rate The speed at which information can be read from a disk. With hard disks, this is typically 5 megabits per second, although new, denser encoding schemes have increased this.

tree-structured directories Directories structured hierachically by DOS using *parent* and *child* directories.

unfragmented Said of a hard disk that has most of its files stored in consecutive sectors, and not spread out over the disk. Such an arrangement allows more efficient reading of data with less time required to move the read/write head to gather the information.

utility A program that performs some useful system or maintenance function, as opposed to an *applications* program.

virtual disk An electronic or "RAM" disk created in memory to mimic a real disk drive, but which is much faster. DOS 3.x and later versions were supplied with VDISK.SYS, a device driver that allows creating multiple virtual disks in memory.

volume The largest hard disk entity that DOS is able to deal with. For example, under DOS 3.3 and later versions a single physical disk can be divided into two or more logical disks created as separate volumes. DOS may see one volume as drive C: and the other as drive D: even though both exist on the same physical drive.

winchester Another name for a fixed disk drive.

WORM Write-once read-many (or mostly). Optical disk technology that allows writing to the disk by the user, although a given section cannot be erased and re-used.

Trademarks

IBM, IBM PC,XT,AT,PS/2, TopView and PC-DOS are registered trademarks of International Business Machines Corporation.

MS-DOS, Windows, and Microsoft are registered trademarks of Microsoft Corporation.

Sidekick is a trademark of Borland International.

Lotus and 1-2-3 are registered trademarks of Lotus Development Corporation.

Intel is a registered trademark of Intel Corporation.

CP/M is a registered trademark of Digital Research, Inc.

DESQview is a trademark of Quarterdeck Office Systems.

WordPerfect is a registered trademark of WordPerfect Corporation.

COMPAQ is a registered trademark of COMPAQ Computer Corporation.

Index

About the Author

A full-time writer since 1970, David D. Busch has twice won "Book of the Year" honors from the Computer Press Association. DOS FOR HARD DISK USERS is his tenth book for the IBM family of computers. He has also written some 1700 articles for magazines ranging from *Computer Technology Review* and *Mini-Micro Systems* to *Personal Computing*.

A contributing editor and monthly columnist in six different computer magazines, Busch has also worked as a newspaper reporter-photographer, as a college sports information director, a photo-posing instructor for a Barbizon-affiliated modeling agency, and as an account executive for a New York-based public relations firm. His non-computer-oriented articles have appeared in publications as diverse as *Adam, Petersen's PhotoGraphic, Income Opportunities*, and *Writer's Yearbook*.

As one of the pioneering personal computer users in 1978, the author collected and published useful DOS tips for early Radio Shack TRS-DOS computers and CP/M machines before turning to MS-DOS in 1982. Since that time, he has emerged as a leading authority on operating system tricks and techniques, chiefly through monthly "DR. DOS" columns in PC Companion Magazine, and DOS-oriented books like DOS CUSTOMIZED. Many of his predictions in magazines like Interface Age as far back as 1980 have since come to pass, including color word processing, memory resident utilities, automatic spelling checkers, outlining, and applications of artificial intelligence to word processing.

After various moves around the United States, the 1970 graduate of Kent State University and his wife are living in his native Ohio with their three children, who range in age from 1 to 19.